THE
UNWED MOTHER

Readers in Social Problems

DONALD R. CRESSEY, CONSULTING EDITOR

DEAN, UNIVERSITY OF CALIFORNIA,
SANTA BARBARA

THE
UNWED MOTHER

EDITED BY

ROBERT W. ROBERTS

HARPER & ROW

Publishers

NEW YORK AND LONDON

HQ
999
U5R6

C-1

Library of Congress Catalog Card Number: 66-12562

CONTENTS

PREFACE

THE ORIGINAL motivation for this volume arose when I was surveying the literature on illegitimacy in preparation for a research project on the unwed mother. At the time, the great volume of literature on the subject suggested a need for the compilation of those writings which appear to be most valid and likely to be of help to those who are interested in the problem but lack the time or the library resources required to read all that has been published.

The actual task of compiling this collection was initiated at the suggestion of Gertrude Yaeger Selznick, of the Survey Research Center, University of California, Berkeley, who saw the need for such a volume and had faith in my ability to complete the task. Without her inspiration and support, my perception of the need for such a volume would have remained a phantasy.

I am indebted to my colleagues, Professors Kermit T. Wiltse, Andrew Billingsley, and Scott Briar, who have helped by their support, encouragement, and intelligent criticisms.

I would also like to express my great appreciation to the secretarial staff at the Research Projects Office of the University of California School of Social Welfare, and especially to Mrs. Leah Smith and Mrs. Miriam Dunbar whose cheerfulness and efficiency helped so substantially in the preparation of this volume.

Finally, I would like to thank my wife, Helen, for her tolerance and comfort during the many weekends and evenings when I was occupied with putting together this work.

ROBERT W. ROBERTS

PART I

The Problem Before Us

Introduction

THE PROBLEM of illegitimacy, although as old as man's social institutions, is one about which much has been written but little is truly known. For most of our history, illegitimacy has been treated as a moral and a legal problem, and society has seemed more interested in punishing the unwed mother and her illegitimate child than in understanding the social, economic, and psychological forces which have placed them in a deviant social position. Indeed, it has been only in the present century that we have attempted to go beyond a moralistic stance to seek insights into a major, and growing, social problem.

If we were to go backward in time three decades or so, a poll of social scientists and psychologists would probably reveal an optimistic belief that the problem of illegitimacy would be solved, or well on the road to solution, by today. The millennium has not arrived. Instead, we find that rather than disappearing, illegitimacy has increased and shows no sign of abating. Although segments of our population have become more understanding and tolerant of the unwed mother and her child, the majority of citizens still see it as an indication of immorality and a threat to the legitimate family system. On the whole, society seems more concerned about the problem and more critical and skeptical of professional efforts to deal with it than ever.

This critical concern is often directed as forcefully at the social welfare programs which attempt to work with the problem as at the unmarried mother herself. If we are to attempt to understand the phenomenon of illegitimacy we must first examine some of the social forces which are con-

3

tributing to this more critical attitude on the part of the public.

The first factor which has undoubtedly fed the public's increased concern is the increase in illegitimate births—both in absolute numbers and as a proportion of all live births. With this increase in the rate of illegitimacy, there has also been a change in the socio-economic characteristics of the unwed mother.

Although the middle-class belief that illegitimacy was something that happened only to the young, the poor, the uneducated, the immoral, and the mentally ill was always overstated, it is less true today than previously. Illegitimacy has invaded our middle-class high schools and colleges, the white collar occupations, and the adult population with a force which has not been known before. While the illegitimacy rates for the lower classes and minority races have slowed their rate of increase and the illegitimacy rate for adolescents has declined, the phenomenon has occurred with increased frequency among the older, better educated, and economically privileged groups.[1] Thus, illegitimacy has become less a subcultural phenomenon and is more threatening to the middle-class institutions which dominate our society. The new immediacy of the problem has surely contributed to society's increased concern about illegitimacy. And, as with other phenomenon such as juvenile delinquency, the concern has often been expressed by the projection of responsibility onto social institutions such as the school and social welfare agencies rather than by an examination of changes in our economic and social systems which are contributing to the social problem. The belief that evil (poverty, ignorance, etc.) produces evil (illegitimacy) is no longer as tenable as before; moreover, the affluent family is threatened by the closeness of illegitimacy and seeks frantically for a scapegoat on which it can release its frustration and anger.

The extent to which society has attempted to use social welfare and ethnic minorities as targets for their wrath has

[1] Clark E. Vincent, *Unmarried Mothers*. New York: The Free Press of Glencoe, Inc., 1961. Also taken from mimeographed material distributed by Clark E. Vincent at the National Conference on Social Welfare, Los Angeles, California, May 26, 1964.

at times reached the proportions of a psychotic delusion. And, as with most delusional systems, there is an initial basis of realistic perception which lends it an aura of plausibility.

The first realistic basis for the public's concern is the rapidly increasing costs of social welfare programs. In the recent past, illegitimacy was less of a problem because, in addition to its dysfunctional aspects, it also served two valid social functions. The first, was a supply of children for economically secure, but infertile, families who constituted a sizable adoption market. The past few years has seen a drastic reduction in the number of couples interested in adoption, and there is now a surplus of adoptable children. Whatever the reason for this, whether because of the shrinkage in the number of couples of childbearing age due to the lower birth rate in the 1930s or because of a disenchantment with parenthood, society is now forced to consider alternate methods of rearing many of the out-of-wedlock children who in prior years were accommodated through the adoption market.

Many of these children are successfully cared for by their natural mothers, with neither tangible nor intangible assistance from the social welfare network. Others, in increasing numbers, become financial dependents of the state via the Aid to Families of Dependent Children program and publicly subsidized foster homes and institutions. Although both of these alternatives often provide inadequate resources for the successful rearing of children, as a budget item they are expensive programs and are frequently attacked by conservative taxpayers.

Quite often the attack upon social welfare expenditures, which is overtly voiced as fiscal concern, is in reality a thinly disguised expression of racial prejudice. The same economic and social forces which have sentenced the vast majority of ethnic minority members to perpetual poverty, have also produced disproportionate rates of illegitimacy. The American Negro, because he is the largest ethnic minority and the group which has suffered the most prolonged and extreme mistreatment, leads the ethnic minorities in social problems and as an object of social criticism and attack.

Attacks on minority groups have increased in recent years. In part this increased attack is in reaction to minority groups' demands for more economic opportunity and social equality. In part the attack has increased because the number of minority members now dependent upon public assistance (whether because they have had illegitimate children or for other reasons) has increased dramatically.

There are several reasons for this increase in economic dependency, especially for the American Negro. While it is not the object of this volume to explore the reasons for this general increase in dependency, it does seem pertinent to explore those reasons which seem directly related to the increased dependency of unwed mothers among ethnic minorities. These reasons apply mainly to the Negro, but are also pertinent for the understanding of other ethnic minorities.

First, during the past quarter century we have witnessed a massive geographical movement of many of these people. Stimulated by World War II, a major exodus occurred from the tenant farms and plantations of the South to the industrial centers of the North and West. This migration was stimulated positively by the need for unskilled labor in industry during the war and by the increased economic opportunity for Negroes in the non-Southern areas of the United States. Migration was stimulated negatively by social oppression and economic exploitation of Negroes in the South. Since this movement began, we have witnessed the introduction of automation and the job market for unskilled labor has shrunk drastically. Thus, many undereducated members of minority groups have been forced to become economically dependent because of the disappearance of acceptable employment. Many unmarried mothers, who formerly worked in factories and service jobs, are now forced to accept economic subsidy from the state.

The movement of Negroes from South to North and West, and from rural to urban areas, has also led to a breakdown of the extended family system. This, in turn, has removed or lessened the resources of economic assistance by the family during periods of temporary unemployment and has meant the loss of child care services which older women in the family often provided while younger unwed mothers worked. Thus, the unmarried mother is more likely to seek public assistance for two reasons: fewer opportunities for employment and fewer resources for child care if she is able to find a job.

These same social changes are rapidly invading the South as farms are increasingly mechanized, as the need for cheap, unskilled (often child) labor diminishes, and as industrialization and automation increase the educational and social skills required for employment.

In the South as in the North, there is a tremendous cultural gap between the educational, economic, and social systems which continue to produce large numbers of ignorant, unsophisticated adults and a changed industrial complex which provides fewer and fewer social positions for them. The matriarchal family of the Negro, which has produced so many illegitimate children, is now dysfunctional to the social system which created it via the institutions of slavery and racial oppression. Having no further economic need of a Negro folk population, the majority culture is now viciously attacking the consequences of the matriarchal family system it created.

Another reason for the increased criticism of Negro illegitimacy is the improved integration of the Negro into the majority social structure. William Goode, in his book, *The Family*, points out that society's condemnation of illegitimacy is based upon a vested interest in the socialization of the child in order to insure its social continuity. As the family is the primary socializing force, the illegitimate child, with only one parent, is at a distinct disadvantage and is less likely to achieve the adequate socialization and psychological integrity that is necessary for complete and successful participation in Western civilization.[2]

Society's concern about a particular child is closely correlated to the importance of his family's position in the social system. If a social group occupies a minor position in the social hierarchy, and if its members fulfill relatively insignificant roles in the social system, then the dominant social group will be less concerned with illegitimacy within that group. However, with increased assimilation into the majority social system, the importance of adequate socialization of individuals becomes of more concern to the society and it becomes

[2] William J. Goode, *The Family*. Englewood Cliffs, N.J.: Prentice-Hall, Inc., 1964.

less tolerant of unmarried parenthood. Thus, the Negro and other ethnic minorities have, by their increased success at integrating themselves into American society, stimulated increased concern about their high illegitimacy rates.

It is because of this same concern for the successful socialization of its children that it is unrealistic to look for a solution to the social problem of illegitimacy in a reform of social attitudes toward the unwed mother and her child. The best knowledge which we have available indicates that a complete family—composed of a sociological father and mother—is necessary to produce an adequately socialized adult. The socially accepted illegitimate child would suffer—as much as the socially stigmatized one—from the deprivation of an intact family experience which appears so necessary for successful participation in Western civilization. If society were to encourage or tolerate illegitimacy it would be contributing to its own demise. It is unlikely that our society will indulge in such suicidal behavior.

Today, American society faces tremendous contradictions between many of its values. Scientific discovery of the emotional damage done by repressive attitudes toward sexuality has contributed to tremendous change in our tolerance of non-marital sexual behavior. However, our attitudes toward birth control and abortion have not been significantly liberalized and the hiatus between the two sets of attitudes has been filled by an increase in illegitimate births. But the optimal solution to the problem of illegitimacy does not seem to lie in the direction of a return to Puritanical sexual attitudes. Instead, the best solution appears to lie in increased dissemination of birth control information, in liberalized abortion laws, and in an attack upon the social inequities that cause the burden of illegitimacy to fall more heavily upon certain disadvantaged social groups.

The success of such an approach requires a more diligent effort to acquire understanding of the social forces which contribute to illegitimate childbearing and a greater dissemination of available knowledge to those who are concerned with the solution of the problem. It is with these challenges in mind that the present volume is presented.

Unfortunately, this volume does not exhaust the supply of

important literature on the subject and limitations of space made the inclusion of many distinguished contributions impossible. Selection was based on several factors. Representative writings of each of the several theoretical schools were selected for inclusion. This often resulted in the elimination of excellent material, simply to avoid duplication of a theoretical position. Also, when it was possible, selection was made in such a way as to include those writings which were based upon empirical evidence. Thus, if several authors had written on a similar perspective or dimension of the problem, the author who based his writings on empirical research was usually chosen over others, though the latter group quite often made the more original contribution of conceptualization.

Although I, as the editor, have tried to be objective in the choice of readings, it was inevitable that my theoretical bias would affect selection. Other editors, with different biases, would have made different selections. My only defense for my decisions is that I carefully surveyed the literature and selected what, in my judgment, were the most reasoned and reasonable viewpoints available—even in cases where the viewpoint of the individual author did not accord with mine.

A Theoretical Overview
of the Unwed Mother

ROBERT W. ROBERTS

Although an exact measurement of the extent of illegitimacy in the United States does not exist, available statistics indicate that illegitimate births have shown a considerable and consistent increase in the past quarter century. It is estimated that the *number* of illegitimate births rose approximately 125 percent (from 89,500 to 201,700) between 1940 and 1957. During the same years the illegitimacy *rate* rose from 7.1 to 20.9 for every 1,000 unmarried females in the population within the childbearing age of 15–44 years. As a *proportion* of all live births, illegitimate births increased from 3.8 percent in 1950 to 4.7 percent in 1957.[1]

Vital statistics also show that illegitimacy occurs disproportionately within certain ethnic minority groups and that it is increasing at a higher rate for these minority populations. While the illegitimacy rate rose from 3.6 for every thousand white women of childbearing age in 1940 to 7.8 in 1955, for non-whites the illegitimacy rate rose from 35.6 to 90.1 during the same years. Thus, despite the inaccuracies reflected in these statistics, it is hard to avoid the conclusion that il-

[1] Statistics taken from: Bureau of Public Assistance, Social Security Administration, U.S. Department of Health, Education, and Welfare, *Illegitimacy and its Impact on the Aid to Dependent Children Program.* Washington, D.C.: April, 1960.

legitimacy is a more major problem among the non-white than the white population.[2]

The figures reported above have been criticized as inaccurate by many authorities, for several reasons. First, fourteen states do not record illegitimate births in their vital statistics. The states which do not record such births tend to be the wealthier and more enlightened states which are believed to have lower illegitimacy rates. These states also provide havens for unmarried mothers who have the resources to leave their home communities in an effort to disguise the illegitimate status of their children. Two, many unwed mothers consciously conceal their unmarried status when they record their child's birth. It is believed that the women who have the economic and social resources to effect such a concealment are likely to be older, better educated, middle-class members of the white race. Three, births among isolated economic and ethnic minority groups (which have high rates of illegitimacy) were probably underreported in vital statistics of the past. Increased efficiency in the recording of vital statistics for such groups has led to reported increase in illegitimacy among certain groups (mainly Southern non-white) which are probably exaggerated.[3]

These various forces, which combine to make the reliability of statistics on illegitimacy questionable, warn us that we must be cautious in interpreting the meaning of these figures as we continue our examination of the problem.

[2] Clark E. Vincent, *Unmarried Mothers*. New York: The Free Press of Glencoe, 1961. Also see, Blanche Bernstein and Mignon Sauber, *Deterrents to Early Prenatal Care and Social Services Among Women Out of Wedlock*. Albany: New York State Department of Social Welfare, 1960; and Jean Pakter et al, "Out-of-Wedlock Births in New York City—Sociological Aspects." *American Journal of Public Health*, Vol. 51, May, 1961.

[3] Bureau of Public Assistance, *op. cit.*, pp. 7–9; and Jane Kronick, "An Assessment of Research Knowledge Concerning the Unmarried Mother," in *Research Perspectives on Unmarried Mothers*. New York: Child Welfare League of America, Inc., 1962.

MAJOR THEORETICAL VIEWPOINTS TOWARD ILLEGITIMACY

Various factors have led to a basic dichotomy in theoretical thinking about the causes of illegitimacy. Like the vital statistics, which show widely varying rates for white and non-white groups, theoretical thinking has tended to develop into two schools, each of which focuses on one or the other ethnic group. Those who argue for a social explanation of the phenomenon tend to look at differences in group rates of illegitimacy and to perceive causes in differing social forces which impose on the various groups. These theoreticians use vital statistics as their foundation and focus on group behavior.

The second school has grown out of the clinical experiences of social workers, psychologists, and psychiatrists and rests upon individual case histories. Their experience has been with a group of unmarried mothers who, for the most part, are white members of the middle or stable working classes. These women subjectively define their unmarried pregnancy as a social or psychological problem and are motivated to request help from community agencies. These unwed mothers are also likely to be interested in relinquishing their illegitimate children for adoption. Many years of experience of working with this group of unwed mothers has led this school to formulate psychological explanations of illegitimacy focused upon intra-psychic factors within individuals.

SOCIAL EXPLANATIONS OF ILLEGITIMACY

Within those who attempt to explain illegitimacy in sociological terms, three theoretical positions may be spelled out. These positions can be summarized under the rubrics of cultural relativism, cultural absolutism, and cultural relationism.

Cultural Relativism

When illegitimacy is looked at from an international or cross-cultural viewpoint, the large differences in the rate with which the phenomenon occurs in various cultural and sub-cultural groups has led one group of social scientists to question that illegitimacy is always a social problem or an indication of social deviation.

Instead, they argue for a position of cultural relativism, which claims that illegitimacy—like many other social phenomena—is subject to the value system of the group within which it occurs and that various cultural groups may not have norms opposed to illegitimacy. Thus, whereas one culture may hold very strongly to the norm of legitimacy, and maintain strong negative sanctions against those who violate the norm, other cultures may have counter-norms which either positively sanction illegitimacy or show an absence of any norm about the phenomenon.

Starting from anthropological observations of widely differing family systems in various parts of the world, they argue that the family is a social institution which shows wide variability between cultures and that some groups have legitimate family institutions which do not require a child to have legally married parents, or a socially responsible father, to obtain legitimate status.

Within complex societies such as the United States, they maintain that sub-cultures exist which have norms about marriage and the family which are different from those held by the majority culture. They explain the higher illegitimacy rates of the lower socio-economic classes and certain ethnic minorities on the basis that these groups hold counter-norms which either positively sanction unwed motherhood or treat it as a morally neutral issue. These theorists also point to the phenomenon of "common-law" marriages among many sub-cultural groups and maintain that a consensual union of the two parents is socially sufficient within their sub-culture and a child of such a union is socially legitimate even if he is not legally legitimate. Oscar Lewis goes one step further and implies that such consensual unions and the closely related phenomenon of illegitimacy may be characteristics of a "culture of poverty" which transcends both national and subcultural boundaries.[4]

The relativistic viewpoint is very prominent among those who have studied the family organization of American Negroes, Mexicans, and various Caribbean cultures.[5]

The American Negro has inspired the most literature in this area. For instance, both E. Franklin Frazier and Gunnar Myrdal hold that historical forces have led to the systematic destruction of the norm of legitimacy among this group and that illegitimacy does not carry a stigma among lower-class Negroes. They trace the development of counter-norms to the institution of slavery wherein marriage was forbidden, promiscuity encouraged, and the mother established as head of the family. This family pattern, they believe, has been perpetuated by the socio-economic enslavement of the Southern Negro since the Civil War, and begins to break down only with the assimilation of folk Negroes into the predominant middle-class culture.[6]

Cultural Absolutism

The second sociological viewpoint sees legitimacy as an absolute norm. First proposed by the eminent anthropologist, Bronislaw Malinowski, this viewpoint maintains that there is a Principle of Legitimacy which is cross cultural.[7] This school postulates that illegitimacy, like incest, is under a universal and inviolate taboo in any society. Cultures and/or sub-cul-

[4] Oscar Lewis, *Five Families.* New York: Basic Books, Inc., 1959.

[5] See Harold T. Christensen, "Cultural Relativism and Premarital Sex Norms." *American Sociological Review,* XXV, No. 1. (February, 1960), pp. 31–39; Oscar Lewis, *op. cit.;* E. Franklin Frazier, *The Negro Family in the United States.* New York: The Citadel Press, 1948; and Hyman Rodman, "On Understanding Lower Class Behavior." *Social and Economic Studies,* VIII, 1959, pp. 441–450.

[6] E. Franklin Frazier, *op. cit.,* and Gunnar Myrdal, *An American Dilemma.* New York: Harper & Row, 1944.

[7] Bronislaw Malinowski, "Parenthood, the Basis of Social Structure," *The New Generation.* V. F. Calverton and Samuel D. Schmalhausen eds. New York: Macauley Co., 1930, pp. 130–146.

tures which have high illegitimacy rates are considered to be sociologically deviant and an understanding of these higher rates depends upon an understanding of the forces which have prevented these groups from conforming to the norm of legitimacy.

William J. Goode, the leading contemporary proponent of this viewpoint, denies the existence of counter-norms which support consensual unions or other forms of unwed mother-hood.[8] Instead, Goode sees an explanation for the differences in illegitimacy rates among various social classes and ethnic sub-cultures in anomie theory. In his brilliant article, "Illegitimacy, Anomie, and Cultural Penetration," he points out that the destruction of native cultures plus the erection of quasi-caste barriers to prevent the full achievement or even complete acceptance of Western standards has led to an incomplete socialization process that permits many ethnic sub-cultures a cultural, but not a social, assimilation.[9] He reasons that only when full assimilation into the majority culture is allowed, with equal access to social rewards and punishment, and where the value system sets norms which are possible of achievement, do we find strong commitments to the Principle of Legitimacy.

Thus, among ethnic minorities, illegitimacy rates drop when their members are given full and equal opportunities for complete acculturation, socialization, and assimilation into the dominant culture.[10] The explanation for differing rates of illegitimacy is thus seen in relation to a breakdown in the socialization process for these groups with higher illegitimacy rates and not in the existence of a set of counter-norms.

[8] William J. Goode, "Illegitimacy in the Caribbean Social Structure," *American Sociological Review*, XXV, No. 1, February, 1960, pp. 21–30.

[9] William J. Goode, "Illegitimacy, Anomie, and Cultural Penetration," *American Sociological Review*, XXVI, No. 6, December, 1961, pp. 910–925.

[10] *Ibid.*

Cultural Relationism

The third sociological position, cultural relationism, is explicated by Clark E. Vincent in his book, *Unmarried Mothers*, and supported in the writings of many others.[11]

The concept of cultural relationism, as originally formulated by Karl Mannheim, was introduced in his development of a sociological theory of knowledge. Rejecting both the relativistic and absolute definitions of knowledge, Mannheim stated that "all of the elements in a given situation have reference to one another and derive their significance from this reciprocal relationship in a given frame of thought."[12]

Clark Vincent, in his application of the concept to illegitimacy seems to hold that the Principle of Legitimacy is universal, but stresses that the phenomenon of illegitimacy is related not only to this principle but to closely related norms as well. That is, a society may, while holding negative sanctions against illegitimacy, at the same time maintain permissive norms about related behavior. Thus, in Vincent's words, there is a "need to consider attitudes and social policy about illicit sexual behavior within the larger social context."[13]

It is in the area of closely related areas of behavior that one finds relativity of values between cultures. It is among those cultures which hold negative norms against both non-marital sexual intercourse and illegitimacy that one finds low rates of illegitimacy. Conversely, cultures which contain contradictory norms—that is, are permissive towards non-marital sexual intercourse and condemning of illegitimacy—will have high illegitimacy rates. Such cultures see the act of illegitimacy and not the act of promiscuity as bad. This implies a contradiction in social goals—and only the most intelligent

[11] Clark E. Vincent, *op. cit.* Also see, William F. Whyte, "A Slum Sex Code," *American Journal of Sociology,* July, 1943, pp. 24–31; Alfred C. Kinsey, Wardell B. Pomeroy, and Clyde E. Martin, *Sexual Behavior in the Human Male.* Philadelphia: W. B. Saunders Co., 1948; and Martha Wolfenstein, "The Emergence of Fun Morality," *Journal of Social Issues,* VII 1951, pp. 15–25.

[12] Karl Mannheim, *Ideology and Utopia.* New York: Harcourt, Brace & Co., 1952, p. 76.

[13] Clark E. Vincent, *op. cit.,* p. 24.

and highly socialized individuals will be able to meet the demands of the two contradictory norms without becoming involved in unmarried parenthood.

Vincent believes that the norms held by the dominant culture in the United States are becoming more permissive about non-marital sexual behavior and sees this shift in our values as accounting for increased illegitimacy among the white population. It can also be reasoned that the higher illegitimacy rates of the lower socio-economic classes and some ethnic minorities can be explained by their more permissive norms regarding sexual intercourse and their less adequate opportunities for socialization.

Furthermore, of those who are "caught" in the conflict and become pregnant out-of-wedlock, those who have the most social sophistication and resources are more likely to resolve the problem via the quasi-approved cultural solutions of abortion or adoption. Thus, according to this viewpoint, it would seem that those individuals and groups who hold a permissive norm in reference to non-marital sexual intercourse, negative norms towards illegitimacy, and norms which oppose birth control, abortion, and adoption will be those who become unmarried mothers and keep their children. Those who hold restrictive norms about non-marital intercourse, negative norms regarding illegitimacy, and more permissive norms about birth control, induced abortion, and adoption are less likely to become unmarried mothers or, if they do find themselves in the predicament, are less likely to keep their illegitimate children.

PSYCHOLOGICAL EXPLANATIONS OF UNWED MOTHERHOOD

The second major theoretical viewpoint which attempts to explain unwed motherhood is psychological in its orientation. Generally, this school of thought holds that unwed motherhood is a symptom of emotional disturbance and must be explained psychodynamically.

As stated earlier, most of the psychological research done

on unmarried mothers has been based on the client populations of social work agencies and psychiatric clinics. Clients
of such agencies tend to be young (often adolescent), white,
middle-class women who subjectively define their out-of-wedlock pregnancy as a problem for which they are motivated
to accept help. Partly because of the adoption market, which
to a large extent is limited to the placement of white infants,
and partly because of the lack of motivation among members
of ethnic minorities and lower-class women to release their
children for adoption, the population groups which have the
highest illegitimacy rates are underrepresented in agency
based samples.

For the most part, psychological theorists have not dis-[x]
cussed the applicability of their findings to the groups with
the highest illegitimacy rates. Sometimes the implication is
that their findings apply to all unmarried mothers, at other
times the authors state that their findings do not hold for
"girls coming from a cultural background where illegitimacy
is more or less socially acceptable."[14]

The various explanations put forth by psychologically
oriented theorists range from rather loosely drawn clinical
impressions to more formally defined research efforts. Many
of the authors find evidence of marked emotional disturbance,
but two recent research efforts questioned whether unwed
mothers show a higher rate of mental illness than the general
population.[15] Most of the research has also shown a high rate
of broken homes in the background of unwed mothers, but
Clark Vincent's recent study revealed that a control group of
single-never-pregnant girls, with socio-economic backgrounds
similar to the unwed mothers being studied, had an almost
identical rate of broken homes in their childhood (35.4 percent for the unwed mothers versus 31.1 for the single-never-
pregnant girls).[16] However, Vincent's sample, like so many
others, was drawn from white, middle-class clients of mater-

[14] Leontine Young, "Personality Patterns in Unmarried Mothers," *The Family*. December, 1945.

[15] Clark E. Vincent, *op. cit.;* and John S. Pearson and Phyllis S. Amacher, "Intellectual Test Results and Observations of Personality Disorders Among 3,594 Unwed Mothers in Minnesota," *Journal of Clinical Psychology*. Vol. XII, No. 1, January, 1956, pp. 16–21.

[16] Clarke E. Vincent, *op. cit.*, pp. 101–102.

nity homes and does not pretend to offer conclusions for the minority groups which have higher rates.

Although definitive research efforts are missing to support the psychological viewpoint as a single-cause explanation, there does appear to be considerable evidence that there is a high rate of emotional disturbance among the unwed mothers studied. It also seems that we can no longer be so cavalier about writing off those groups who have historically suffered extremely high illegitimacy rates by "explaining" their behavior as due to a difference in cultural norms. Recent research in the new specialty of social-psychiatry forces us to question some of our old answers about these groups. Specifically, the two major studies done in New Haven and midtown Manhattan have shown that those segments of our population which have high illegitimacy rates also have high rates of mental illness.[17] These studies alone are enough to make us question an oversimplified explanation of illegitimacy as due simply to "cultural relativity" and demand that we at least consider the possibility that high illegitimacy rates are indicative of a high degree of social and emotional disorganization.

A SUGGESTED RESEARCH APPROACH

What appears to be needed is a long-term, collaborative research effort between the social and psychological theorists. An indicated first step would be for an empirical examination of the attitudes and behavior expressed toward illegitimacy by the various geographic, economic, and ethnic strata of our society. Such a sample should include single-never-pregnant women and married mothers as well as unmarried mothers. It is only by such a systematic exploration that the question of the possible relativity of values toward illegitimacy can be answered.

[17] See August B. Hollingshead and Frederick C. Redlick, *Social Class and Mental Illness*. New York: John Wiley and Sons, 1958; and Thomas S. Langer and Stanley T. Michael, *Life Stress and Mental Health*. New York: The Free Press of Glencoe, 1963.

If such research showed that certain groups do hold counter-norms, the problem would be defined—for these subcultural groups at least—as exploring the ways and means of offering these groups opportunities for more complete acculturation to the dominant norms, more adequate socialization, and a fuller assimilation into the core culture.

If such research shows that the Principle of Legitimacy is universal, then we would have to concern ourselves with the question of why there are differing rates of conformity to the norm. The culturally relativistic viewpoint would be considered and an answer would be looked for in the possibility that norms pertaining to closely related behavior such as non-marital sexual intercourse, birth control, abortion, and adoption were significantly related. Another possibility is that these groups, as well as individuals from the majority culture, have shared experiences which have led them to a state of alienation from, or rebellion against, the dominant value system.

The third approach would be to look at the individual factors which have produced personality problems that have prevented these unwed mothers from conforming to the values which they collectively hold. Gross possibilities which suggest themselves are idiosyncratic experiences which have caused individuals to fail to internalize the particular norm of legitimacy (superego defects), insufficient personality strength to control sexual impulses (inadequate ego strength), or overly strong unconscious conflicts which dominate the rational components of the personality (the possibility of unsuccessful resolution of the Oedipal conflict which results in unconscious acting out of incest phantasies suggests itself as one possibility).

In summary, it appears that each of the outlined theoretical positions is based on enough factual evidence to warrant a consideration of its possible validity. Each position needs further empirical testing on its own merit. But equally merited is the possibility that illegitimacy, like so much other human behavior, is not a single-cause phenomena. It seems more likely that while either psychological or sociological forces may be sufficient to produce illegitimacy in specific cases, it is their combination which leads to high illegitimacy rates among certain segments of the population. That is, the various social and psychological forces which lead to a weak consensus with the Principle of Legitimacy, permissive sexual norms, and damaged personalities fall unevenly among the population, accounting for higher illegitimacy rates among disadvantaged segments of our population.

PART II

Cross Cultural Perspectives on the Unwed Mother

Parenthood—The Basis of Social Structure

BRONISLAW MALINOWSKI

The anthropologist [is] . . . a useful helpmate of the student of modern conditions. He studies human cultures and the organization of societies within the widest compass of human experience. He can provide the background of comparative knowledge against which all modern problems must be discussed. He should be able to lay down the laws which define the constitution and nature of the family and parenthood. He should be able to demonstrate how certain elements vary, disappearing in some societies, hypertrophied in others, while yet the fundamentals of relationship between parents and children remain stable and universal. These fundamentals are the true constituent elements of marriage, parenthood and the family. Their discovery, definition and establishment is the real task of scientific anthropology. . . .

THE FUNCTIONAL PROBLEM OF KINSHIP

The functional anthropologist regards facts as being of equal value whenever they really loom large in native life and

REPRINTED WITH editorial adaptations, from *The New Generation,* edited by V. F. Calverton and Samuel D. Schmalhausen (1930), pp. 129–143, by permission of the publisher. (Copyright, 1930, by The Macaulay Company.)

25

social organization, irrespectively of whether they are drab or amusing—whether they appear strange or familiar from the European point of view. And when these facts consistently appear together, when they obviously form part of an organic whole, the functional anthropologist is not prepared to tear this organic whole to pieces and then to place the torn fragments on an evolutionary scale. The questions usually asked are: is promiscuity the original institution from which marriage and the family gradually developed; or, on the contrary, are the family and monogamous marriage the starting point, and communal kinship and sexual laxity only temporary aberrations? These questions are for us irrelevant and fictitious.

The real question is: What is the relation between the family and clan—between individual and classificatory kinship? These are not stages which succeed each other, and can be found here and there, accidentally mixed or overlapping. It is absurd to regard one of them merely as a "survival," the other as an innovation. They are two aspects of kinship which always appear in conjunction, though the clan or classificatory side is sometimes almost in abeyance. But since they work side by side they must fulfil functions which are, on the one hand related, on the other certainly not identical. These distinct functions must be discovered and defined. The first and capital problem of primitive kinship is therefore to establish the relation between the family and the clan, between individual and classificatory kinship. By solving this problem we shall be able to arrive at a clear conception of kinship—to define it functionally in a way which covers the two phases and assigns to each its respective place in culture.

With this problem, that of classificatory terminologies is obviously intimately connected. If we cannot explain them as a monstrous linguistic fossil, as an encumbrance always dragging one stage behind in evolution; if we have to regard them as live parts of language; we shall have to ask again: what is the function of the classificatory principle of terminology? What is there in the actually existing social conditions of primitive mankind which these terminologies express and with which they are correlated?

Mother-right and father-right again cannot possibly be stages or shadows of stages. Each of them is always associated with its opposite or correlate. They are the two sides of the big system which defines filiation in each community. The real problem is: why does such a system always involve an overemphasis of one side, that of the mother or of the father; what does this overemphasis really mean, and what serviceable part does it play in social organization? And here it is easy to see that, since motherhood is biologically the far more important fact, it is the paternal side of kinship which presents the problematic facet of the case. Interesting customs such as the *couvade,* psychological problems such as relate to the ignorance of fatherhood and its social consequences, are among the problems which must also be functionally solved. And, once we embark upon questions of filiation and the counting of kinship, we are faced directly by the whole complex of problems concerning derived kinship, that is, the contribution of clans and moieties to the cohesion of society; the function of collective solidarity; the function of exogamy and of group-reciprocity.

These are the pieces of our puzzle and on the whole most of them seem so disconnected, so ill-fitting, that the natural reaction of the explaining mind was to cut them up into proper shapes and regard them, either as stages of fragments of compound cultures, trait-complexes or *Kultur Kreise.*[1] To the functionalist, however, the relatedness of the various aspects and institutions is the most important characteristic of culture, and here the universal coexistence, the dovetailing, the

---

[1] The anthropological reader of this essay will have noticed that the contributions of the so-called Historical or Diffusionist School have received but small attention in my argument. As a matter of fact they have been almost insignificant, both in quantity and quality. The treatment of the family and kinship by the American School is sound, but it is not historical, it is comparative, I should almost say functional. Here belong the contributions of Lowie, Goldenweiser, Gifford, Kroeber, Wissler and Dorsay and the few but sound remarks scattered through the writings of E. Sapir. Graebner's and Schmidt's method of regarding father-right and mother-right, clanship and the individual family as independent cultural traits belongs, on the other hand, to the type of cultural surgery which is incompatible with the functional treatment of human institutions. Fortunately Schmidt and Koppers are inconsistent, and in their last big work (*Der Mensch aller Zeiten*), following E. Grosse, they treat the elements of kinship as organically connected parts of a bigger unit, and even try to correlate them with economic, environmental and political factors.

obvious many-sidedness of kinship, makes us see in all the facts of sexuality, marriage, family and clanship one integral institution: the Procreative Institution of mankind.

THE INITIAL SITUATION OF KINSHIP

What is the main function of this big institution? The obvious answer is—the propagation of the species, but it is easy to see that the continuity of culture is as deeply involved in kinship as is the continuity of the race. Let us start with the biological fact, since that is the more tangible and definite. What is the procreative unit in human society? The answer is so obvious, the fact that one male must be married to one female in order to produce offspring is so patent, that the answer that it is the human family, consisting of mother, father and child which is the procreative unit, appears at first sight an unnecessary truism.

It may come as a shock therefore to the man in the street when he is told that it is really around this question that most learned anthropological discussions center and that, even now, there is a profound disagreement in the views held. Thus in the latest voluminous discussion on the question we are told that "the clan like the family is a reproductive group and not a political organization," and again, "We must dismiss entirely from our minds the notion that, while the patriarchal family is a sexual group depending upon certain intimate relations, reproductive and economic, the clan is a group resting upon some other principle; that while the one is a reproductive group, the other is a social or political organization."[2] Obviously these statements are paradoxically worded, for the author patently does not intend us to assume, what in fact he actually says, that under the clan system group babies are conceived in collective copulation and brought forth out of a communal womb in an act of joint parturition. Whatever might be the similarity between the clan and the family, the sexual relations as well as the reproductive conditions within the clan are carried out by single pairs.

[2] R. Briffault, *The Mothers*, Vol. 1. New York: The Macmillan Company, 1927, pp. xvi, 591.

The only way in which we can plausibly interpret the above contention is that the author does not really dispute the fact that biological procreation happens in pairs, but merely discounts the validity of this biological fact as regards ties of kinship and social relationship. He regards, in other words, zoology as not relevant for social organization. It would be possible to imagine that since human instincts are almost indefinitely plastic, the communally constructed clan can completely replace the biologically constructed family. Though the child is produced by one man and woman only, if this child were brought immediately under the control of a group of fathers and mothers, the early influences which shape its kinship ideas and kinship theories would be collective and not individual.

If we thus reformulate Mr. Briffault's extravagant statement it opens before us the real problem of Kinship.[3] The statement becomes reasonable. But of course this does not mean that it is true.

We have thus to open the question of what the *initial situation* of kinship really is. Is the child actually born into the clan or into the family; is it brought directly under the influence of groups or of individuals? Is there such a thing as "group-motherhood" or "group-fatherhood" or have we always only individual mothers and fathers, and that not only in the biological, but also in the cultural and social sense of the words?

In laying down the study of the *Initial Situation of Kinship* as the capital problem of kinship, in demanding the exact analysis of the sociological configuration of the earliest experiences, we are doing, somewhat tardily, for social anthropology what psychology has been doing for the study of the mental development of the individual in general; nor is it only psychoanalysis which forces us back to the cradle in order to study

---

[3] This indeed is the way in which it has been framed by Rivers: "A child born into a community with moieties or clans becomes a member of a domestic group other than the family in the strict sense." This point of view has also been expressed by the same author in his hypothesis of group-motherhood and in his whole conception that in the early stages of development of society the clan filled that place in social organization which the family occupied afterwards.

the formation of complexes and the charging of the Unconscious with most of its subsequent drives! Behaviorism, in showing that it is the conditioning of reflexes or, as I should prefer to say, the molding of innate dispositions, which matters most, is also leading us back to the study of the period when this molding takes place on the largest scale. Above all, the most important contribution to modern psychology and social science, the Theory of Sentiments propounded by Shand and McDougall, demands that all human values, attitudes and personal bonds be studied along the line of development, with special consideration of the earliest periods.

The concept of the *Initial Situation of Kinship*, which I first introduced in my article on Kinship in the 14th edition of the *Encyclopaedia Britannica*, places the emphasis on the study of the first stages of kinship sentiments. And, indeed, if the study of any and all human sentiments must be done along the life history of the individual, in a biographical treatment so to speak, this must be done in the case of kinship above all things. Because in kinship the most typical and the fundamental process is that in which biological facts are transformed into social forces, and unless this be understood well, the whole question is placed on a false foundation and we get the chaos of controversy with which we are faced at present

It is hardly necessary, perhaps, to add that in laying down the problem of the Initial Situation we are doing more than merely introducing a concept and a terminological entity. In doing this we are really opening a number of definitely empirical questions referring to the cultural transformation of the biological elements, sex, maternity and fatherhood; we are focusing our argument on the linking-up of courtship, marriage and kinship; last, but not least, we are demanding a clear answer to the question as to the relation between procreation, domesticity and the legal or political aspects of kinship.

Let us then proceed to the analysis of the Initial Situation of kinship and try, through a comparative survey along the widest range of variations, to see whether some general principles can be established with reference to it.

INDIVIDUAL MATERNITY AS A CULTURAL AND SOCIAL FACT

Maternity is the most dramatic and spectacular as well as the most obvious fact in the propagation of species. A woman, whether in Mayfair or on a coral island of the Pacific, has to undergo a period of hardship and discomfort; she has to pass through a crisis of pain and danger, she has, in fact, to risk her own life in order to give life to another human being. Her connection with the child, who remains for a long time part of her own body, is intimate and integral. It is associated with physiological effects and strong emotions, it culminates in the crisis of birth, and it extends naturally into lactation.

Now what is it that the advocates of "group-motherhood" want us to believe? Neither more nor less than that, with birth, the individual link is severed and becomes merged in an imaginary bond of "collective motherhood." They affirm that such powerful sociological forces are at work, such strong cultural influences, that they can override and destroy the individual attitude of mother-to-child. Is this true? Do we really find any sociological mechanisms, which succeed in severing the mother-child relationship, dumping each into the group of collective mothers and collective children? As a matter of fact all these hypotheses are pure figments and, looking at facts . . . [we are] led to the conclusion that maternity is as individual culturally as it is biologically. The point is of such capital importance, however, that we must look more in detail at the arguments by which individual maternity has been challenged by such writers as Rivers and Briffault.

They have alleged that communal suckling, the frequent and indiscriminate adoption or exchange of infants, joint cares and joint responsibilities, and a sort of joint ownership of children create an identical bond between the one child and several mothers, which would obviously mean that every mother would have also a group of joint children. In these views there is also implied the assumption that conception, pregnancy and childbirth, which obviously are individual and not communal, are completely ignored by society as irrelevant factors, and that they play no part in the development of maternal sentiments.

Let us examine the implication of the group-motherhood hypothesis first, and then decide whether a communal game of share and exchange in children and infants is, or ever could have been, played.

Now, in the first place, it is a universal fact that conception, pregnancy, childbirth and suckling are sociologically determined; that they are subjects of ritual, or religious and moral conceptions; of legal obligations and privileges. There is not one single instance on record of a primitive culture in which the process of gestation is left to nature alone. Conception, as a rule, is believed to be due as much to spiritual as to physiological causes. Conception, moreover, is not a process which is allowed to take its natural course as a result of prenuptial intercourse. Between the freedom of sexual life and the freedom of becoming a mother a sharp distinction is drawn in all human societies including our own, and this is one of the most important sociological factors of the problem and to it we shall presently return.

Most important of all, a legitimate, socially approved of conception must always be based on an individual legal contract—the contract of marriage.[4]

Once conception has taken place the prospective mother has always to keep taboos and observe ceremonial rules. She has to abstain from certain foods and carry out lustrations; she has to undergo more or less complicated pregnancy ceremonies; she has to wear special decorations and clothes; she is regarded sometimes as holy, sometimes as unclean; last, [but] not least, she is very often sexually tabooed even to her own husband. All these ceremonial, moral and legal rules are, by the very nature of the facts, individual. Their motive is invariably the welfare of the future offspring. Most of them establish individual ties between the prospective mother and

[4] In order to avoid possible misunderstandings I should like to remind the reader that plural marriages such as polygyny and polyandry, are always based on an individual legal contract between one man and one woman, though these contracts may be repeated.

her future offspring. Maternity is thus determined in antici-' pation by a whole cultural apparatus of rules and prescriptions, it is established by society as a moral fact, and, in all this, the tie of kinship between mother and child is defined by tradition, long before birth, and defined as an individual bond.

At the crisis itself, that is at birth, the ceremonies of purification, the idea of special dangers which unite mother and child and separate them from the rest of the community, customs and usages connected with midwifery and early lactation—this whole cultural apparatus continues to reaffirm and to reshape the bond of maternity, and to individualize it with force and clearness. These anticipatory moral influences always put the responsibility upon one woman and mark her out as the sociological or cultural mother over and above her physiological claims to the title.

All this might appear to refer only to the mother. What about the child? We can indeed completely discount Freud's assumption that there is an innate bond of sexual attraction between mother and child; we must reject further his whole hypothesis of "the return to the womb." With all this we have to credit psychoanalysis with having proved that the earliest infantile experiences, provided that they are not completely broken and obliterated in childhood, form a foundation of the greatest importance for the later individual relationship between the child and its mother.

Now here again, the continuity between prenatal cares, the earliest infantile seclusion of mother and child, and the period of lactation, which in native society is much longer than with us, the continuity of all these experiences and their individual unity is in primitive societies as great as, if not greater than, with us.

And this is the point at which we have to deal with the unprofitable assumption of communal lactation. In the relatively small savage communities where there occur perhaps one or two childbirths in a year within reach of each other the idea of mothers synchronizing conception and pregnancy and clubbing together to carry out lactatory group-motherhood, at the greatest inconvenience to themselves, the babies and the whole community, is so preposterous that even now I cannot think how it could ever have been promulgated by Dr. Rivers and upheld by Mr. Briffault.

As to a "communalizing" adoption, in the first place, even where it is most frequent, as in certain Polynesian and Melanesian communities, it simply substitutes one maternity for another. It proves undoubtedly that cultural parenthood can override the biological basis, but it does not introduce anything even remotely like group-maternity. In fact the severance of one bond before another is established is a further proof of the individuality and exclusiveness of motherhood. In the second place the custom of indiscriminate adoption is prevalent among a few savage societies only.

We can thus say that motherhood is always individual. It is never allowed to remain a mere biological fact. Social and cultural influences always indorse and emphasize the original individuality of the biological fact. These influences are so strong that in the case of adoption they may override the biological tie and substitute a cultural one for it. But statistically speaking, the biological ties are almost invariably merely reinforced, redetermined and remolded by the cultural ones. This remolding makes motherhood in each culture a relationship specific to that culture, different from all other motherhoods, and correlated to the whole social structure of the community. This means that the problem of maternity cannot be dismissed as a zoological fact, that it should be studied by every field-worker in his own area, and that the theory of cultural motherhood should have been made the foundation of the general theory of kinship.

THE PRINCIPLE OF LEGITIMACY AND THE RIGHT TO SEXUAL FREEDOM

What about the father? As far as his biological role is concerned he might well be treated as a drone. His task is to impregnate the female and then to disappear. And yet in all human societies the father is regarded by tradition as indispensable. The woman has to be married before she is allowed legitimately to conceive. Roughly speaking, an unmarried mother is under a ban, a fatherless child is a bastard. This is by no means only a European or a Christian prejudice; it is the attitude found amongst most barbarous and savage peoples as well. Where the unmarried mother is at a premium and her offspring a desirable possession, the father is forced upon them by positive instead of negative sanctions.

Let us put it in more precise and abstract terms. Among the conditions which define conception as a sociologically legitimate fact there is one of fundamental importance. The most important moral and legal rule concerning the physiological side of kinship is that no child should be brought into the world without a man—and one man at that—assuming the role of sociological father, that is, guardian and protector, the male link between the child and the rest of the community.

I think that this generalization amounts to a universal sociological law and as such I have called it in some of my previous writings *The Principle of Legitimacy*.[5] The form which the principle of legitimacy assumes varies according to the laxity or stringency which obtains regarding prenuptial intercourse; according to the value set upon virginity or the contempt for it; according to the ideas held by the natives as to the mechanism of procreation; above all, according as to whether the child is a burden or an asset to its parents. Which means according as to whether the unmarried mother is more attractive because of her offspring or else degraded and ostracized on that account.

Yet through all these variations there runs the rule that the father is indispensable for the full sociological status of the child as well as of its mother, that the group consisting of a woman and her offspring is sociologically incomplete and illegitimate. The father, in other words, is necessary for the full legal status of the family.

In order to understand the nature and importance of the principle of legitimacy it is necessary to discuss the two aspects of procreation which are linked together biologically and culturally, yet linked by nature and culture so differently

[5] Compare article s.v. *Kinship* in the *Encyclopaedia Britannica*, 14th edition; also *Sex and Repression* (1927) and Chapter VI of *The Family Among the Australian Aborigines* (1913). In this latter the relevant facts are presented although the term is not used.

that many difficulties and puzzles have arisen for the anthropologist. Sex and parenthood are obviously linked biologically. Sexual intercourse leads at times to conception. Conception always means pregnancy and pregnancy at times means childbirth. We see that in the chain there are at least two possibilities of a hiatus; sexual intercourse by no means always leads to conception, and pregnancy can be interrupted by abortion and thus not lead to childbirth.

The moral, customary, and legal rules of most human communities step in, taking advantage of the two weak links in the chain, and in a most remarkable manner dissociate the two sides of procreation, that is sex and parenthood. Broadly speaking, it may be said that freedom of intercourse though not universally is yet generally prevalent in human societies. Freedom of conception, outside marriage is, however, never allowed, or at least in extremely few communities and under very exceptional circumstances.

Briefly to substantiate this statement: it is clear that in those societies, primitive and civilized, where prenuptial intercourse is regarded as immoral and illegitimate, marriage is the *conditio sine qua non* of legitimate children—that is children having full social status in the community.

In the second place, in most communities which regard prenuptial intercourse as perfectly legitimate, marriage is still regarded as essential to equip the child with a full tribal position. This is very often achieved without any punitive sanctions, by the mere fact that as soon as pregnancy sets in a girl and her lover have to marry. Often, in fact, pregnancy is a prerequisite of marriage or the final legal symptom of its conclusion.

There are tribes again, where an unmarried mother is definitely penalized and so are her children. What is done under such conditions by lovers who want to live together sexually and yet not to produce children is difficult to say. Having had in my own field-work to deal with the case in point, I was yet unable to arrive at a satisfactory solution. Contraceptives, I am firmly convinced, do not exist in Melanesia, and abortion is not sufficiently frequent to account for the great scarcity of illegitimate children. As a hypothesis, I venture to submit that promiscuous intercourse, while it lasts, reduces the fertility of women. If this side of the whole question still remains a puzzle it only proves that more research, both physiological and sociological, must be done in order fully to throw light upon the principle of legitimacy.

There is still one type of social mechanism through which the principle of legitimacy operates, and that is under conditions where a child is an asset. There an unmarried mother need not trouble about her sociological status, because the fact of having children only makes her the more desirable, and she speedily acquires a husband. He will not trouble whether the child is the result of his love-making or not. But whether the male is primed to assume his paternity, or whether child and mother are penalized, the principle of legitimacy obtains throughout mankind; the group of mother and child is incomplete and the sociological position of the father is regarded universally as indispensable.

THE CONTROL OF SEXUALITY
BY PARENTHOOD

Liberty of parenthood, therefore, is not identical with liberty of sexual intercourse. And the principle of legitimacy leads us to another very important generalization, namely, that the relations of sexuality to parenthood must be studied with reference to the only relevant link: marriage, conceived as a contract legitimizing offspring.

From the foregoing considerations, it is clear that marriage cannot be defined as the licensing of sexual intercourse, but rather as the licensing of parenthood.

Since marriage is the institution through which the inchoate, at times even disruptive, drives of sex are transformed and organized into the principal system of social forces, it is clear that sexuality must be discussed, defined and classified in relation to marriage. From our point of view we have to inquire as to what is its function in relation to marriage.

We have first to inquire, is chartered and limited sexual liberty subversive and destructive of marriage and family; does it ever run counter to these institutions? Or, on the contrary, is regulated and limited intercourse outside matrimony one of those cultural arangements which allow a greater stability of marriage and the family, of easier adjustment within it, and of a more suitable choice of partner?

It is obvious that once we erect chastity as a positive ideal, once we accept the Christian principle of monogamous marriage as the only decent way of regarding this institution, we have prejudged all these questions and stultified the whole inquiry. And it is astounding how even those who attack the institutions of Christian morality and marriage and regard themselves as absolutely free of preconceptions, still remain under the influence of the ideal or at least of its pretenses. Thus all sociologists, from Bachofen to Briffault, were inclined to regard communistic orgies, relaxations of the marital tie, forms of prenuptial freedom, as "survivals," as traces of a primeval sexual communism. That, I think, is an entirely wrong view, due to an involuntary tendency to regard sexual intercourse outside marriage as something anomalous, as something which contravenes marriage; a view directly implied in our Christian ideal of monogamy.

Let us look at facts in the correct perspective; see, that is, how sexuality is related to marriage in various primitive communities. Let us first classify the various types of regulation in relation to marriage. Those communities where virginity is a prerequisite of decent and legal marriage, where it is enforced by such surgical operations as infibulation; where wives are jealously guarded and adultery is a rigorously punished offense—those communities present no problem to us. There sex is as absolutely subordinated to marriage as in the Christian monogamous ideal, and far more so than in our Western practice. But such communities are comparatively rare, especially at a primitive level, and generally we find some form of customary license outside marriage.

Here again we must distinguish with direct reference to marriage, which really means to parenthood. Prenuptial license, that is, the liberty of free intercourse given to unmarried youths and girls, is by far the most prevalent form of chartered freedom, as well as the most important. What is its normal course and how is it related to marriage? Does it as a rule develop habits of profligacy; does it lead to a more and more promiscuous attitude?

lawful as wives or lovers; where the taboos of occupation, of status, of family and of special occasions considerably restrict the opportunities of intercourse; in communities where there exists the severest code of conduct in public and private, imposed upon husband and wife, brother and sister, and people standing in definite kinship relations—in such communities it is clear that repression acts with at least as great a force as with us. And this means that the forces of reaction against the trammels and restraints imposed by society are very powerful. Thus sex, throughout humanity, is regulated; there are restrictions as well as liberties and the institutions which allow of the latter can only be understood in their function when we refer them to the fundamental procreative institutions—those of family and marriage.

We see, therefore, that parenthood and marriage furnish the key to the functional understanding of regulated sexuality. We see that sexual regulations, the liberties and the taboos, constitute the road to marriage and the way of escape from its too rigid bonds and consequent tragic complications. The sexual impulse has to be selective in human as well as in animal communities, but its selectiveness under culture is more complicated in that it has to involve cultural as well as biological values. Trial and error are necessary and with this is definitely connected the interest in variation and impulse towards novelty. To satisfy the fundamental function of sex we have the institution which makes full sex, that is parenthood, exclusive and individual. To satisfy the correlated selective components of sex, we have the dependent institutions of regulated license. To sum up, we have found that parenthood gives us the key to marriage, through the principle of legitimacy, and that marriage is the key to a right understanding of sexual customs. It may be added at once that the dissociation of some sexual experiences from the primitive idea of marriage, coupled with the real interrelation of the two, yields to the sociologist an interesting background for the consideration of modern problems of sexuality, marriage and divorce.

Illegitimacy in the Caribbean
Social Structure

WILLIAM J. GOODE

Over a generation ago Malinowski enunciated a principle which he said amounted to a universal sociological law, that "no child should be brought into the world without a man— and one man at that—assuming the role of sociological father. . . ."[1] This rule is not based on the social disapproval of premarital or extramarital sexual freedom. Malinowski's Trobrianders, for example, indulged in considerable sex play before marriage, but were shocked at illegitimacy. Rather, the rule expresses the interest of the society in fixing responsibility for the child upon a specific individual. Marriage, therefore, is not primarily the legitimation of sex, but the legitimation of parenthood.[2] Whether Malinowski's principle is indeed a universal sociological law has not been analyzed, except to

REPRINTED FROM *The American Sociological Review,* Vol. XXV, No. 1 (February, 1960), pp. 21–30, by permission of the author and the publisher. (Copyright, 1960, by The American Sociological Association).

[1] Bronislaw Malinowski, "Parenthood, the Basis of Social Structure," in V. F. Calverton and Samuel D. Schmalhausen, editors, *The New Generation,* New York: Macaulay, 1930, pp. 137–138.

[2] Malinowski was puzzled as to how the Trobrianders could be sexually so free without numerous illegitimates, especially since they denied any connection between sexual intercourse and pregnancy and took no contraceptive precautions. It was not until W. F. Ashley-Montagu's *Coming Into Being Among the Australian Aborigines,* London: Routledge, 1937, that the solution seemed to be clear.

See also M. F. Ashley-Montagu, *The Reproductive Development of the Female,* New York: Julian, 1957.

the degree that the recurring debate as to whether the "nuclear family" is universal implicitly includes that principle.[3] It seems safe enough to claim at least that all societies have family systems and that possibly a sociological father is required everywhere.[4]

ILLEGITIMACY IN THE CARIBBEAN

Malinowski's principle is not refuted by data from the United States or Western Europe, where illegitimacy rates range from perhaps four or five per cent to about eleven per cent.[5] However, in the Caribbean area illegitimacy rates are often over fifty per cent, as Table 1 shows.

Under such conditions, doubt may be raised as to whether a "sociological father" exists, and indeed various writers have spoken of a "matrifocal family."[6] Certainly so high a rate of

[3] For a recent discussion of this point, see Melford E. Spiro, "Is the Family Universal?" *American Anthropologist,* 56 (October, 1954), pp. 839–846.

[4] The most notable case which raises doubts is the Nayar of Malabar Strait. See K. M. Panikkar, "Some Aspects of Nayar Life," *Journal of the Royal Anthropological Institute,* 48 (July–December, 1918), esp. pp. 260 ff; E. Kathleen Gough, "Changing Kinship Usages in the Setting of Political and Economic Change among the Nayar of Malabar," *Journal of the Royal Anthropological Institute,* 81 (Parts I and II, 1951), pp. 71–88. Gough's latest report ("The Nayars and the Definition of Marriage," *Journal of the Royal Anthropological Institute,* 89 [1959], p. 31) asserts that Nayar marriage does establish paternity legally. Another possible case is the Minang-Kabau; see E. N. Loeb, "Patrilineal and Matrilineal Organization in Sumatra, Part 2," *American Anthropologist,* 36 (January–March, 1934), pp. 26–56.

[5] In Iceland, illegitimate births constituted 27.9 per cent of live births in 1950, and the rate in Stockholm and a few other areas in Sweden has remained at about 15 per cent in recent years. Cf. Meyer Nimkoff, "Illegitimacy," *Encyclopaedia Britannica,* 1954.

[6] "One of the regularities of social organization, which has appeared in the literature from Herskovits to Henriques, is the concept of the 'matrifocal' family." Vera Rubin, "Cultural Perspectives in Caribbean Research," in Vera Rubin, editor, *Caribbean Studies: A Symposium,* Jamaica: Institute of Social and Economic Research, 1957, p. 117. Such comments are often applicable as well to one period in the development of the Negro family in this country. Cf. E. Franklin Frazier, *The Negro Family in the United States,* New York: Dryden, revised edition, 1948, Part 2, "In the House of the Mother."

deviation would suggest that the norm, if it does exist, might have a very different meaning than in a society in which the rate is less, say, then ten per cent. But we must keep in mind that Malinowski was stating a proposition about a *cultural*

TABLE 1.   Illegitimacy Rates in Selected Caribbean Political Units

Political Unit	Year	Per cent
British Guiana	1955	35
French Guiana	1956	65
Surinam (excluding Bush Negroes and aborigines)	1953	34
Barbados	1957	70
Bermuda	1957	30
Dominican Republic	1957	61
Guadeloupe	1956	42
Jamaica	1954	72
Antigua	1957	65
Martinique	1956	48
Trinidad and Tobago	1956	47
Grenada	1957	71
Puerto Rico	1955	28
Haiti	—	67–85

a All figures except those for Puerto Rico, British Guiana, Surinam, Dominican Republic, Trinidad and Tobago, Grenada, and Haiti were taken from the United Nations Year Book Questionnaire for the years in question. Data were furnished to the U.N. by the statistical offices of the country, and contain all the errors of their own registration procedures. Data for other countries, excluding Haiti and the Dominican Republic, were kindly furnished by the Caribbean Commission. The Dirección General de Estadística of the Dominican Republic graciously sent me the figure for 1957. I have found no recent figure for Cuba; presumably it was 30 per cent in 1939. For Surinam, Rudolf van Lier, *Samenleving in ein Gransgebied*, 's-Gravenhage: Martinus Nijhoff, 1949, p. 287, gives 70 per cent for 1940. The rate has also dropped in British Guiana from the 41 per cent reported in 1946 in *British Guiana Annual Report of the Registrar-General, 1954*, Georgetown, Demerara, British Guiana, 1956, p. 9. I have found no official figure for Haiti. Bastien reports two-thirds for Marbial (Remy Bastien, *La Familia Rural Haitiana*, Mexico: Libra, 1951, p. 85); George E. Simpson reports about 85 per cent for one Haitian area in "Sexual and Family Institutions in Northern Haiti," *American Anthropologist*, 44 (October-December, 1942), p. 664.

element: he asserted that the *norm* would be always be found, not that the members of the society would obey it under specified conditions.

It is precisely with reference to Malinowski's principle that many students of the Caribbean have taken an opposing position—without developing its implications for family theory.

The claim has often been made for various Caribbean lands that when a couple is living together in a consensual union "the family may be said to exist in much the same way as it does in peasant communities throughout the world,"[7] and the child therefore suffers no disadvantage from being illegitimate.[8] Henriques, also writing about Jamaica, comments that there is no moral sanction against "concubinage," by which he means a man and woman keeping house together and raising children, and even claims that respectable black people would rather have their daughter become mistress or concubine to a white or fair colored man than marry a black one.[9] Otherwise put, the consensual union is the marriage form of the lower classes in the Caribbean, and is "sociologically as legitimate" as a legal union. It is, in short, a "cultural alternative," as permissible a way of founding a family as any other.[10] If this interpretation is correct, Malinowski's principle would be erroneous, and one of the apparently major functions of the father would have to be redefined as unessential.

Comments similar to those given above about Jamaica have been made about other Caribbean areas. Herskovits and Herskovits make a similar claim for Trinidad, noting what a "false perspective on the thinking of the people is given by the application of legal terms such as 'legitimate' and 'illegitimate' to the offspring."[11] Similarly, they assert that "there is no social disability imposed by the community because of legitimacy or illegitimacy."[12] The common-law marriage is for many the accepted form.[13]

With respect to Haitian children of a placée union which

[7] T. S. Simey, *Welfare and Planning in the West Indies,* Oxford: Clarendon Press, 1956, p. 15.

[8] "The fact of illegitimate birth is one completely taken for granted. An illegitimate child does not consider himself disadvantaged. . . ." *Ibid.,* p. 88.

[9] Fernando Henriques, *Family and Colour in Jamaica,* London: Eyre and Spottiswoode, 1953, pp. 87, 90.

[10] "Thus, the matrifocal family . . . is a subcultural norm. . . ." John V. Murra, "Discussion," in *Caribbean Studies, op. cit.,* p. 76.

[11] Melville J. Herskovits and Frances S. Herskovits, *Trinidad Village,* New York: Knopf, 1947, p. 17.

[12] *Ibid.,* pp. 82–83; see also p. 107.

[13] Lloyd Braithwaite, "Social Stratification in Trinidad," *Social and Economic Studies,* 2 (October, 1953), p. 125.

is legalized, of a legal union, or of a union outside of an existing marriage the claim is made that "none of these classes of children are at any special social disadvantage."[14] With reference to the forms of Haitian unions: "In the main, especially in the countryside, socially sanctioned matings which do not enjoy the approval of the Church endure as long and hold as respected a place in the community. . . ."[15] In a parallel vein, Bastien remarks that when a man has "good intentions" with respect to a girl, but does not have enough money with which to marry, he may "establish himself" with the girl, with marriage as a publicly acknowledged, later goal, but does not thereby "incur the scorn of the community."[16]

In Martinique, we are told, in place of the rule of legitimacy, which is absent here, other values have emerged such as ingroup solidarity, status equality, and conviviality, which express family organization.[17] There is "no unequivocally preferred type of bond between parents."[18] The legitimate and illegitimate share the same status.

Although the illegitimacy rate in Puerto Rico is lower than in the areas noted above, here too the claim has been made that the rule of legitimacy fails. It is said of the consensual union that it is "a cultural alternative," that is, marriage is split into two culturally permissible alternatives.[19] Similarly, ". . . the prevalence of consensual unions ought to be considered in terms of local lower-class conceptions of what is considered 'moral.' " It is not that the lower class prefer illegal behavior, but that consensual unions are not seen as immoral.[20] It is asserted, too, that "the consensual union is con-

[14] Melville J. Herskovits, *Life in a Haitian Valley*, New York: Knopf, 1937, p. 118.

[15] *Ibid.*, p. 106.

[16] Bastien, *op. cit.*, pp. 72–73. However, Bastien also presents the prestige rankings of the three forms of matings.

[17] Mariam Kreiselman, *The Caribbean Family. A Case Study in Martinique*, Columbia University, Ph.D. thesis, 1958, pp. 271, 292.

[18] *Ibid.*, p. viii.

[19] J. Mayone Stycos, *Family and Fertility in Puerto Rico*, New York: Columbia University Press, 1955, p. 110. I assume here the meaning of "culturally equivalent" or "normatively equal."

[20] Sidney W. Mintz, "Cañamelar, The Subculture of a Rural Sugar Plantation Proletariat," in Julian Steward *et al.*, *The People of Puerto Rico*, Urbana: University of Illinois Press, 1956, p. 377.

sidered a binding marriage truly cemented at the birth of the first child."[21]

At first glance, then, Malinowski's rule of legitimacy is refuted. A substantial number of societies in the West appear not to accept the norm. If this is the case, then several fundamental notions in family theory would have to be discarded.

Yet a closer examination of these and other reports prove conclusively that the norm exists, since in fact marriage is the ideal, and those who violate the rule do suffer penalties. The fact that perhaps a majority of certain of these populations do live in unions outside marriage, at some time in their lives, does not change the normative status of the rule. On the other hand, as we shall later indicate, Malinowski's rule must nevertheless be reformulated.

Let us first look more closely at Jamaica. As against the assertion that illegitimacy is not stigmatized, we note the opposing facts. Both upper- and middle-class opinion is set against "concubinage."[22] The priests may shame the couple about the matter. When a young girl is found to be pregnant, her family is angry.[23] Few men (Rocky Roads) allow their women to bring their illegitimate children into the union, if they do marry.[24] In the same community, illegitimate children are subjected to more physical rejection and pressures of sibling rivalry.[25] Moreover, as individuals move through the life cycle, an increasing proportion are actually married, a phenomenon which would be inexplicable if the consensual unions were backed by a set of alternative norms. This process is illustrated by the proportions of persons ever married by selected ages in the major areas of the British West Indies, as shown in Table 2.[26] Thus, though the average British West

[21] Robert A. Manners, "Tabara: Subcultures of a Tobacco and Mixed Crop Municipality," in *The People of Puerto Rico, op. cit.*, p. 144.

[22] Henriques, *op. cit.*, pp. 87, 164.

[23] *Ibid.*, p. 88. See also Edith Clarke, *My Mother Who Fathered Me*, London: Allen & Unwin, 1957, p. 99; and Kreiselman, *op. cit.*, p. 189.

[24] Yehudi Cohen, "Structure and Function: Family Organization and Socialization in a Jamaican Community," *American Anthropologist*, 58 (August, 1956), p. 669.

[25] *Ibid.*, p. 672.

[26] G. W. Roberts, "Some Aspects of Mating and Fertility in the West Indies," *Population Studies*, 8 (March, 1955), p. 223. The figures for Jamaica in Table 2 presumably refer to 1943.

Indian ages at marriage are among the highest in the world (for example, for Jamaica, 34.1 years for males; for Barbados, 31.7, and for Grenada, 33.0[27]), most individuals do marry. In sum, these various mating forms are "not regarded as alternative forms of conjugal associations between which any individual was free to choose."[28]

TABLE 2.   British West Indies: Per Cent of Males Ever
Married by Age, 1946

Age	Jamaica	Barbados	Windwards	Leewards
20–24	10.1	8.5	4.1	4.0
25–34	21.0	37.6	27.6	27.3
35–44	41.9	61.7	54.9	53.4
45–54	55.0	70.8	68.2	63.7
55–64	66.3	75.2	78.4	75.5
65 and over	74.7	85.2	83.1	78.9

Similarly, in Trinidad, a couple may finally marry after living together for some time, "for the position it gives the family." Among other things, "marriage is . . . a prestige phenomenon in terms of social or religious values." Though a couple will usually begin life together as "keepers," "such an episode is outside correct procedure." The unmarried keeper woman wears no ring, and only the married woman is called *Madam*.[29] Many people who rise in class find that their new rank is incompatible with the type of union they once

[27] *Ibid.*, p. 205. More fundamental data are the actual expressions of norms and ideals, to be found in Judith Blake's *Family Structure: The Social Context of Reproduction*, Ph.D. thesis, Columbia University, 1959, a study of the lower class Jamaican family. It is the first detailed investigation of the mechanisms through which the norms lose much of their coercive power. For a preliminary report from this study, see Blake, "Family Instability and Reproductive Behavior in Jamaica," *Current Research in Human Fertility*, New York: Milbank Fund, 1955, pp. 24–41.

[28] Clarke, *op. cit.*, pp. 77–78. It is significant that Clarke and Blake, who appear to be the only investigators to take seriously the Jamaican's *own* normative statements, assert unequivocally the normative underpinnings of a legal marriage.

[29] Herskovits and Herskovits, *op. cit.*, pp. 82, 84, 87, 93–94.

entered. Moreover, when working-class women quarrel, one may point out that the other is not properly married.[30]

Although the case of Haiti seems more complex, the same conclusion seems inescapable. The prestige from the legal, Church union is of sufficient significance to "motivate weddings at which the children and even children of the principals act as attendants."[31] The legal union cannot be broken as easily as the plaçage. When the unmarried girl becomes pregnant, she is beaten.[32] The woman in a placée union cannot demand as much from her man, and her children have no right to the name of the father.[33] Most persons would prefer to marry, and this is especially true of women.[34] Contemporary pressures are increasing the proportion who marry, but some gradations of prestige remain.[35] The plaçage is not stable: "perhaps three-fourths of the peasant men, and possibly more, have or have had at one time one or more mates in addition to a legal wife or *femme caille*."[36] "The consciousness of their social inferiority so troubles . . . [them] . . . that few resist the temptation to explain the cause of their situation. . . ."[37]

In Martinique, too, parents are angry at the pregnancy of the unmarried girl, who may have to leave her home. When talking about the consensual relationships of others, the term "concubine" is used. Many men will promise marriage, but deceive the girl. In a few reported cases of girls having babies,

---

[30] Lloyd Braithwaite, "Social Stratification in Trinidad," *Social and Economic Studies*, 2 (October, 1953), pp. 125, 126.

[31] Herskovits, *op. cit.*, pp. 106, 107.

[32] *Ibid.*, p. 110; George Eaton Simpson, "Sexual and Familial Institutions in Northern Haiti," *American Anthropologist*, 44 (October-December, 1942), p. 665.

[33] Herskovits, *op. cit.*, pp. 116, 119.

[34] Simpson, *op. cit.*, pp. 655, 658.

[35] Rhoda Metraux, *Kith and Kin*, Ph.D. thesis, Columbia University, 1951, pp. 197, 205–209.

[36] Simpson, *op. cit.*, p. 656. The *femme caille* shares her consort's house. Bastien, *op. cit.*, p. 73, gives three main categories of unions, in order of social rank: (1) marriage; (2) a union established with the idea of later marriage; and (3) the ordinary plaçage, some forms of which involve several women living apart from one another.

[37] Bastien, *op. cit.*, p. 73.

the parents pretended that the children were their own.[38] The consensual union is easily dissolved, and no social obligations are incurred by entering it.[39]

Perhaps more conclusive for Martinique is an important finding, which grew out of an effort to understand the *fête*. In possibly every study of illegitimacy in the Caribbean, people are described as saying—most researchers have accepted this assertion—that they cannot marry because they cannot afford the wedding feast, without which the ceremony is a mockery. The couple will be laughed at later. The "cost of the wedding" is not the church expenses; in every country the Catholic Church (or others, where they are important) has offered nearly free weddings—but with rare acceptance. A few observers have doubted that the expense of the *fête* was the crucial item, even though it is substantial, emphasizing rather that the *fête* is an expression of community solidarity, a *rite de passage,* and a community validation of the union. Kreiselman is unique among observers in offering and, within limits, testing the hypothesis that most persons who can afford to live *en ménage* can also afford a *fête* and therefore a marriage, but that most who do not marry early or later do not have the same rank.[40]

Whether the rank differences among people of a lower stratum are so crucial, and whether a broad sample of stable consensual unions would show that it is mainly those of equal status who marry, remains to be seen. But if this is the case even in Capesterre (Martinique), the relationship shows that the rule of legitimacy holds there. For the rule has as a major function the prevention of unions between wrong lineages, and in nearly every society the rules of marriage serve to confine legal unions mainly to men and women of equal rank.[41]

[38] Kreiselman, *op. cit.,* pp. 189, 223, 201, 191, 188.

[39] *Ibid.,* p. 231. All unions involve social obligations, of course, but the fact that the investigator makes this observation underlines the lack of community support for this type of union.

[40] *Ibid.,* pp. 221–231. After a long consensual union, may marriage occur because the man and woman come to have the same rank?

[41] Perhaps the Natchez were an exception. See Kingsley Davis, "Intermarriage in Caste Societies," *American Anthropologist,* 43 (July-September, 1941), pp. 382 ff. Of course, a "free courtship system" achieves the same end; and one may date a person whom one may not marry without censure.

In Puerto Rico, there is social disapproval of the consensual
union, even though the sanction does not necessarily lead to
conformity. Fathers become angry when their daughters
elope, and almost everyone pays "lip service" to the superiority
of marriage.[42] People may say that they get married in order
to baptize the children.[43] Girls have "idealized feelings" about
marriage ceremonies,[44] and often the girls' parents request or
insist upon legal unions.[45]

Two-thirds of both men and women in a national sample
of Puerto Rico said that a consensual union is a bad life for
a man, and over 80 per cent of the respondents made the same
assertion for women.[46] Perhaps a more penetrating test of the
normative status of the consensual union may be found in the
attitudes expressed about a *daughter* entering a consensual
union: only 7.4 per cent of the men and 5.5 per cent of the
women admitted that this arrangement would either be "all
right" or that "it's up to her; doesn't matter."[47]

We are similarly told that in British Guiana the children
born outside wedlock "are not sharply differentiated by any
stigma of illegitimacy," while the consensual union is a "socially sanctioned one," and "part of the lower-class tradition."[48]
Once again, however, we can note that parents are angry at
the daughter and beat her when she becomes pregnant while
still in the home. An unmarried mother will usually ask another person to take her illegitimate child to church for

---

[42] Stycos, *op. cit.*, pp. 108, 110–111.

[43] Eric R. Wolf, "San José: Subcultures of a 'Traditional' Coffee
Municipality," in *The People of Puerto Rico, op. cit.*, p. 220. In Puerto
Rico, the girl is usually a virgin when she enters a consensual union.
Bastien makes the same claim for the Marbial area in Haiti, but to my
knowledge no observer of other Haitian areas has done so; and Bastien is
inconsistent. See Bastien, *op. cit.*, pp. 64, 65, 72.

[44] Mintz, *op. cit.*, p. 378.

[45] Elena Padilla Seda, "Nocora: The Subculture of Workers on a
Government-Owned Sugar Plantation," in *The People of Puerto Rico,
op. cit.*, p. 293.

[46] Paul K. Hatt, *Backgrounds of Human Fertility in Puerto Rico*,
Princeton: Princeton University Press, 1952, p. 127.

[47] *Ibid.*, p. 64. I would suppose, however, that the percentage would
be much less on the mainland of the United States.

[48] Raymond T. Smith, *The Negro Family in British Guiana*, New
York: Grove Press, 1956, pp. 109, 149, 182.

baptism.[49] And, although the scholar here quoted agrees with
a turn-of-the-century French writer on the Congo who asserted
that among the Bavili "birth sanctifies the child," a man's
"outside" children in British Guiana do not rank equally with
his legitimate children, and not all of a woman's children
remain with her in a new marital union.[50] Moreover, only the
married woman is called "Mistress," while her marital rights
are clearer and more secure.[51] Marriage confers a different
status on the woman. Women wish to marry, and after they
have begun to have illegitimate children they understand that
they can achieve this status only by gambling that a quasi-
marital union may develop into a marriage.[52] Finally, most
people do marry eventually, and the legal, monogamic union
is clearly the ideal.[53]

DIFFERENTIAL INTENSITY OF NORM
COMMITMENT

Several conclusions and problems emerge from such a
confrontation of general assertions with specific observations.
In order to proceed to further related propositions, these conclusions may be summarized: (1) Unequivocally, Malinowski's Principle of Legitimacy holds even for these societies,
for which various observers have asserted that it did not hold.
Birth out of wedlock is not a "cultural alternative." There is
no special approval of the consensual union, no "counter-
norm" in favor of such a union. Of course, the parental anger
aroused by a clandestine pregnancy will not be repeated when
the girl has entered a consensual union. Nevertheless, in none
of these societies does the unmarried mother or her child
enjoy the same status as the married mother and her legitimate children. A union based on a marriage enjoys more

[49] Ibid., pp. 126, 145, 132.
[50] Ibid., pp. 102, 120, 156, 178.
[51] Ibid., pp. 179–180; see also pp. 59, 148–149.
[52] Ibid., p. 138. The highest illegitimacy rate occurs among births to
females 15–19 years of age; British Guiana, Annual Report . . . , op.
cit., p. 9.
[53] Ibid., Chapter 5.

respect than do other types of unions. (2) Equally clear, however, is the corroboration of another principle: that the degree of norm commitment varies from one segment of the population to another. Not only do some individuals reject particular norms, but the members of some strata are less concerned than those of others about given norms.[54] (3) A more specific inference from the latter principle is also corroborated, namely, that the lower social strata are less committed than the middle or upper strata to a variety of family norms, in this instance that of legitimacy,[55] and also obey them less.

More important, however, is a reformulation of Malinowski's principle. As stated, it gives too little emphasis to the real foundation on which it rests, and ignores the differences in norm commitment among different strata, doubtless because neither problem was important in the societies with which Malinowski was concerned. The principle in fact rests primarily upon the function of status placement, not that of locating a father as "protector": the bastard daughter of a count is still illegitimate even if he "protects" her. Violation of the norm creates some status ambiguity with respect to the child, the parents, and the two kin lines. Consequently, (4) commitment to the norm of legitimacy will be greater among the strata *or* kin lines which enjoy a higher prestige, or in which concern with the kin relation is higher. Although in general this concern is more marked in the upper strata, in every stratum there will be *some* family lines which possess "traditions," pride, a sense of kin identity, and so on. Illegitimacy rates can be expected to be higher among the lower strata in all societies. (5) Correlatively, to the extent that a

[54] Thus, one can find individuals who specifically reject marriage for one reason or another in all these societies. However, the empirical question is: what percentage of the society or stratum? In our society, too, any public opinion poll will locate a few such individuals.

[55] There is substantial literature on this point. See, e.g., William J. Goode, *After Divorce,* Glencoe, Ill.: Free Press, 1956, Chapters 4 and 5; Ruth S. Cavan, *The Family,* New York: Crowell, 1953, Chapters 5, 6, and 7; and William F. Whyte, "A Slum Sex Code," *American Journal of Sociology,* 49 (July, 1943), pp. 24–31. For other data relevant to the subsequent discussion, see Herbert Hyman, "The Value Systems of Different Classes . . . ," in R. Bendix and S. M. Lipset, editors, *Class, Status, and Power,* Glencoe, Ill.: Free Press, 1953, pp. 426–442.

given society possesses a high proportion of lower strata families who are concerned little or not at all with their lineage, that society will exhibit a higher total rate of illegitimacy than it would have if the proportion were lower.

Given a high rate of illegitimacy, two further inferences may be made. (6) The actual amount of stigma suffered by the average illegitimate child cannot be great, relative to legitimate children in his same stratum and neighborhood. (7) The "matrifocality" of the Caribbean family is merely the result of the mother being left with her children, by either a casual lover, a consensual partner, or husband. The "matriarch" who is in charge has power precisely because no other adult of her generation is there to exercise it. Very likely a different personality configuration as well as a different self-image can and sometimes does develop from this experience.[56] The loyalty of children to the mother is stronger under such a system, since the father is not likely to be around during much of the infancy and youth of the off-spring.[57]

On the other hand, early in the union, or continuously when the father remains in the union, the male behaves in a fashion which might be called "patriarchal" in the United States. It is possible that some observers have been misled, in their evaluation of the mother's power, by a false image of male behavior in such patriarchal societies as Japan, China, and India, where in fact the older mother is likely to have great authority in the home even when she pays considerable overt deference to the male head of family.

---

[56] Nor should the matter of *self-selection* be forgotten. Given the social option, some individuals will find this role more congenial and choose it against other alternatives.

[57] Although almost every writer points to "some" consensual unions which have "lasted as long as" legal ones, the instability of both types seems indubitable, and consensual unions are less stable; see R. T. Smith, "Family Organization in British Guiana," *Social and Economic Studies,* 1 (No. 1, 1953), p. 101; Simpson, *op. cit.,* p. 656; Braithwaite, *op. cit.,* p. 147; Seda, *op. cit.,* p. 293; Mintz, *op. cit.,* p. 375; Stycos, *op. cit.,* p. 119; Simey, *op. cit.,* p. 16. (Kreiselman, by contrast, asserts stability for both types: *op. cit.,* p. 180.) That matrifocality is by default has been noted by others, e.g., Kreiselman, *op. cit.,* p. 282; Simey, *op. cit.,* p. 43; Braithwaite, *op. cit.,* p. 147.

ROLE BARGAINING AND ILLEGITIMACY

An "explanation" of these high rates may properly take two directions. One of these would widen our empirical perspective to include other areas of the world, especially the country south of the Rio Grande where high illegitimacy rates are found, and locate the cultural elements which are common to them. In a related paper, I am making such an analysis, with special reference to the culture structure of a society and conformity to its norms. This analysis seeks to answer the question: in what types of societies are high rates found?

The second direction is to focus on the more immediate social forces which create a high illegitimacy rate in the Caribbean. It may be granted that the lower norm commitment in the lower strata of this area would, other things being equal, decrease conformity. Intensity of norm commitment, however, is only one element in the decision to risk pregnancy. The social pattern of primary importance is that the young woman in her courtship behavior must make essentially an *individual role bargain*. This apparent contrast with courtship patterns which produce low illegitimacy rates requires only little attention.

By "making an individual role bargain," I refer to the fact that in any role relationship both ego and alter are restricted in what services they may agree to perform for one another, by the expectations of others and thus by the sanctions which others will apply. For example, father and daughter owe, and feel they owe, certain obligations to one another, and in part these obligations are met because of the rewards and sanctions which either can direct toward the other. However, even if both of them are willing to agree to a different set of obligations—say, those appropriate to lovers—there is a "third layer" of persons who have role relationships with either ego and alter, or both of them, and who will act to force both of them to perform properly. These actions include pressures on ego or alter to punish the other for improper performance.

All courtship systems are market systems, in which role

bargains are struck. They differ from one another with respect to the commodities which are more or less valuable on that market (beauty, personality, kinship position, family prestige, wealth) and who has the authority to do the marketing. Modern Western societies seem to constitute the only major historical civilization in which youngsters have been given a substantial voice in this bargaining (Imperial Rome might be added by some historians). Even in the U.S., however, where this trend is most fully developed, numerous studies have shown that youngsters make their choices within a highly restricted market, with respect to age, race, religion, social class, and so on. Precisely because courtship systems are bargaining systems, apparently hypergamous marriages (the woman marries upward in class) usually are, in most societies, unions in which a high ranking on one or more variables (wealth, beauty) is traded for a high ranking on other variables (power, prestige, race).[58] As a consequence, most marriages occur between individuals of like rank, or at least like bargaining power,[59] whether youngsters or their elders have the greater authority to conduct the bargaining process. When one party has much less bargaining power, he may be unable to pay as much as the other demands, or will have to pay much more than another family with greater bargaining power.

Although these principles hold with respect to both the choice of marital partner and the decision to marry at all, they are upheld, as is any market system, by a set of community-wide or stratum-wide set of agreements about *what* is valuable and *how* valuable those characteristics are, and a set of corresponding pressures which prevent the individual from paying too much. In our society, for example, even if a middle-class girl is willing to bear a child outside of marriage, usually her parents will oppose this behavior strongly because she would be giving more than need be under the operating market system.

[58] See Davis, *op. cit.*, p. 386.

[59] Of course, the principle of least interest operates in courtship as in marital conflict; the individual who is more deeply in love has less bargaining power. Willard Waller and Reuben Hill, *The Family: A Dynamic Interpretation*, New York: Dryden, 1953, pp. 190–192.

By contrast, what is striking in the Caribbean community studies are the anonymity and isolation within which the decision is made to enter a union, and the fact that under those social conditions the girl has little chance of being married at all unless she is willing to risk a union outside of marriage. Not only does she become pregnant without her parents' knowing that she is courting, but she is also likely to enter the consensual union without any prior ritual or public announcement.[60]

A synthesis of the factors of importance in the decision to marry or to enter a consensual union can be made from the existing studies (although in many cases needed data are lacking because the appropriate questions were not asked[61]). Especially important are the following five points:

1. The class pattern of marriage has been suggested above. This may be clarified here by noting that not only do middle- and upper-class individuals marry (though of course males from those strata may have mistresses whom they do not marry), but that most members of the lower strata also marry eventually. Some lower-class persons never enter a consensual union, but begin their conjugal career by a wedding. Others begin with a consensual union, but marry sooner or later, usually after the male has somewhat improved his social position. In certain communities which seem to enjoy a higher social standing, a substantial majority of all marital unions are legal.[62]

2. Kreiselman's finding for Martinique concerning marriages between persons of similar rank can be extended to every Caribbean community. Notwithstanding the frequently voiced assumption to the contrary, many fine distinctions of prestige are made within the lower class, in spite of its apparent homogeneity to the (usually White) outside observer.[63] If there were no other index, we could rely on the fact that

[60] Smith, *op. cit.*, pp. 101, 137.

[61] For Jamaica, as noted in footnote 28, the most complete synthesis has been made by Blake, *op. cit.*

[62] E.g., Orange Grove reported in Clarke, *op. cit.*; Better Hope reported in Smith, *op. cit.*; and apparently San José as reported in Wolf, *op. cit.*

[63] For example, although Smith, *op. cit.*, pp. 218–220 *et passim*, refers to a lack of status differentiation, his detailed descriptions show considerable differentiation.

certain members of the lower class do marry without entering a consensual union.[64] However, other data are also available, for example, the higher ranking of unskilled laborers with *steady* jobs. Granted, these differences are less sharp or refined than the gross differences between upper and lower strata, but within the narrower class horizon of persons in the bottom stratum they may nevertheless loom large. From this fact, we can suppose that when marriage does occur, the man and woman are more likely to be "rank equals," within the more generalized terms proposed above—which include not merely family prestige but also personal qualities such as beauty.[65]

3. Given a system in which consensual unions are common, it follows that the punishments for entering them cannot be severe, and the rewards for marrying cannot be great. (This proposition is an inference from a well-known principle of social control.) Consequently, the girl's parents or relatives (there is no extended kin group which acts as a unit) are punished or rewarded very little if, in turn, they make or fail to make her behavior conform to "ideal" norms.

4. In the Caribbean, there is no "free" adolescent courtship system such as our own, in which an as yet ineligible male is permitted to approach an immature girl, under the protection of her relatives and peer group. Many or most of the men she first meets are ineligible because of the great cost of a wedding. Most of them have not accumulated enough wealth to finance the formal union and to support its subsequent requirement of a higher level of living than a consensual union.[66] Consequently, the girl's first love and sex contacts occur away from home, and without the knowledge of the family. These first contacts take place essentially in social anonymity, so that she must make the best bargain

[64] See, for example, Smith's description (*ibid.*, pp. 169–170) of a formal engagement; Seda's comment that parents may insist on a wedding ceremony (*op. cit.*, p. 293); and Clarke, *op. cit.*, pp. 85–88.

[65] Here the variable of rank is generalized, of course, and Kreiselman's observation (*op. cit.*, p. 278) from Martinique is extrapolated to the rest of the Caribbean.

[66] Cf. Clarke, *op. cit.*, pp. 78, 99; Herskovits and Herskovits, *op. cit.*, p. 84.

she can, without the family's support.[67] Parental anger, reported in most studies, is at least in part a reaction to the knowledge that the girl has entered the world of adulthood without parental permission and has acted independently while presumably still a child.[68]

5. The Caribbean girl with unusual qualities may be able to demand marriage. However, the average girl has little chance at marriage, early or late, unless she is willing to gamble that a more permanent union will grow from one relationship or another. Without reliable data on the number of unions in the average individual's life, we cannot state what these chances are. Motherhood lowers the girl's value in the market, but if she does not produce a child for the man with whom he is living, or with whom she has a liaison, her chance of a stable union is low.[69] The decision to marry, within the existing social structure, is his rather than hers, and she gains more from marriage than he does. Consequently, as noted previously, it is the women who press toward marriage, while they must take the only road which can—and, apparently, eventually does—lead to marriage. Meanwhile, however, a woman may have children by several men, and may leave some or all of them with her parents or relatives when entering a new union[70]—a practice often resulting in the "grandmother" family. The widespread adoption pattern in the Caribbean is in part a method of taking care of these children. Ideally, a man wants only his own children in his home, especially if he is marrying.

---

[67] Kreiselman, *op. cit.*, p. 99; Herskovits and Herskovits, *op. cit.*, p. 88; Smith, *op. cit.*, pp. 109, 137, 145.

[68] Smith, *op. cit.*, p. 145, makes this point clearly, citing a common statement, "If you want to play a big woman go find yourself a man."

[69] At the same time a pregnancy may frighten him away, as being too great a burden to assume. Clarke, *op. cit.*, pp. 75, 91, 100–102; Smith, *op. cit.*, p. 138. Blake, *op. cit.*, also reports this fact.

[70] Herskovits and Herskovits, *op. cit.*, pp. 104–105, 131; Clark, *op. cit.*, p. 91; Smith, *op. cit.*, Chapter 4.

SUMMARY

Although Malinowski's Principle of Legitimacy has been called into question by several students of the Caribbean, the detailed descriptions of family and courtship patterns in that area show that it is generally valid. Derived from societies in which conformity to this norm was high, however, the principle requires revision. This should emphasize status placement rather than "paternal protection," and should specify the lower strata as the part of the society in which deviation from the norm is greatest. In addition, revision of the principle should note the weaker norm commitment in these strata, and the resulting lowering of both punishment for deviation and reward for conformity.

The "matrifocal" Caribbean family is a product of an unstable family pattern, in which the mother or grandmother is often in power because no father is there. The courtship pattern is anonymous, so that the young girl must make the best bargain she can, which usually means that she must be willing to risk pregnancy in order to establish a basis for a more stable union. Eventually, most individuals do enter a marriage. The girl is not protected by her relatives or peers in this bargaining. Thus, though the Principle of Legitimacy is valid, it must be revised. It has also been shown how courtship relations in the Caribbean may lead to a high illegitimacy rate, even when the norm of legitimacy is accepted.

Cultural Relativism and
Premarital Sex Norms

In noting that behavioral standards vary over time and from society to society, William Graham Sumner made the now classic statement: "The mores can make anything right." By this he meant that moral problems are interpreted differently by different societies—that questions of right and wrong are relative to the particular culture in which the behavior occurs. This theory has been labeled *cultural relativism*. It challenges the notion of absolute standards of judgment to be applied uniformly regardless of time or place.

But there has been little quantitative research to test the

REPRINTED FROM *The American Sociological Review*, Vol. XXV, No. 1 (February, 1960), pp. 31–39, by permission of the author and the publisher. (Copyright, 1960, by The American Sociological Association.)

Slightly revised version of a paper read at the Fourth World Congress of Sociology, sponsored by the International Sociological Association, September, 1959.

In an earlier paper prepared for the Fourth International Seminar on Family Research, held at Wageningen, Holland, two years ago, the writer presented certain preliminary data on the sex norms of the same cultures treated here and sketched in his "theory of value relevance." Since that time, more data bearing on the problem have been gathered and the analysis has been extended. The present report is a continuation of the previous one, and it is expected that still others will follow.

See Harold T. Christensen, "Value Variables in Pregnancy Timing: Some Intercultural Comparisons," in Nels Anderson ed., *Studies of the Family*, Gottingen, Germany: Vanderhoeck & Ruprecht, 1958, Vol. III, pp. 29–45.

theory of cultural relativism, especially as applied to modern Western societies. Furthermore, the tendency has been to stop with a simple noting of attitudinal and behavioral differences, without pinning down the relativism of the *consequences* of these differences. For example, it is well known that some societies are rather restrictive and others very permissive regarding premarital sexual behavior;[1] but there is almost no information as to whether this behavior has the same or different *effects* (in terms of mental health, subsequent social behavior, or both) across these contrasting types of societies.

This paper is an attempt to illuminate further the notion of cultural relativism by applying it to differing sets of premarital sex norms. Since premarital pregnancy can be reliably measured by use of a method known as "record linkage,"[2] whereas most other levels of sexual behavior are more elusive, the focus here is upon this phenomenon.[3] We are interested in both regularities and variations among the cultures studied, with special reference to the consequences of premarital pregnancy.

Specifically, it is hypothesized that the more permissive the culture regarding sexual matters, the greater will be the incidence of premarital pregnancy, *but the lesser will be the effects of such pregnancy as pressure either for hasty marriage or for subsequent divorce*. It is further hypothesized that certain aspects of premarital pregnancy *are not culturally relevant*.

SEX NORMS IN THREE CULTURES[4]

In order to treat culture as a variable, we have made identical observations in three widely divergent areas. The

[1] See e.g., George Peter Murdock, *Social Structure,* New York: Macmillan, 1949, pp. 260–283.

[2] For descriptions of this method, see Christensen, *loc. cit.;* and Harold T. Christensen, "The Method of Record Linkage Applied to Family Data," *Marriage and Family Living.* Vol. 20, February, 1958, pp. 38–43.

[3] It is expected that the questionnaire and interview data that were collected to throw light upon other aspects of sexual behavior in these same cultures, will eventually be reported also.

[4] For more detailed descriptions of these differing sex norms, see Christensen, "Value Variables . . . ," *op cit.,* pp. 30–35.

first is the state of Utah, where the Mormon Church is dominant and premarital sex norms tend to be extremely conservative, almost to the point of being puritanical. Here, religion is a motivating force in the lives of most people, and the religious interpretation of premarital sexual intercourse is that it is an extremely grievous sin. Waiting until marriage for sexual intercourse—"keeping the law of chastity"—is regarded as one of the highest of virtues.[5]

The second is the state of Indiana, which in many ways is typical of the United States as a whole. It is centrally located and heterogeneous in culture. It is approximately an average state in size, in rural-urban distribution, in population numbers and composition, and in various social indices such as median income, school attendance, and marriage, birth, and divorce rates. The "chastity norm" is a part of the prevailing culture in Indiana as in most of the United States—in prescription even if less so in practice. And there are religious incentives, promoted by a variety of denominations, which give support to the sexual mores.

The third location is Denmark, which, like all of Scandinavia, has a long tradition of sexual intercourse during the engagement. This goes back three or four centuries at least, in spite of efforts by the State Lutheran Church to establish a chastity code.[6] In this connection, it is important to point out that, although most Danes have their names on the church records, they seldom attend church services. Except for a few, religion in Denmark is not a strong motivating force in the lives of the people. Croog notes the importance of understanding the *ring engagement*—which has almost the status of a formal marriage, including rights to sexual intercourse, and obligations to marry if pregnancy results—as background for

[5] In this connection, it is interesting to recall Kinsey's finding to the effect that religiously devout men and women participate less in all socially disapproved forms of sexual behavior. He regarded religion as being the "most important factor in restricting premarital activity in the United States." See Alfred C. Kinsey et al., *Sexual Behavior in the Human Female.* Philadelphia: Saunders, 1953, pp. 324, 686–687, and *passim.*

[6] Cf. K. Robert Wikman, *Die Einleitung der Ehe,* Aabo, Finland: Acta Academiae Aaboensis, XI, 1937; and Georg Hansen, *Saedelighedsforhold Blandt Landbefolkningen i Denmark i det 18 Aarhundrede,* Copenhagen: Det Danske Forlag, 1957.

interpreting sexual behavior in Denmark. He also explains how this pattern of sexual freedom is spreading to include the more informal "going steady" relationships; and how these practices are encouraged by a liberal clergy, by welfare laws which make abortion and unmarried motherhood relatively easy, and by the facility with which premarital sexual behavior can be rationalized since "everyone is doing it."[7] Svalastoga cites five recent empirical studies to support his claim that: "Coitus before marriage may now safely be considered the rule and chastity the exception in Scandinavia."[8]

Thus these three areas have widely different norms regarding premarital sexual behavior. At the one extreme is Utah, dominated by a homogeneous culture and conservative religious tradition. There, the moral condemnation of premarital sexual intercourse under all circumstances has the support of strong supernatural sanctions. At the other extreme is Denmark, with a liberal tradition in sexual matters, and a religious membership, which, though homogeneous is only nominal. There, premarital sexual intercourse, if accompanied by love and the intent to marry, tends to be an accepted practice. Somewhere in between these two extremes lies Indiana, with norms more moderate, more variable, and yet somewhat typical of the country of which it is a part.

INCIDENCES OF PREMARITAL CONCEPTION

For any accurate measure of premarital conception, one needs to know three quantities: abortion among the unmarried, both spontaneous and induced; illegitimacy, that is, birth outside of marriage; and the number of weddings that are preceded by pregnancy.[9]

[7] Sydney H. Croog, "Aspects of the Cultural Background of Premarital Pregnancy in Denmark," *Social Forces*, 30 (December, 1951), pp. 215–219.

[8] Kaare Svalastoga, "The Family in Scandinavia," *Marriage and Family Living*, Vol. 16, November, 1954, pp. 374–380; quotation from p. 337.

[9] Strictly speaking, early birth within marriage provides the only available accurate measure of premarital conception. Some unmarried women

Unfortunately, there are no available statistics to enable us to make comparisons on the relative numbers of abortions.

With regard to illegitimacy, official statistics for 1955, which are typical of recent years, show the per cent of all births occurring outside of wedlock to be .9 for Utah, 2.9 for Indiana, and 6.6 for Denmark. (See Table 1 on page 66.) Thus, in these societies, illegitimacy increases with each advance in the sexual permissiveness of the culture.

Although illegitimacy rates can be obtained from published statistics for whole populations, it has been necessary to conduct sample studies for measures of the premarital conceptions which end in postmarital births.[10] As a consequence, the following analysis relies heavily upon the writer's earlier record linkage studies of Utah County, Utah, and Tippecanoe County, Indiana, and his more recent parallel investigation of Copenhagen, Denmark. The Utah County data were derived by comparing marriages occurring during the years 1905–7, 1913–15, 1921–23, and 1929–31 with birth records for four years following each wedding, in order to find the date of the first birth. This process yielded 1,670 cases. The Tippecanoe County data were derived by taking marriages which occurred during the years 1919–21, 1929–31, and 1939–41, matching them with the birth records searched for five years following the wedding, and finally checking against the divorce records to discover which marriages ended in failure. The result consisted of 1,531 cases involving a first child, with 137 of these cases terminating in divorce. The Copenhagen data were derived by taking every third marriage which occurred during a single year, 1938, eliminating cases involving remarriage and those in which the wife was thirty or more years of age,

---

have abortions and illegitimate births; the term "premarital" hardly describes them. Yet, since it is likely that the majority of such women later get married, no great violence is done in using the concepts in this way. In Denmark, for example, one study has shown that by age six well over half of all children born out of wedlock are then living with their mother who has since been married—in most cases to the child's father. See "Den Familiemaessige Placering af Børn Født Uden For Aegteskab," *Statistisk Maanedsskrift,* Vol. 30, No. 9, 1954, pp. 193–195.

[10] Denmark has published nation-wide statistics on this phenomenon, but the United States has not.

TABLE 1. Selected Indices of Premarital Conception

| | United States | | Denmark | |
Indices	Utah County, Utah	Tippecanoe County, Indiana	City of Copenhagen	Entire County
I. Illegitimacy rate[a]	.9	2.9	11.2	6.6
II. Premarital conception rates[b]				
A. Child born within first 6 months of marriage	9.0	9.7(10.0)[c]	24.2(31.1)[c]	32.9(34.9)[c]
B. Child born within first 9 months of marriage	30.9	23.9(26.1)[c]	30.5(39.3)[c]	44.3(48.5)[c]

[a] Per cent of all births occurring outside of wedlock. Calculations based upon official reported statistics for the year 1955.
[b] Per cent of marital first births occurring within six and nine months of the wedding, respectively.
Figures in the first three columns are from the Utah County, Tippecanoe County, and Copenhagen studies described in the paper. Fourth column figures were derived from the *Statistisk Aarbog 1956*, Copenhagen: Bianco Lunos Bogtrykkeri, 1956, Table 25, p. 35, and are for the calendar year 1955.
[c] Figures in parentheses are adjusted indices, derived by using only those births which occurred during the first four years of marriage as the base for calculation. This adjustment is for the purpose of making the figures comparable in this respect with the Utah indices shown in the first column.

and then checking both birth and divorce recordings for sixteen years following the wedding. These steps provided a sample of 1,029 cases involving a first child, with 215 ending in divorce.

These samples from three cultures are not, of course, strictly comparable. They were drawn in slightly different ways and have somewhat different compositions. Nevertheless, the contrasts reported below are of sufficient magnitude to suggest at least tentative answers to the problem posed.

From Table 1, it may be observed that the same general pattern holds for this phenomenon as was previously noted for illegitimacy. The six months index, which is a sure minimum measure of premarital conception, makes the clearest comparison. It shows the lowest incidence of premarital pregnancy in Utah, a somewhat higher incidence in Indiana, but a considerably higher incidence in Denmark. The nine months index is less valuable since it includes unknown numbers of postmarital conceptions.[11] The higher rate for Utah than for Indiana may simply reflect the tendency to earlier postmarital conceptions in Utah.[12]

These findings may be viewed as validation for our earlier labelings. In these cross-cultural comparisons, behavior has been found to be consistent with attitudes; and, attitudes *plus behavior* have differentiated Utah and Denmark at opposite ends of a continuum describing premarital sex norms, with Indiana in between.

An interesting contrast between Copenhagen and the whole of Denmark can be seen by comparing the last two columns of Table 1. Copenhagen shows higher illegitimacy rates than the national figures, but relatively low rates of premarital conception. Though interpretation of the contrast takes us beyond available data, we hazard a guess: Copenhagen, being

[11] The normal period of uterogestation in human beings is 266 days, or slightly less than nine calendar months. Furthermore, premature births would cause a number of early postmarital conception cases to be included in this index.

[12] See Figure 1 of the present paper, where Utah is shown to have proportionately more conceptions *at the time of marriage* than Indiana. Of course, some of these may actually be premarital by a day or so, but the other explanation for the Utah-Indiana differential seems more plausible to the writer.

metropolitan in character, reflects the more liberal sex culture, including a sophistication which discourages rushing
into marriage just because of pregnancy; thus, it is possible
that disproportionately more premaritally pregnant couples
in Copenhagen either put off marriage until after the child
is born or elect against it entirely. An alternative possibility
is that women with an illegitimate pregnancy tend to move to
Copenhagen sometime before the child is born.

ASSOCIATED FACTORS

Not only does the incidence of premarital pregnancy differ
from culture to culture, as demonstrated above, but it varies
among certain sub-groups within each culture. As shown in
Table 2, there are strong and consistent tendencies for pre-

TABLE 2.   Factors Associated with Premarital Conception[a]

| | Per cent of First Birth Premaritally Conceived[b] | | |
Factors	Utah County, Utah	Tippecanoe County, Indiana	Copenhagen, Denmark
Wife's age at marriage			
Young group[c]	14.4	13.2	29.0
Older group	7.7	5.7	15.1
Type of ceremony[d]			
Civil	16.6	21.0	37.0
Religious	1.1	9.9	13.5
Husband's occupation			
Laborer	17.9	16.0	30.0
All other	8.6	7.2	18.2

[a] All factor differences were found to be statistically significant in all three
samples.
[b] As used here: per cent of marital first births within the first 196 days of marriage
(Utah and Indiana), or within the first 182 days of marriage (Denmark).
[c] This group was defined in the Utah sample as aged 20 or under, in the Indiana
sample as aged 24 or under, and in the Danish sample as aged 23 or under.
[d] In the Utah sample, the division is not strictly civil-religious, but rather non-
temple-temple. Since the most orthodox Mormons marry in one of the temples, this
group would represent the most religiously motivated of the religious marriages. But
the non-temple group, though mostly civil marriages, would include *some* religious
marriages—where these did not take place in a Mormon temple.

marital conception to be higher with young age at marriage in contrast to the older ages, with a civil wedding in contrast to the religious ceremony, and with a laboring occupation in contrast to the more skilled and professional ways of earning a living. Each of these differences was found to be in the same direction and to be statistically significant for each of the three cultures studied, which is evidence of certain cross-cultural regularities.

Perhaps youth gets into difficulties of this kind because of its lack of sophistication. Furthermore, since premarital pregnancy encourages earlier marriages than couples otherwise would undertake, marriages of this sort are certain to involve more of the younger-aged persons. The higher proportions of premarital pregnancy among those who have a civil wedding may possibly be explained by a relative lack of religious influence in the lives of these people, plus an attempt on the part of those who become pregnant to hurry the wedding and to avoid the judgment of the church or the scorn of fellow church members. The disproportionately high premarital pregnancy percentages for persons in the laboring occupations may largely be due to the greater sexual permissiveness found in the lower social classes, plus their relative lack of education. But, whatever the complete explanation, there is the strong suggestion here that broad cultural norms may be to some extent overruled by the operation of other factors.[13]

EFFECTS UPON TIMING OF THE WEDDING

The tendency to be philosophical about a premarital pregnancy when it happens, so as not to be stampeded into a marriage, seems to be much more characteristic of Denmark than of Indiana or Utah. It is suggested, perhaps, by the higher Danish illegitimacy rates.

[13] Of course, these factors also have cultural content, but they—and possibly many others—seem not to be confined by the limits of an area or a society; hence the suggestion of cross-cultural regularities.

But even stronger evidence is presented in Figure 1, which has been constructed from estimated dates of conception calculated by counting back 266 days from each date of birth. It may be noted that, whereas in the Utah and Indiana samples the modal time of conception is one lunar month after marriage, in the Danish sample it is five lunar months *before* the marriage. As a matter of fact the Danish data show

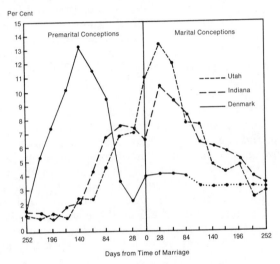

FIGURE 1.   Pregnancy inception as related to time of marriage: a cross-cultural comparison. Data are for births occurring during the first nineteen lunar months of marriage and are expressed as percentages.

many more couples conceiving about five months before the marriage than at any other time; in that culture, therefore, premarital conception coupled with subsequent delayed marriage must be considered as the norm. The Indiana curve is bimodal, with the peak for premarital conceptions at two lunar months prior to marriage—suggesting a tendency to get married as soon as possible after the second menstrual period has been missed and the doctor's positive diagnosis has been given. The Utah curve starts low and moves up regularly until the time of marriage and immediately thereafter, when it is the highest of all three.

The fact just noted is further evidence of Utah's pattern of early conception following the wedding. Of the three cultures here compared, Utah has not only the lowest rates of premarital conception but the highest rate of *early* postmarital conception.

Apparently, in Denmark there is little pressure to hurry marriage merely because of pregnancy.[14] In Indiana the tendency is to marry immediately after the pregnancy is definitely known so as to hide the fact from the public. Couples who have premarital sexual intercourse in Utah, on the other hand, seem to hurry marriage because of that fact alone, without waiting for pregnancy to force them into it (religious guilt is a sufficient sanction once the "law of chastity" has been broken).[15]

As Kinsey has pointed out, "The psychologic significance of any type of sexual activity very largely depends upon what the individual and his social group choose to make of it."[16] Since in Danish culture there is less stigma placed on premarital conception and on illegitimacy than in Indiana, and especially in Utah, the differences in timing pattern for the wedding once pregnancy has occurred may be explained in cultural terms.

EFFECTS UPON THE DIVORCE RATE

This type of explanation may also apply to possible variations in divorce rate differentials of premarital pregnancy

---

[14] In attempting to explain this situation to the writer, several Danish scholars have pointed to the current great housing shortage in Copenhagen—which means waiting for a place to live, thereby discouraging any rush into marriage. When reminded that the figures used here are for 1938 marriages, however, these observers were quick to admit that the argument doesn't apply, since there was little housing shortage then.

[15] Although this latter explanation is speculative, it is plausible. Chastity is so stressed in Mormon culture that the religiously oriented offender may panic and try to ease his conscience by getting married.

[16] Kinsey, *op. cit.*, p. 320.

versus postmarital pregnancy cases. We would hypothesize that the more liberal the culture the *less* likely is premarital pregnancy to be followed by divorce. This hypothesis is tested with data from the Indiana and Danish samples.[17]

For Tippecanoe County, it has been reported earlier that the divorce rate is significantly higher for premarital than postmarital pregnancy couples.[18] For marriages occuring in Copenhagen during 1948, Holm has shown that, with age controlled, the divorce rate is not significantly different for couples bearing a child within the first nine months of marriage than for all other cases.[19] At first glance, this seems to bear out our hypothesis.

It is to be noted, however, that Holm did not compare premarital pregnancy cases with postmarital pregnancy cases, as was done for Tippecanoe County, but rather with all non-premarital pregnancy cases, including childless couples. Since those who become divorced are less likely to have children than those who do not,[20] the inclusion of childless cases in the non-premarital pregnancy category would raise the divorce rate for that category and, in this way, would obscure the true comparison. What is needed is a comparison between divorce rates of premarital and postmarital pregnancy cases; for unless non-conceivers are excluded, it is impossible to determine the effects of conception timing.

Table 3 is designed to compare the Copenhagen and Tippecanoe County samples concerning possible effects of premarital and postmarital pregnancy upon the divorce rate. As noted above, these two samples are not strictly comparable,

[17] Unfortunately, in our Utah sample record linkage was limited to marriage and birth data; whereas in the Indiana and Denmark samples divorce data were also include.

[18] Harold T. Christensen and Hanna H. Meissner, "Studies in Child Spacing: III—Premarital Pregnancy as a Factor in Divorce," *American Sociological Review*, Vol. 18, December, 1953, pp. 641–644.

[19] Henry F. Holm, Actuary for the City of Copenhagen's Statistical Office, *Statistisk Maanedsskrift*, 33, No. 4, 1957, Table 12, p. 117.

[20] In the writer's Copenhagen sample of 1938 marriages, for example, 57.0 per cent of the childless marriages ended in divorce or separation as compared with 20.9 per cent of the fertile marriages. A primary explanation for this differential is that many of the divorces occur relatively soon after the wedding, before the couple has decided to start a family.

TABLE 3. Divorce Rate Comparisons by Interval to First Birth
(For Births Occurring Within 5 Years of the Wedding)

Classification	Copenhagen, Denmark			Tippecanoe County, Indiana		
	Number of Cases	Number Divorced	Per Cent Divorced	Number of Cases	Number Divorced	Per Cent Divorced
Interval between marriage and first birth						
(1) 0–139 days (premarital pregnancy, marriage delayed)	176	60	34.1	71	14	19.7
(2) 140–265 days (premarital pregnancy, marriage hurried)	129	31	24.0	276	39	14.1
(3) 266 days–4.99 years (post-marital pregnancy)	572	111	19.4	1184	84	7.1
Percentage difference between divorce rates						
(4) between lines 2 and 1			42.1			39.7
(5) between lines 3 and 2			23.7[a]			98.6[a]

[a] No direct formula has been located for testing the statistical significance of this intersample difference between differences in proportions. However, an approximate equivalent test is to consider $p1 - p2 < p3 - p4$ (where $p1 = 24.0$, $p2 = 19.4$, $p3 = 19.4$, and $p4 = 7.1$). When the p-values are changed according to the arcsine transform, they have been placed on a comparable scale and the use of the normal probability table is permitted. This procedure yields a probability for a one-tailed test of .12.

Alternatively, we may approximately test $\frac{p1}{p2} < \frac{p3}{p4}$ if we assume $\frac{p1}{p2} - \frac{p3}{p4}$ is normally distributed, and use an approximate variance formula. Since the hypothesis is stated in terms of the greater ratio for the United States than for Denmark, a one-tailed test is permissible, yielding a probability of .038. There is no way to evaluate the assumption of a normal distribution for this test.

but they are approximately so.[21] It seems probable that the following generalizations are at least tentatively justified:

(1) In both populations there is the clear tendency for the divorce rate to fall as the length of interval between marriage and first birth increases. This means that premarital pregnancy cases are more likely to end in divorce than are postmarital pregnancy cases,[22] and that those premarital pregnancy couples who delay marriage for a considerable time after the knowledge of pregnancy have the highest divorce rate of all—in Denmark as well as Indiana.

(2) The *relative* difference in divorce rate between premarital pregnancy couples who hurried marriage and those who delayed it is essentially the same for both populations. Thus, Copenhagen figures show a 42.1 per cent difference between these two rates as compared with a difference of 39.7 per cent in Tippecanoe County, an intersample difference that is not significant.

The facts that both samples show substantially higher divorce rates for couples who delay marriage after knowledge of pregnancy and that the differentials in this respect are about the same in the two cultures suggest universal tendencies for certain pregnant couples to marry under the pressure of social responsibility (for example, sympathy for the

[21] See descriptions of the two samples, above. Calculations for Table 3 are based uniformly on cases having a first child born within five years of the wedding. Although absolute divorce rates cannot be compared across the two samples—since they would be influenced in distinctive ways by differential emigration and differential lengths of time of exposure to the divorce possibility—there seems to be no good reason why the *relative* rates by pregnancy timing cannot be compared.

[22] There is an interesting parallel finding from the Copenhagen data: marriages in which the wife had borne an illegitimate child previously showed a divorce rate of 45.7, as compared with 20.9 for childbearing marriages where she had not. A partial explanation, of course, may be that a selective factor is operating, which may mean that the least stable personalities are the ones most likely to become pregnant before marriage and also to be divorced later. But another possibility is that, through such things as resentment about the necessity to marry, guilt feelings, and poor preparation and unsuitable personality matching because of a hasty or pressured marriage, the premarital pregnancy may itself help to bring about divorce. In the Tippecanoe County study, the writer controlled other divorce-producing factors, through matching, and still found premarital pregnancy to be significantly associated with high divorce.

lover, consideration for the future child, or parental influence). The data also suggest that, statistically speaking, such "shot gun" marriages do not turn out well.

(3) The *relative* difference in divorce rate between postmarital pregnancy couples and the premarital couples who married soon after the discovery of pregnancy is four times greater in the Indiana sample (98.6 per cent compared with 23.7 per cent), an intersample difference that by some tests is statistically significant. (See note to Table 3.)

The fact that the postmarital pregnancy divorce rate is lower in both cultures is evidence that premarital pregnancy—even when associated with an early wedding—tends generally to make marriage's survival chances less than even. This may be because some marriages take place under pressure from others and are therefore accompanied by resentment, or because in their haste to escape public scorn the couple marries without adequate preparation, or in the absence of love, or in the face of ill-matched personalities. But the fact that the postmarital-premarital pregnancy divorce rate differential is substantially less in Denmark, gives strong support to our hypothesis. It seems probable that in Denmark, where sexual relations outside of marriage are more or less accepted, premarital pregnancy will have less negative effect upon marriage than in Indiana, where it is expected that sexual intercourse and pregnancy be confined to marriage.

SUMMARY AND THEORY

Premarital sex norms in Utah, Indiana, and Denmark stand in sharp contrast—with Utah being very conservative or restrictive, and Denmark being extremely liberal or permissive. As might be expected, therefore, premarital pregnancy rates were found to be lowest in the Utah sample and highest in the Danish sample, with the difference being considerable. Furthermore, certain consequences of premarital pregnancy were found to vary from culture to culture. Thus permissive Denmark, at the time of the study, showed the longest delay between premarital conception and the wedding, and the smallest divorce rate differential between premarital pregnancy and postmarital pregnancy cases.[23] In all three cultures the same factors were associated with premarital pregnancy: namely, young age at marriage, a civil wedding, and a laboring occupation.

In some respects our data give support to the idea of cultural relativism. It has been shown that both the rates and effects of premarital pregnancy are to a considerable extent relative to the cultures involved. The most liberal culture was found to have the most premarital pregnancy, but also the least negative effects therefrom; in Denmark there is less pressure than in the American cases either to speed up the wedding or to resort to divorce when premarital pregnancy occurs. Thus, the relationship is not simply a matter of how premarital pregnancy affects subsequent behavior, considered in a vacuum, but rather how it affects this behavior in the light of particular norms. Cultural norms represent an intervening variable.

But there are also *regularities* among the cultures studied. In all of them, pregnancy usually takes place within marriage. In all of them also, premarital pregnancy is found to be associated with young age, a civil wedding, and a laboring occupation. Finally, the Indiana-Denmark comparisons reveal a parallel phenomenon of higher divorce rates for premarital pregnancy than for postmarital pregnancy cases. These rates are especially high, and in similar magnitude within both cultures, for couples who delay marriage until just before the child is born. Forced marriage, in other words, seems to work against marital success regardless of the culture. All of this

[23] As noted above, divorce rate comparison does not include the Utah sample since data were not available. It is believed, however, that the Utah divorce rate differential (between premarital and postmarital pregancy cases) probably is the greatest of the three areas—because premarital sexual intimacy is most strongly condemned there.

This unestablished assumption can be argued by an analogy. The drinking of alcoholic beverages is also strongly condemned in Utah (and in the rest of Mormon culture). Research shows that Mormon college students have the lowest incidence of drinking among religious groups, but that, of the drinkers, Mormon students have a very high rate of alcoholism. This suggests that cultural restrictions can lower the incidence of the condemned practice, but that for those who indulge, the negative effects are apt to be extreme. Cf. Robert Strauss and Selden D. Bacon, *Drinking in College.* New Haven: Yale University Press, 1953, *passim.*

suggests the existence of certain universals which are to some extent independent of the cultural variable.

The present analysis is concerned with *inter*cultural comparisons. The next step is to see if the theory applies to the *intra*cultural level, that is, when interpersonal differences are taken into account. We hypothesize both regularity and variability at that level also, with personal values having very much the same effects as cultural norms are found to have in this report.

PART III

Psychological Perspectives on the Unwed Mother

Personality Patterns
in Unmarried Mothers

LEONTINE R. YOUNG

The psychology of the unmarried mother—what she is like and why she becomes an unmarried mother—is an infinitely complex question. Its roots are deeply embedded in those powerful emotions of early childhood which form the basic pattern and structure for the individual's total life. Far more than most, this specific problem represents a direct expression of early fantasies and emotional conflicts. Perhaps this very directness has contributed to confusion about the unmarried mother. Clearly, she is a human being who like all other human beings responds dynamically to her particular life situation, but, also clearly, she chooses one common and specific response, having an out-of-wedlock child.

Unless we are to assume that illegitimacy may spring from any haphazard combination of motives and circumstances, there must be certain defined emotional patterns that lead to the creation of this problem. Anyone who has observed a considerable number of unmarried mothers can testify to the fact that there is nothing haphazard or accidental in the causation that brought about this specific situation with these specific girls. On the contrary, there is an inevitability about

REPRINTED FROM *The Family*, Vol. XXVI, No. 8 (December, 1945), by permission of the author and the publisher, The Family Service Association of America. (Copyright, 1945, by The Family Service Association of America.)

the chain of emotions climaxing in this action which rivals the old Greek tragedies. It is not coincidence that one almost never finds a girl, however intelligent or educated, who has thought of contraceptives or has ever considered the possibility of an abortion as a solution to her problem.

One girl indeed, who because of physical disability was entitled to a therapeutic abortion, avoided the certain insistence of her doctor on such action by concealing her pregnancy until she knew it was too late to perform the operation —this in spite of the fact that she knew childbirth might well cost her her life. Another girl, coming to an unmarried mother agency for assistance from a state some distance away explained that she had first heard of the agency several years before through a subscription letter to her employer and had remembered the name. She thought she must have had a "premonition."

These illustrations could be duplicated indefinitely and they all point to the purposefulness of the girl's behavior, her determination, however unconscious, to have not just a baby but specifically a baby out of wedlock. That a legitimate child is not what she desires and is, in fact, in most cases, at least at this point in her life, definitely unwanted can be seen in the many situations where a girl turns from a reliable fiancé or boy friend to become pregnant by a casual acquaintance who she knows will take little interest and less responsibility. Married women having an out-of-wedlock child are particularly enlightening in this respect, since many of them have failed during years of married life to have a child but become pregnant very quickly—sometimes after having had intercourse only once or twice—by a man other than their husband. While the factor of possible sterility of the husband has not been sufficiently studied to eliminate it, actually the frequency of this situation gives ample indication that sterility of the man is hardly a probable explanation. Interesting and illuminating in this connection was the case of a girl married for over a year to a serviceman who had been sent overseas about six months before she became pregnant by a man many years older than herself. She and her husband had wanted very much to have a child before he went away, but she could not become pregnant. They went to a doctor who, after examining both of them, stated that the husband was perfectly normal but that the girl would need an operation before she could bear a child. She decided to wait until her husband's return from the war before undergoing so serious an operation. A few months after her husband's departure she met this older man whom she knew very briefly, had intercourse with him only twice, and promptly became pregnant.

This leads logically to the question of what combination of factors and circumstances, what personality patterns underlie this problem. Are there common elements in the backgrounds of these girls? Are there common trends and tendencies in their personality structures despite the individual variations, the unique quality of any single human being? What of particular significance in their family situations or their life histories casts light upon the development and direction of these personality patterns? Is there any correlation between their family backgrounds and the circumstances surrounding conception, and in turn any direct relationship with their decision about the baby? Obviously only a careful and detailed study of a large number of cases could give any final answer to such questions but even a limited survey can elicit the broad outlines, can highlight consistencies and inconsistencies, can define probabilities.

For this purpose a random sample of 100 cases from an unmarried mother agency has been studied. They represent in intelligence, education, social and economic background rather wide variations; if anything, as a group they are above average in intelligence. No attempt has been made to select particular kinds of cases, but two specific groups have been excluded. Adolescents have not been included because psychologically and often environmentally their problems differ from those of the older girl. Thus, the ages of those studied range from 18 to 40. Second, girls coming from a cultural background where illegitimacy is more or less socially acceptable have been excluded. Because of cultural influence these girls may have quite different personality patterns, may have little or no internal conflict about the baby, and may face quite a different situation, socially, economically, and psychologically from that of the girl who must rebel against training and accepted social standards if she is to be an unmarried mother. The 100 cases have been studied with particular relation to four points: family background, circumstances surrounding conception, the mother's decision about the baby, and the quality of the girl's present relationships to both family and other people. It was immediately apparent that almost all the girls had come from two or three general types of family patterns and that this family pattern determined to a very large extent the pattern of her personality and the direction of her life experiences. What were the kinds of family situations in which the early lives of these 100 girls had been molded?

DOMINATING MOTHERS

Thirty-six of them came from homes where the mother was definitely the dominant personality and the father either was a weaker person or was emotionally cut off from the children to a greater or lesser degree. To the girls of this group the father was all too often a stranger, the man who paid the bills but was not allowed, or did not attempt, to share intimately in the lives and feelings of his children. The mother on the other hand, dominated her daughter's life to an unhealthy degree, was usually possessive and often rejecting and sadistic. While there were 36 variations of this pattern, they were variations of degree not of kind, variations in expression not in essential quality. This family situation had left its indelible mark upon the girl. Without exception she was overly dependent upon her mother and both resented and embraced that dependency. She was constantly involved in the conflict between her love and her hate for her mother. Most of the girls expressed openly one side of the conflict, some of them their hate for the mother, some of them their love for her, but not one of the group gave any indication that she was conscious of both the love and the hate. They spoke of their mothers as real people whatever their feelings might be, but they talked of their fathers in vague shadowy terms, never resentful, often idealized, so that except for brief flashes the fathers never seemed real at all.

With these unhappy parental relationships, how did these

36 girls feel about the fathers of their babies and what was their relationship to these men? Eighteen did not know the fathers at all in a social sense. They had met the boys in casual, unconventional fashion, "pick-ups" or "blind dates." One girl had asked a strange boy on the street for directions to find her way and then had spent the evening with him. Three girls said they had been drinking too much and remembered nothing of the incident and of course nothing concerning the man. Two other girls who had similarly blacked out all recollection of the sexual experience insisted that they had been given knockout drops by men strange to them. It would be easy to say that these latter girls were simply lying to protect themselves, but there is no indication that this is so. Indeed, the probabilities are that they have either wholly or partially blotted out their recollection of the incident. In any case the casual nature of the relationship is clear. Of the remaining 18 girls, 9 had known the alleged father but had had only a brief acquaintance with him and a very superficial relationship to him. Typical is the girl who met a man on her summer vacation, knew him for about a month, and had sexual relations with him only during the last two weeks. The other 9 girls had known the alleged fathers for periods varying from two or three months to more than a year.

Only one man continued to keep in touch with the girl after she became pregnant or indicated that the relationship had any continuing meaning to him. None of the 9 girls had had a happy, satisfying relationship with the man. One girl said frankly that she had never felt comfortable with her baby's father, had never really liked him, and had never enjoyed the sexual relationship with him. She herself could not explain why she had continued to see him and had become pregnant by him. In brief, none of these 36 girls had enjoyed a happy relationship with the man. Only the rare girl spoke of him as an individual and as a person who had any meaning to her. The majority ignored his very existence as if only the actuality of the baby proved that he had ever been there at all.

There is a striking similarity between the girl's relationship to her own father and her relationship to the father of her baby. One cannot escape the conclusion that she is in one sense seeking her own father and that the father of her baby is truly a kind of biological tool, unimportant to her as a person in his own right. Her lack of interest in him is a natural and inevitable outcome and not a deliberate evasion of her feeling for him. In situations like this the case worker's attempt to bring the alleged father into the picture can only be both irrelevant and damaging.

With this relationship or lack of relationship to the baby's father, how did these 36 unmarried mothers feel about their babies and what decision did they make? It is scarcely strange in the light of their warring emotions that they had mixed and conflicting feelings about the baby. Certainly few of them wanted the baby in a mature and adult fashion. In this sense it is interesting to note that all their conflict centered around the fact of a baby, never around the developing personality of a child. The obvious fact that a baby becomes a child was ignored and was for them at the time quite irrelevant.

They had conceived and borne this baby for definite, unconscious purposes of their own, and the problem was now how to achieve those purposes with the baby as the tool. It may safely be said that where the girl's mother would take the baby and the girl home, she was not likely to consider any other plan. And this was true regardless of how unhappy that home had been and would continue to be. One can only assume that giving a baby to her mother represented one of those unconscious purposes. With this one action the girl expressed both her hate and her love for the mother. What better revenge could she devise against a rejecting mother than to bear an illegitimate child and place the responsibility for him upon her mother's shoulders? And in what more complete way could she express her love for and her dependency upon her mother, and assuage her guilt toward her mother, than to give the mother her baby, a tangible evidence of her deep, unconscious tie as well as a symbol of her own desire to be again an infant cared for by the mother?

One girl from this group who is bitterly antagonistic toward a very rejecting and hostile mother had spent months with her baby in a maternity shelter trying to force her mother to take the baby home. She refused to make any other plans and, when it became necessary for her to move, she took a room and settled down with the baby, prepared to continue this endurance contest until her mother capitulated. She is blindly and stubbornly acting out the drama of her love and her hate for that mother. When it was clear that a girl's mother would not accept the baby, she nearly always planned to place the infant for adoption. Nor did she show any great conflict about this decision; the conflict did not lie primarily in this area at all. Of the 36, 27 placed their babies for adoption, 7 took the babies home to their mothers, 1 placed her baby in a foster home, and one infant died at birth. From this group a pattern begins to emerge.

DOMINATING FATHERS

In contrast to the family background of these 36 girls, 15 others came from homes where the father was the dominating personality and the mother was the weaker or less aggressive person. In 8 of the cases the parents were foreign born and had brought with them to this country a cultural pattern of male dominance in the home. All these girls expressed fear or resentment, usually both, toward their fathers. Most of them described the father as a stern, unsympathetic person whose chief role in relation to the children was that of disciplinarian. He was overly strict in his demands upon them, had no understanding of their needs as opposed to his wishes, and in some of the cases was very abusive. The mother was described usually as a rather ineffectual person who rarely attempted to oppose her husband's authority. Five of the girls were very protective toward their mothers, since in these families the father was openly abusive not only to the children but to the mother as well. Four of them referred to their mothers as "just like a sister to me" but there was little indication of real closeness or warmth in their relationship. Six of them said little at all about their mothers, who emerged from their scattered and brief descriptions as shadowy figures with little reality. Seemingly they were rather cold women and certainly they had no discernibly close relationship to their daughters. It was noticeable with this group that neither parent emerged with the clarity and strength typified in the mothers of the first group, but at least the father in most of the cases were described as a person. None of these 15 girls had had a happy home life or had known close, satisfying relationships with either parent. Ten of them had left home, but 5 had continued to live at home despite the unhappiness and conflict in the home situation.

When one considers the nature of their relationship to their own fathers, it is scarcely surprising to discover that their experiences with the fathers of their babies were not happy. None of them knew the man well or had known him for any considerable period of time. Eleven of them had known him on a rather casual basis for periods of time varying up to a few months, and 4 had known him little or not at all. Superficially, at least, this pattern looks very little different from that of the previous group. Actually the majority of these girls showed more awareness of the man, however casually they may have known him, than did most of the girls of the first group. Observing them one got the impression that they were trying unconsciously either to deny their own fathers by picking a virtual stranger or to re-experience with a lover much the same kind of masochistic relationship they had had with their fathers.

The kind of men these girls had selected was significant. If he was more than the faceless, haphazard choice of an evening or a week end, he was quite likely to be a later edition of those same traits that the girl had so feared and resented in her father. Jane had a domineering brutal father who forced his entire family to submit to his tyrannical will. The father of her baby was a boy of a different nationality background, violently disapproved of by Jane's father who had forbidden her to see him. This boy was crudely callous of her feelings, domineering in his attitude, and at times physically abusive. When she became pregnant, he did nothing to help her. Jane had another boy friend, a quiet reliable boy, who came to see her in the maternity shelter and wanted to marry her. Jane refused him and her explanation to the social worker was startlingly frank. She liked him but she did not love him because "he was too good to her." It was her baby's father that she loved. Few cases were so extreme but again the difference was one of degree not of principle.

These girls had a more difficult time coming to a decision about the baby than those of the first group. Some of them wavered until the last possible moment, seeking vainly to compromise with the inevitable exigencies of their own life situations of which they were from the first aware. Their alternatives seemed to be less definitive, less predetermined by their own psychology than those of the first group. They did not show the strong need, so evident in the girls of the first group, to give their babies to their mothers. Some of them, usually in those cases where their relationship to their fathers had not been too destructive, were able to place more value on the baby as an individual in his own right.

Of these 15 girls, 11 placed their babies for adoption. Three of these 11 girls expressed no feeling for the baby, surrendered the child with no indication of indecision, and said frankly that they wanted only to be rid of the responsibility. Two of these 3 girls had denied any feeling for their fathers almost to the point of sweeping him out of existence, and the third expressed only hatred and contempt for her father. The other 8 both wanted and did not want their babies and, caught in an emotional tug-of-war, did not find it easy to make a definite and final decision. They were more conscious of wanting than of rejecting the baby, and they tended to throw the responsibility for their decision upon the cruel inflexibility of their reality circumstances, circumstances which because of their very reality could successfully cloak the underlying rejection. Four girls out of the group kept their babies. One placed her child in a private boarding home, 2 took jobs and kept their babies with them, and 1 went home with her child.

BROKEN HOMES

Not surprisingly, the largest group of girls, 43, came from broken homes. This in itself tells a familiar story but not its particular relevance to this specific problem. Closer study of the individual situations reveals that in 22 of the cases the father was gone, either through death, separation, or divorce, and the mother had been the dominant influence and authority. Twelve of those mothers had clearly been dominating, sadistic, and openly rejecting, and all of them had been to some extent rejecting of their daughters. In 8 cases the mother was gone and the father was the parent taking responsibility for the children. Five of those fathers had been definitely rejecting, had been openly abusive or coldly indifferent, and had taken little responsibility for their daughters as they grew older. None of the 8 girls had had a close or happy relationship with their fathers. In 11 cases both parents were gone, and the girl had been brought up by relatives or in foster homes. All too often the relatives did not welcome the responsibility and these girls knew little but insecurity and rejection. In 2 cases the parents were separated but both saw the girl and took an active if scarcely wise part in her care. In each instance the child was caught in the conflict between the parents. There is obviously a striking similarity in the family patterns of the 30 girls who came from homes where either the father or the mother was gone with those families which though unbroken were dominated by the mother or the father, and that similarity extended to the lives of the girls themselves.

Of the 22 girls coming from homes where the father was gone, only 6 had known the baby's father for any length of time. Fourteen of these girls placed their babies for adoption, 3 took them home to their mothers, 1 placed her child in a private boarding home, and 2 girls married the fathers of their babies. The other 2 babies died at birth.

Of the 8 girls coming from homes where the mother was gone, 4 knew the baby's father well and 4 knew him only casually. Four of these girls kept their babies, 3 placed the child for adoption, and 1 baby died. Of the 11 girls coming from homes where both parents were gone, only 1 knew the baby's father well, and this girl insisted that the boy had given her knockout drops in order to rape her. Six of these girls placed their babies for adoption, 2 returned with the babies to the homes of the respective aunts who had brought them up, and 3 babies died at birth. The 2 girls caught in the conflict between their parents both knew the fathers of their babies very well and both placed the babies for adoption.

OTHERS

Six girls out of the 100 had family backgrounds differing from the previous patterns observed. One girl was adopted and the adoptive parents had seemingly been overindulgent with her and were dominated by her. It is probable that beneath this parental indulgence lay some rejection of her, but the relationships were never clear. The other 5 came from homes at least outwardly stable but these girls discussed their families so little that the web of family emotions remained effectually obscure. However, all 6 girls shared in some measure one characteristic: they tended to dominate their parents and anyone in a position of authority to them to achieve their own purposes. They gave little of themselves, felt little obligation to others, and were stony firm in their determination to carry out their own wishes.

All these 6 girls knew the fathers of their babies but except for 2, only rather casually. One of the girls had lived for some months as the supposed wife of her baby's father. When she became pregnant, the man arranged for an abortion and provided the money. She took the money, led the man to believe that she had had the abortion, then left him and had the baby without his knowledge. She placed the child immediately for adoption, the only plan that she ever considered. One can see here clearly the determination to have the baby as a fulfilment of an unconscious fantasy, to eliminate the man from any part in this, to carry into action a set and predetermined plan, but the total picture with its interlocking familial relationships remained obscure. Three of the girls placed their babies for adoption and 3 placed them in foster homes.

SOME INFERENCES

While it would be rash indeed to attempt any far-reaching and dogmatic conclusions at this point, yet from this study there are some facts ascertainable. Certainly there are common elements in the backgrounds of these girls. Most con-

spicuous is the fact that none of them had happy, healthy
relationships with their parents. Whatever the particular
family situation, the conflicting feelings of love and hate
remained a basic and potent source of unhappiness and
trouble. Almost equally noticeable was the dominance of
mother, the strength and the pervasiveness of the role she
played in this complex drama. Fifty-eight out of the 100 girls
had known mothers who controlled their lives and their emotional development to an extent that could only result in
damage to the whole structure of their personalities. The
degree of that damage seemed to be in direct proportion to
the power and destructive quality of that control. In other
words, the more dominating, the more sadistic, the more
rejecting the mother, the sicker and more hopeless was the
girl. Nor was the lot of the 23 girls who had known dominating and rejecting fathers much happier. Since fathers do
not normally assume the direct care of the children, it is
more difficult in these cases to evaluate what part was played
by the seemingly weaker, more submissive mother or by the
woman caring for the child. But one thing is clear, in all but
17 cases the girl came from a home dominated by one parent,
and the girl's relationship to that parent was a battleground
on which a struggle whether of greater or lesser intensity was
fought, and the baby was an integral part of that struggle. Not
even in the 17 cases can we safely conclude that no such
pattern is present, since relatives can play the role of parents
and a dominating or rejecting aunt can in the end be not too
different from a dominating or rejecting mother.

To discuss common trends in the personality patterns of
100 girls can be a snare and a delusion, but certain traits are
obvious even from the surface. All these girls had fundamental problems in their relationships with other people.
Some of them could not carry on even superficial contacts
successfully; others did well with casual acquaintances and
friends but were unable to enter into a close or intimate relationship with anyone. It was noticeable that these difficulties
occurred with both men and women, although the quality of
the relationships might differ. The problems followed them
into their work and few of them were able to use more than
a small part of their native intelligence and ability.

One of the most frequent tendencies to be found in their personality patterns was that of self-punishment. Almost none of the cases was completely free of it and with many of them it represented the major force in their lives. So deeply ingrained and so powerful was this force that often the girl would permit nothing and nobody to interfere with its self-destructive progress.

All of these girls, unhappy and driven by unconscious needs, had blindly sought a way out of their emotional dilemma by having an out-of-wedlock child. It is not strange that one finds among them almost no girl who has genuinely cared for or been happy with the father of her baby. Less than one-fourth of the group had even known the man well enough to make him a real person and only a scattered handful of these made even a pretense of caring for him in any adult fashion. The girls dominated by their mothers even more than the others seemed to reduce the man to the position of a tool, a kind of biological accessory without reality or meaning as a person. Some of them could not even permit themselves to remember his existence. This was less true of those dominated by their fathers. Rather they chose men who must inevitably hurt and humiliate them and then either submitted masochistically or fought a bitter futile battle to revenge themselves upon these men.

None of these violent neurotic conflicts are helpful ingredients in creating a good mother. These girls had wanted a baby but a baby without an accompanying husband, a baby that might somehow serve as a solution for unconscious strivings and conflicts. Sixty-six of them had placed their babies for adoption and, whatever the reality pressures, these girls must have recognized unconsciously that the baby was not the solution sought nor could ever be the answer to their torturing needs. Since 7 babies died at birth, only 27 of the girls kept their babies. Out of these 27, 8 were seemingly normal enough people to develop real love for their children, to see them not as helpless infants to be possessed but as individuals with rights and needs of their own, and to make the best plans possible for their care. The other 19 girls made very destructive plans for their babies, plans which took no account of the rights and needs of the child and which promised little but disaster for both the mother and the baby. These girls were still striving to achieve the impossible, to find through tenacious possession of the baby an answer to their own unconscious conflicts and anger.

Clearly, if the case worker is to give effectual help to the unmarried mother in relation to this all-important decision about the baby, she must not only be aware of these unconscious patterns but must know how to utilize them to the best interests of both the mother and the child. The writer is well aware that to generalize about unmarried mothers, as about any group of human beings, may be both rash and misleading. This study does not pretend to touch more than the surface manifestations of this intricate and difficult problem. It is frequently guilty of oversimplification but it would not have been otherwise possible to separate some of these major threads from the total pattern. The unmarried mother as a person might be said to be an endlessly unique variation of certain fundamental personality patterns that extend indeed far beyond the confines of this specific means of expression.

Psychodynamic and Clinical Observations in a Group of Unmarried Mothers

JAMES P. CATTELL, M.D.

It is well known that women with all types of behavior patterns and many varieties of emotional disorder become unmarried mothers. Motivation to the specific experience of unmarried motherhood depends to some extent on the degree of emotional illness and the personality of the patient. There is a growing volume of literature on clinical investigations and psychodynamic formulations of some of these problems. In the present study, it is hoped that some of the earlier observations and concepts may be supplemented with data on a somewhat larger case material.

The setting of this investigation is a privately endowed maternity home in New York City. Fifty-four consecutive referrals were seen once or twice in psychiatric consultation. The social workers provided a concise history of patients in most instances. The group ranged in age from 15 to 39 years and represented a reasonable cross section of the community in terms of socio-economic background and education.

Personality evaluation or diagnostic classification was made on the basis of historical data, present clinical status, and functioning in the residence hall. A diagnosis of character

REPRINTED FROM *The American Journal of Psychiatry*, November, 1954, pp. 337–342, by permission of the author and The American Psychiatric Association.

disorder was based on evidence of passive-aggressive or passive-dependent functioning, some degree of emotional immaturity, the prominence of such ego defense mechanisms as acting-out, denial, displacement, reaction formation, and the pursuit of some magical resolution of problems. A diagnosis of anxiety, depressive or conversion reaction, was made whenever there were leading symptoms of that nature. Schizophrenia was diagnosed in patients in whom the primary symptoms of the disorder obtained. The pseudoneurotic category was used to designate those who, in addition, had numerous neurotic mechanisms, gross emotional dysregulation, and chaotic sexuality. The other subcategories of schizophrenia were used according to the standard criteria. Patients with character disorder were differentiated from those with pseudoneurotic schizophrenia on the basis of the primary symptoms of schizophrenia and pan-neurotic symptoms in the pseudoneurotic group. The psychopathology in the character disorder group was quantitatively less severe and qualitatively less ramified.

The following distribution of diagnoses was found: character disorder, 30; neurotic reaction, 7 (anxiety, depressive, and conversion); schizophrenia, 17 (pseudoneurotic, 7; other types, 10).

One schizophrenic patient was rejected on psychiatric grounds and another had to be sent to a psychiatric hospital after admission because of an acute psychotic episode. The other 15 patients with this diagnosis continued to term without acute emotional complications, though in contrast with the nonschizophrenic group, there were obvious differences in ego strength and ability to cope with reality. In most instances, these deficiencies had been present in many areas for most of the patient's life. A great majority of the schizophrenic group had a history of a broken home (loss of one or both parents by death, divorce, separation, or mental illness years before the pregnancy), and a higher incidence of recognized or evident mental illness in the family was noted. The responses of these patients to environmental vicissitudes were usually rigid, unrealistic, and there was an illogical expectation that problems would be resolved by the magical effects of certain behavior. The relationship of such patients to a parent or parent-surrogate was often one of extreme dependency, to the point of psychological addiction, and the emulation of parental behavior or defiance of parental mores was carried out on a very concrete basis. Sexuality in this group was chaotic and the motivations to intercourse were usually vague and unreal, as was the relationship to the putative father. The latter was often a casual acquaintance who was repudiated by the patient with the advent of pregnancy, or an older man, often married, who fulfilled the role of understanding father in the patient's literal dramatization of this wish. These men lost interest in the patient with pregnancy or proposed continuation of the relationship after the child had been placed for adoption. A majority of the schizophrenic group planned to keep the child in contrast with only a minority of the nonschizophrenic group. These plans were formulated in some instances on the basis of regarding the child as a supplementary ego to be completely possessed, who would be a dependable and lifelong source of love for the patient. Some planned to keep the child as a lever to facilitate the legalizing of the illicit relationship with the married man. Others were pressured by not too healthy mothers to bring the child home, either to fulfill a need in the life of the mother or to insure a firm tie between patient and the home with a mother-daughter-grandchild group as a substitute for the father-mother-child domestic role. Some patients had little apparent interest in a continued social and sexual relationship with the man, using him only to sire a child and then to have the child without the problems of living with a man. The patient's father could be retained in fantasy to complete the triangle.

Many other real or apparent determinants of behavior could be mentioned for this group. To some extent, these obtain in association with the chaotic thinking, emotionality, and sexuality which are so evident in these patients.

The 37 nonschizophrenic patients demonstrated much more flexibility in coping with reality despite variable disturbances in the nature of character disorder or neurotic illness. There were qualitative and quantitative differences in reactions in contrast with the schrizophrenic group, including more inclination to abstract, logical responses, and less tendency to the use of denial, acting out, displacement and projection in the concrete, literal sense. The ability to initiate and sustain emotional relationships was much better, often despite numerous traumatic experiences. It is possible to achieve a better understanding of the psychodynamics of these patients inasmuch as one can more clearly establish some meaningful sequence of environmental experiences and the patient's reaction to them. Multiple determinants of behavior continued to obtain but one could differentiate the primary factors more easily from the accessory ones.

A majority of the patients with character disorder or neurotic illness had a history of a broken home, though the percentage was not as great as in the schizophrenic group. However, there was striking evidence of distortion and disturbance in the patient's relationship to her father in almost all of the group. The patient had had little or no opportunity to achieve concepts of the role of father, husband, or man in the domestic and social milieu. In those instances in which the patient had grown up in a intact home, the father was usually a passive, ineffectual person who either resignedly tolerated the girl as another inexplicable female or idolized her in a somewhat seductive manner. Some of the fathers were unpredictable strangers to the patients in the sense that they were seldom at home when the patient was, or, having functioned as a father for a period, would suddenly lose interest in the home and move in with another woman. Concepts of a stable, responsible man of the house and father of the family were difficult to crystallize. A few of the fathers and some of the step-fathers were brutal, exploitative, or seductive in their attitude toward the patient. The mothers or mother-surrogates of patients in this group introduced further complexity into the patient's discovering her own identity and gaining concepts of the mother-wife-woman role in life. These women, with or without husbands present, usually "wore the pants of the family," assuming many of the male prerogatives in domestic and community activities. In some instances, there was a possessive, harsh, demanding attitude toward the patient, a cool attitude of rationalized neglect, or a begrudging acceptance of an unruly child who seemed alien to the family. One factor, noted with striking regularity in this group, was a feeling of not belonging, not having a close emotional bond with someone, and compensatory activity to achieve a feeling of being loved. This feeling of a lack of love was predominantly based on reality factors rather than individual emotional deficit and social retirement. However, negative attitudes toward family were, for the most part, repressed and denied and appeared only obliquely in various types of displacement or acting-out behavior.

The relationship to the putative father varied from real or invited rape by an unknown to a 10-year affair with a married man. Some were boy-friends or "rebound" boy-friends, following the termination of another relationship. Many of these men had a façade of tender devotion and deep interest in the welfare of the patient, but an underlying exploitative and irresponsible behavior. The patients often denied the presence of these fairly obvious characteristics in the men and responded to the superficial aspects they wished to see. In many instances, the putative father was several years older than the patient and fulfilled some of the fantasies of the ideal father. Only in exceptional cases did the putative fathers offer emotional or financial support after pregnancy was recognized. Several of the patients preferred not to inform the men of their plight and a few refused assistance. Inasmuch as many of the patients had a lifelong experience of rejection or repudiation, some probably expected the pattern to continue and, to some extent, may have invited it. A vague recognition of some of the unconscious incestuous connotations of the relationship was another factor in arranging for desertion by the putative father. A few quickly shifted emotional interest to another man in an effort to deny the entire experience.

Some of the other motivations to intercourse and impregnation included emulation of sexual behavior of important persons in the life of the patient as well as defiance of family and social mores. Curiosity and confusion about sexuality was a fairly common determinant, while sexual pleasure motivated some whose relationships were more protracted. Though most of the patients were aware of the possibility of impregnation without contraception, many felt that this did not apply to them, that they would be magically protected, a further example of denial. Intercourse and child-bearing were

considered by some as a magical route to maturity and a resolution of problems. A number spoke of their wish and need to continue a relationship with the man and feared sexual refusal would drive him away. Some women wished to force married men to seek divorce and wed them.

After a period of ambivalence during pregnancy, most of these patients decided to place the child for adoption. With those who decided to keep the child, there was often defiance of family wishes for adoption and a few hoped to attract the man to marriage. Manifest evidence of the more primitive motivations to keeping the child, as seen in the schizophrenic group, was not striking, though such material might be revealed with more intensive investigation.

A comparison of behavior and of various determining factors in the actions of younger and older adolescent age groups and young adult and adult age groups revealed more likenesses than differences. The majority of the patients in all age groups were bound to a parent or parent-surrogate with adolescent ambivalence about dependency, defiant resentment, and some confusion about emotional relationships. Just as each patient had a unique set of motivating factors, each age group showed certain differences from the others. There was some evidence of increasing incidence of emotional disability and psychopathology proceeding from the younger to the older groups.

There were no significant physical or emotional complications in this group in specific relationship to the puerperium. There were 2 stillbirths and in each there was some question of attempted interference with drugs early in the pregnancy. Another patient delivered a viable infant in the seventh month of gestation but the child died a few minutes later. The patients were delivered in various hospitals, either as ward or private patients. The gross infant mortality rate for this group, including the premature infant who died, is 5.55%. This does not compare unfavorably with the infant mortality rate of 3.36% at a large medical center.[1]

There are numerous problems in the technique and appli-

[1] Annual Statistical Report of the Obstetrical Service for 1952. Sloane Hospital for Women, Columbia-Presbyterian Medical Center, New York, 1953.

cation of psychotherapy in a maternity home setting. Patients have a number of pregnancy-specific problems relating to hospitalization, plans for the child, attitude toward putative father, and future plans for self. In addition, there are the personality-specific problems of much greater magnitude and more subtle connotation. On a more superficial level, these include attitudes toward family, friends, and self, and some of the meaningfulness of behavior in terms of acting-out, displacement, and other mechanisms. Other issues of character structure and symptom formation on a more profound level would require much more extensive investigation and intensive treatment. An effort was made to help the social workers limit the goals of treatment in view of the short time available and the heavy case-load. In treating patients who were quite disturbed emotionally, it was suggested that most of the efforts be confined to pregnancy-specific problems and even these proved too formidable to be adequately handled by some patients. Concerning some of the other patients, it was suggested that ventilation of the more superficial aspects of personality problems could be facilitated, with an occasional comment by the worker on some of the possible meanings of behavior in present-day terms.

Despite the obvious need for therapy and the efforts of the staff, a majority of the patients seemed averse to any opportunity for clarification of personality problems during or after the pregnancy. They cherished their defenses, however unsuccessful they had proved to be, and were eager to return to the *status quo*. This was a further reason for limiting the goals of therapy and for suggesting that defenses should be left intact unless something better could be offered.

The role of the social worker in this setting is most difficult in view of the circumstances noted above as well as in association with countertransference and subjective emotional reactions of the worker.

DISCUSSION

An attempt to organize and integrate clinical and psychodynamic material on any sizable group of patients is a humbling and arduous task which will increasingly occupy the student of clinical research in psychiatry. The problem is compounded as one approaches such a widely ramified issue as unmarried motherhood. Excellent reports of smaller groups have been presented by Bernard,[2,3] Clothier,[4] Deutsch,[5] Kasanin and Handschin,[6] Reider,[7] and others.

Space limitations preclude use of much of the fascinating and extensive case material; however, the sample is as large and unselected as possible.

The individual is seen as the emergent, integrated product of his basic endowment, his nursery and early childhood experiences in the family, and his response to them, as well as the impact of subsequent biological, social, and other experiences at a given time in his development. Clinical data suggest that in some individuals there may be an inherent deficiency in potential for integration, with a low threshold to stimuli from within and without and inability to cope with environmental vicissitudes. The needs of different individuals may vary remarkably from birth, and various techniques of care, love, and training are applicable to various persons for optimal facilitation of integrated development. To the extent that much of the development of the concepts of oneself, of the sexual differences, of the behavior of male and female, husband and wife, father and mother, are based on passive emulation, especially during the early years, the relative intactness of the family is most necessary. The importance of the father and mother fulfilling their respective roles, as seen in this culture, is paramount.

It must also be noted that evidence of certain dynamic

[2] Bernard, V. Psychodynamics of unmarried motherhood in early adolescence. Nerv. Child, 4:26, October, 1944.

[3] Bernard, V. Needs of unmarried parents and their children as seen by a psychiatrist. Read at National Conference of Social Work, Atlantic City, April 1948.

[4] Clothier, F. Psychological implications of unmarried parenthood. Am. J. Orthopsychiat., 3:531, July 1943.

[5] Deutsch, H. The Psychology of Women, Vol. II. New York: Grune & Stratton, 1945.

[6] Kasanin, J., and Handschin, S. Psychodynamic factors in illegitimacy. Am. J. Orthopsychiat., 11:66, January 1941.

[7] Reider, N. The unmarried father. Am. J. Orthopsychiat., 18:230, April 1948.

mechanisms varies according to the relative intactness of the personality of the patient. Those with integrative disability, low threshold to stimuli, and disordered thinking processes, equivalent or tantamount to primary process thinking, usually present much more material in terms of regressive or fixated mechanisms and chaotic sexuality. These factors must be considered in formulating psychodynamic mechanisms in relation to a specific patient or to a special symptom such as unmarried motherhood.

The somewhat bold attempt to use diagnostic categories in this study was prompted by a wish to obtain a better understanding of the problem in a relatively unexplored area and to indicate certain possibilities as to goals of therapy. It was astonishing to discover, upon tabulation of the material, the distribution of diagnoses: 30% of this group of 54 were diagnosed schizophrenic. It is quite possible that other investigators might have made a somewhat different interpretation.

Schizophrenia in an unmarried mother may make a difference in the decision to admit or to keep her on the rolls of a given agency or maternity home. This material demonstrates that of 17 patients with this diagnosis, all but 2 were cared for through parturition. The others made a variable adjustment and the very fact of recognizing the illness facilitated understanding and flexibility in the staff. It was possible to warn the social workers to be cautious about pursuing emotionally-charged material that, once recognized, might not be dealt with adequately in the short time available. Thus, it must be emphasized that, despite integrative deficiency and emotional disability of variable severity, these patients have therapeutic and social assistance in a maternity home.

The numerous motivations to keep the child have been touched on and have been well described in the literature. The reality awareness of the schizophrenic is impaired and may be quite evident in unrealistic, vague plans about keeping the child. It has been noted that a large majority (70%) of the nonschizophrenic patients selected adoption for the child, while a small majority (54%) of the schizophrenic patients decided to keep the child. The extent to which staff members are able to influence this decision, or should try to influence it, is a matter for further investigation.

Several of the investigators noted above have reported remarkable results with psychotherapy conducted over a reasonable period in family agencies, clinics, or private practice. The unmarried mother, especially in adolescence or early adulthood, has manifest evidence of personality difficulty, usually with other more chronic problems. If sufficient facilities were available and various agencies dealing with unmarried mothers were adequately coordinated, it might be possible to have more of these patients enter psychotherapy. Technique and goals of therapy would vary according to the patient's integrative capacity. This could be a definite contribution to preventive and therapeutic psychiatry and might obviate recidivism. A 5-year follow-up study of a sizable group of unmarried mothers, with and without psychotherapy, would further help in clarifying this and many other of these problems.

Are We Still Stereotyping
the Unmarried Mother?

ROSE BERNSTEIN

The theory of out-of-wedlock pregnancy currently accepted among social workers and members of other helping disciplines is that it is symptomatic and purposeful, an attempt by the personality to ease an unresolved conflict. The extent to which we are committed to this point of view can be seen in some typical excerpts from the literature.

The caseworker should recognize that pregnancy for the unmarried woman is a symptom of underlying emotional difficulty. (She) is a person who solves her emotional problems through acting out, as exemplified by the pregnancy.[1]

We recognize unmarried motherhood as a symptom of a more pervading personality difficulty.[2]

Her illegitimate pregnancy is the result of an attempt to solve certain emotional conflict. . . . [3]

REPRINTED FROM *Social Work,* Vol. 5 (July 1960), pp. 22–38, by permission of the author and the publisher. (Copyright, 1960, by The National Association of Social Workers, Inc.)

[1] Margaret W. Millar, "Casework Service for the Unmarried Mother," *Casework Papers 1955.* New York: Family Service Association of America, 1955, p. 93.

[2] Louise K. Trout, "Services to Unmarried Mothers," *Child Welfare.* Vol. 35, No. 2, February, 1956, p. 21.

[3] Jane K. Goldsmith, "The Unmarried Mother's Search for Standards," *Social Casework.* Vol. 38, No. 2, February, 1957, p. 69.

[The unmarried mother] . . . has failed to attain a mature pattern of adaptation to the demands of her social reality.[4]

. . . everything points to the purposeful nature of the act. Although a girl would . . . not plan consciously . . . to bear an out-of-wedlock child, she does act in such a way that this becomes the almost inevitable result.[5]

The popular magazine articles have been echoing this point of view.

In many situations it is a useful approach. The results of treatment are often dramatic and gratifying when a girl is able to make use of help in understanding and dealing with some of the underlying problems related to her out-of-wedlock pregnancy. However, in contacts with residents in a maternity home, and particularly in reviewing material for a study, one becomes concerned about the limited applicability of this theory in a number of cases. One has the impression that in some situations factors other than, or in addition to, underlying emotional pathology have been of greater significance; that emphasis on a single point of view has prevented us from seeing other essential aspects of the experience and, correspondingly, has resulted in a limited treatment offering. This has seemed a good time, therefore, to re-examine the theory and look at other hypotheses which might be applicable in our work with unmarried mothers.

SOCIAL MORES

By and large, unmarried motherhood in our society is looked on as the violation of a cultural norm. It should therefore be possible to isolate and identify the norm in question. But this is not easy. For one thing, it is not clear whether the offended norm is the taboo against extramarital relations or against bearing a child out of wedlock. We point to the symptomatic nature of the pregnancy ("there are no accidental conceptions"), but in speaking of prevention we are

[4] Irene M. Josselyn, M.D., "What We Know About the Unmarried Mother." Paper read at National Conference of Social Work, June 1953.

[5] Leontine Young, *Out of Wedlock*. New York: McGraw-Hill Book Co., 1954, p. 22.

unable to clarify what we are trying to prevent—unsanctioned sex experience or out-of-wedlock pregnancy.

Some communities are more or less resigned to wide-spread sexual experimentation (among teen-agers) yet indignantly aroused and condemning when such experimentations result in out-of-wedlock pregnancy.[6]

If one observes public reactions today, one can hardly escape the conclusion that it is not so much the sexual relationship to which we object as the fact of the baby.[7]

Actually we are not dealing with a single norm, but with a multiplicity of norms which will vary according to cultural and ethnic groups, social or educational sophistication, peer practices, and so forth. These norms will vary not only from one girl to another but also for the same girl, according to the group she is most strongly related to at a given period in her life. The girl whose group or family loyalties at the age of seventeen preclude sexual experience may be safer from out-of-wedlock pregnancy at that time than she is at the age of twenty-two, when her major satisfactions may reside in a group whose climate sanctions or invites such activity.

Our society has been undergoing a change in its sexual behavior. The relaxation of taboos which usually accompanies the upheavals of war has been accelerated in the last two generations by the development of a widely publicized psychology. Permissiveness, self-expression, sexual adjustment, and freedom from inhibition have become in some quarters the marks of the well-adjusted American. The idea of extra-marital sex experience is accepted among many college students; among some groups its practice is almost a social *sine qua non*.

However, the professed code of behavior has not kept pace with the changing practices, and the ideal of chastity and marriage continues to be cherished along with other cultural fictions.[8] As long as the violation of the professed value is conducted with a decent regard for secrecy or is not other-

---

[6] Lola A. Bowman, "The Unmarried Mother Who Is a Minor," *Child Welfare*. Vol. 37, No. 8, October, 1958, p. 13.

[7] Leontine Young, *op. cit.*, p. 6.

[8] For an extended discussion of this problem *see* Max Lerner, *America as a Civilization*. New York: Simon & Schuster, 1957, pp. 657–688.

wise detected, society is content to accept the implied and overt contradictions resulting from the gap between our professed and operational codes.

Most adults sooner or later arrive at some sort of equilibrium in this cultural tightrope-walking act within which their satisfactions and their consciences manage a reasonably peaceful coexistence. For the young person searching for standards such a balance is not so easily achieved. When those from whom her standards are to be derived—the guardians of our social mores—are operating on more than one set of values, it is not surprising that she herself should question the validity of the professed code. The realism in the seemingly cynical "It's just that I was unlucky enough to get caught" cannot be lightly dismissed.

The uncertainty in our point of view as professional people may well be a reflection of the confusion in the society in which we participate and the role to which the community assigns us as social workers. As members of contemporary society we tolerate the original sexual activity. In deriving our social attitudes from the society that fosters the agencies we represent, we are expected to deplore the activity when confronted with its outcome. Identified with the unmarried pregnant girl who must hide from a censuring community, we reach out to comfort and counsel her. In addition we have our own private views to deal with. To say that a girl is in some respects an inevitable casualty of social change would almost make it appear that we approved of her sexual activity. We are uncertain as to what stand we should take toward extramarital sex experience, or whether we wish to take a stand at all. Yet a noticeable increase in the incidence of illegitimate births compels our attention. We are indeed on the multiple horns of a dilemma.

The extension of unmarried motherhood into our upper and educated clases in sizable numbers further confounds us by rendering our former stereotypes less tenable. Immigration, low mentality, and hypersexuality can no longer be comfortably applied when the phenomenon has invaded our own social class—when the unwed mother must be classified to include the nice girl next door, the college graduate, the physician's or pastor's daughter. In casting about for an appropriate explanation for her predicament we find it more comfortable to see the out-of-wedlock mother as a girl whose difficulty stems from underlying, pre-existing personality problems. We are forced into the position of interpreting the situation primarily in terms of individual pathology, failing to recognize the full extent to which the symptom may be culture-bound. We do, when pressed, acknowledge the possible influence of cultural factors, but in the main we do not tend to incorporate these elements significantly into our thinking.

There are no ready answers to this perplexing question, but as social workers we cannot adequately deal with the problem of the unmarried mother unless we see it within the framework of our conflicting mores. We must make room in our thinking for factors in the social scene—not only as they contribute to unwed motherhood, but also as they color the girl's reaction to her out-of-wedlock status in pregnancy.

It is understandable that we should incline toward a theory of underlying pathology as the cause of unmarried motherhood. Frequently, when we see the illegitimately pregnant girl, she presents a picture of severe disturbance. Guilt, panic, suspicion, and denial are not uncommon reactions. More often than not she will give a history of deprivation in primary relationships. However, if we are to assess correctly the sources and appropriateness of these reactions, we must take into consideration the circumstances under which we are seeing them. Two compelling factors in these circumstances are the crisis itself and the specifics of pregnancy and maternity. They are important not only for their diagnostic meaning but also because of their implications for practice in our work with unmarried mothers.

CRISIS

We know that in a crisis situation current functioning may be disrupted, past vulnerabilities exposed, and hitherto manageable conflicts stirred up. Earlier feelings of guilt, deprivation, and the like may be reactivated. The unmarried pregnant woman, seen at a point of crisis, may exhibit a whole range of disturbed reactions. To be sure, each girl will experience

her unwed motherhood in accordance with her basic personality make-up and will integrate it into her own patterns of
reaction and behavior. However, crisis can produce distortions
of one's customary patterns, and we cannot assume that her
reactions in a crisis situation represent her characteristic
mode of adaption to reality any more than we can say that
an acute pneumonia is characteristic of a person's physiological endowment, even though he may have some pulmonary
susceptibility. A girl may become an unmarried mother because she has had pre-existing problems, or she may be
having problems because she is an unmarried mother. Her
behavior may be a true reflection of underlying emotional
pathology, or it may be an appropriate response in an anxiety-
producing situation. She may be manifesting primarily a
resurgence of the latent guilt and unresolved conflicts which
are ingredients in all human adjustment and which have
been stirred up under acute stress.

Unmarried mothers as seen in a maternity home appear to
experience these crises in stages, with periods of relative
calm between, rather than in an unbroken line. Each girl
seems to have her own pattern of stress alternating with
well-being. For each the crisis-precipitating factor seems to
be different at different times. It may be related to elements
in the pregnancy. ("The emotional crises of pregnancy are
produced mainly through stimulation by biological processes
within the mother. . . .")[9] or it may result from news of the
baby's father, her own parents, or some other external source.
Our knowledge and experience are rather limited in this area.
Perhaps we should be directing some of our efforts toward
learning to recognize the signs of these crises, in order to
anticipate and prepare for them if possible—to know when
intervention is indicated and when the potentials for self-
healing inherent in crisis situations had best be left to do their
own work; to try to understand so that we may learn to deal
with the rhythms of crisis in the unmarried mother.

A recognition of the crisis factor in unmarried motherhood should give us pause in our routine use of psychological

[9] Gerald Caplan, M.D., from a lecture delivered in Cleveland, June
1953, to the first annual convention of the National League of Nursing.

testing of the resident in a maternity home, and in the requirement for prescribed casework interviews. One may hope that it will prompt us to interpret with great caution the results of projective tests and questionnaires, devices which appear to be taking on increasing importance in the diagnosis of unmarried mothers. Personality traits registered at a time of crisis, though applicable to the time and circumstances under which the tests are administered, can be interpreted in only a limited way as ongoing characteristics of the unmarried mother, individually or as a group. (The provocative nature of some of the test questions might also be considered.) Otherwise we are likely to emerge with a personality picture that does not fit the observations of many of us who are seeing unmarried mothers in their day-to-day living.

Note some conclusions from a recent study:

> . . . acting out anti-socially is a primary characteristic of the unwed mother. . . . There does not appear to be much difference between the unwed mother and other delinquent females.
> The unmarried mother is bitterly hostile . . . more so than all patient groups. . . .
> They are unfitted for psychotherapy because they deny problems and in their defensiveness appear aloof and independent, thus rejecting help and their basic dependency needs.[10]

PREGNANCY AND MOTHERHOOD

It is generally accepted that the experience of pregnancy can contain elements of crisis even for the married woman. "So-called 'normal pregnant women' might be highly abnormal, and even if they are not, they are anxious to a degree beyond that of the so-called 'normal non-pregnant female.' "[11] "Particularly during the first pregnancy women are apt to suffer terrifying dreams and phantasies of giving birth to a

---

[10] Edmund Pollock, "An Investigation into Certain Personality Characteristics of Unmarried Mothers." Unpublished doctoral dissertation, New York University, 1957, pp. 103, 110, 141.

[11] J. C. Hirst and F. Strousse, "The Origin of Emotional Factors in Normal Pregnant Women," *American Journal of Medical Sciences.* Vol. 196, No. 1, July, 1938, p. 98.

dead or misshapen child."[12] With the additional pressures to which the unmarried pregnant woman is subjected, we should not be surprised to see an intensification of the reactions which in her married counterpart we are prone to accept with tolerant indulgence. In themselves they are not necessarily signs of severe pathology. By the same token, the "normal deviations" of adolescence should figure prominently in our assessment of the meaning of out-of-wedlock pregnancy in the teen-ager.

Pregnancy and parturition constitute a continuing experience in physiological and emotional change. Each period seems to have its biological characteristics and typical emotional concomitants. There is still much uncharted territory in our knowledge of this psychobiological phenomenon, but obstetricians, psychiatrists, and others working with married pregnant women are becoming increasingly interested in the importance of these factors. As members of a helping discipline we have an obligation to incorporate into our work with the unmarried mother whatever relevant information is available. We may not be able to apply it very specifically as yet, but recognition of the significance of such factors can influence the ways in which we respond to a girl's reactions, the areas in which we offer help, and the manner in which we offer it.

It can affect our decision whether to reassure or to explore for deeper meaning at a given point. It may influence our interpretation of a girl's dependent leaning toward her mother or a mother-person. It will have a bearing on our reaction to her apprehensiveness about her growing attachment to a baby which she must relinquish—the ease with which we can help her to accept herself as a prospective mother and experience pregnancy and motherhood in as constructive a way as possible. It will have much to do with the strength we can lend her in the face of a separation from her baby, so that she can liberate and experience her feelings of motherliness toward her child. The "some day if I marry and have a baby *of my own* . . . ," inadvertently voiced by many girls

[12] Florence Clothier, M.D., "Psychological Implications of Unmarried Parenthood," *American Journal of Orthopsychiatry*. Vol. 13, No. 3, July 1943, p. 541.

who will be surrendering their babies, should give us pause as to its implications regarding their efforts to prepare for the interruption of a biological process which does not readily lend itself to alteration by social stricture.

For most unmarried mothers this is a first experience in motherhood and as such it may be an important influence in the image a girl establishes of herself as a mother-person. Part of our goal should be to help her emerge from it with as positive an image of herself as a mother as her personality and circumstances will permit. To do this we need to be ready, at appropriate points, to de-emphasize the unmarried, socially deviant aspect of her experience and accentuate its normal motherhood components. In fact we may well ask ourselves whether, in failing to exploit the full possibilities of motherhood for the unmarried mother, we may not be encouraging the blocking out of large areas of affect in her experience in maternity, whether she is surrendering her baby or keeping it.

In general, it might be well to examine our uncritical assumption that for the mother who must relinquish her child early separation is invariably indicated. Perhaps we need to consider the possibility that there are differences in the rates at which biological ties between mothers and babies are loosened, just as there are differences in the strength of these ties; that variations in the timing of the separation may therefore be indicated; that a premature separation may be as injurious as indefinite temporizing; and that perhaps the community has a responsibility to furnish the resources whereby such individual differences can be provided for.

If we see illegitimate pregnancy primarily as a symptom of underlying emotional pathology, we are likely to interpret much of an unmarried mother's behavior in similar terms. We will be on the alert for signs of pathology and will undoubtedly find them; one wonders whether we may not sometimes even be guilty of promoting the "self-fulfilling prophecy."[13] In trying to assess the nature and degree of disturbance, no matter how skillfully we proceed we may turn valid exploration into inappropriate probing, and find ourselves contributing to the very disturbance we are trying to diagnose.

[13] Robert K. Merton, *Social Theory and Social Structure.* Glencoe, Ill.: The Free Press, 1957, pp. 421–426.

The extent to which pathology orientation can skew our thinking can be illustrated in two fairly typical experiences we are likely to meet in our work with unmarried mothers, namely, "denial" and planning for the baby.

DENIAL

The unmarried mother's use of "denial" is a source of some concern to social workers. We tend to see it in her efforts to delay her admission to the maternity home, in her remaining in ordinary clothing beyond the appropriate time, in her reluctance to discuss plans for the baby just yet, in her unwillingness to talk. This may well be a denial of sorts, but is it bad?

Unless a girl is seriously disturbed, it is a fairly safe guess that she is not denying to herself the *fact* of her pregnancy. The question then is, what is she denying, and to whom? Is she expressing the feeble hope that there may have been an error in diagnosis after all (a not uncommon reaction in married women), or could she be trying to minimize the implications of her abandonment by the baby's father? She may be struggling with the problem of maternal affect, seeking to protect herself psychologically from a growing interest in a baby she may have to give up.

In assessing the meaning of denial it might be well to take cognizance of our own role in fostering it. As agents of the community, we offer the unmarried pregnant girl anonymity in a protected shelter; we provide out-of-town mailing addresses; we encourage her to deny her maturity by plans for the early placement of her baby, so that she can resume her place in the community as though nothing had happened. What we interpret as pathology may be the girl's valid use of a healthy mechanism to protect herself in crisis from a threatening reality. She is behaving the way society requires, in order to avoid permanent impairment of her social functioning. There are times when the girl who does not deny should perhaps be of greater concern to us than the one who does.

PLANNING FOR THE BABY

Our assumption that illegitimate pregnancy is invariably rooted in personality pathology has led us to accept uncritically certain further assumptions deriving from the basic one, namely:

1. That the same neurotic conflict which resulted in the out-of-wedlock pregnancy will motivate the girl in planning for her baby.

"Her decision about the baby is based not upon her feeling for him as a separate individual but upon the purpose for which she bore him."[14]

2. That adoption is the preferred plan for the babies of unmarried mothers.

"It is not an unwarranted interference with the unmarried mother to presume that in most cases it will be in the child's best interests for her to release her child for adoption. . . . The concept that the unmarried mother and her child constitute a family is to me unsupportable."[15]

3. That the girl who relinquishes her baby is healthier than the one who keeps hers.

No doubt many girls who should be relinquishing their babies are keeping them. Conversely, it may well be that some girls who are relinquishing their babies should keep them. One mother may be giving up her baby for reasons as neurotic as another's who keeps hers. However, if we are committed uncritically to the assumptions outlined here, we are less likely to give the adoption plan the thorough-going exploration that we devote to the plan to keep the baby, nor are we likely to examine the extent to which factors in the girl *and* in society are responsible for making one plan more desirable than another.

Actually we do not have enough verified data regarding the long-range outcomes of either plan to substantiate one as-

[14] Leontine Young, *op. cit.*, p. 199.
[15] Joseph H. Reid, "Principles, Values, and Assumptions Underlying Adoption Pratice," *Social Work*. Vol. 2, No. 1, January, 1957, p. 27.

sumption over the other. In the meantime we are subscribing to a point of view which states in effect that the presence of neurotic conflict automatically cancels out the validity of an impulse which is biologically determined. A mother, married or unmarried, may be severely neurotic in her motivation toward motherhood and still be substantially maternal. If we fail to take cognizance of this, we are taking only a partial view of the problem and are likely to give the unwed mother an incomplete or distorted service in the various aspects of her problem.

Technically we may claim that our underlying point of view does not influence us and that each girl is allowed to make her own decision regarding her baby. And technically this is probably correct in most cases. But the subtle communication of our essential attitude cannot be denied—as observed by one girl who felt she was being pressured into surrendering her baby: "It's not what Mrs. K says exactly, it's just that her face lights up when I talk about adoption the way it doesn't when I talk about keeping Beth."

SUMMARY

In our emphasis on a single theory of causation with regard to unmarried motherhood we are overlooking other important aspects of this phenomenon. As a result we may be depriving ourselves of meaningful diagnostic perceptions and failing to make full use of the rich treatment possibilities inherent in the experience for the girl. The additional factors of social mores, crisis, and the specifics of pregnancy and motherhood are offered for consideration here. They are presented not as substitutes for the currently accepted theory of underlying emotional conflict as causative in out-of-wedlock pregnancy, but rather as added dimensions which can extend our horizons and increase the effectiveness of our work in this area. Nor are these factors thought of as relevant for all unmarried mothers. It is hoped that they may be evaluated and applied with the same diagnostic discrimination, and on as individual a basis, as any theory.

If we are to help the unmarried pregnant woman to weather

her experience with a minimum of damage, and if possible exploit it as a point of departure for her maturing as a woman, we must help her understand what is happening to her in terms of her personal psychological make-up, her biological experience, and the social world of which she is a part. To do this we must be ready to accept multiple theories of causation; we need to explore without bias as many of the relevant ingredients as we can identify, and bring them all to bear in our effort to understand and help her. We must be ready to divest ourselves of some of the stereotyped images of the unmarried mother to which we have uncritically committed ourselves, and to recognize the conflicts in our own roles as social workers in relation to this problem.

We need to search for ways of broadening our knowledge and applying it more meaningfully in diagnosis and treatment of the unmarried mother. We need to think in terms of hypotheses to be truly tested rather than closed systems of explanation for which we are impelled to find substantiating evidence.

PART IV

Sociological Perspectives on the Unwed Mother

Social Level and Sexual Outlet

ALFRED C. KINSEY

WARDELL B. POMEROY

CLYDE E. MARTIN

PATTERNS OF BEHAVIOR

Within any single social level there are, of course, considerable differences between individuals in their choice of sexual
outlets, and in the frequencies with which they engage in each
type of activity. The range of individual variation in any level
is not particularly different from the range of variation in
each other level. Within each group, each individual pattern
is more or less duplicated by the patterns of individuals in
every one of the other social levels. Nevertheless, the frequencies of each type of variant are so different for different
social levels that the means and the medians and the general
shapes of the frequency curves for the several groups are perfectly distinct. Translated into everyday thinking, this means
that a large proportion of all the individuals in any group
follows patterns of sexual behavior which are typical of the
group, and which are followed by only a smaller number of
the individuals in other groups.

If the mean or median frequencies for each type of sexual
activity, at each social level, are brought together in a single
chart (Figures 2 and 3) it becomes possible to see what

REPRINTED FROM *Sexual Behavior of the Human Male,* 1948, pp. 374–
378, by permission of the authors and the publisher. (Copyright, 1948,
by W. B. Saunders Company.)

material differences there are in these patterns of behavior. Each horizontal line, followed across the chart, epitomizes the story of one social level. It is, as it were, a silhouette, a profile representing the essence of the group's attitudes on matters of sex, and the translation of those attitudes into overt sexual activity.

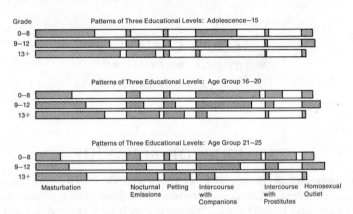

Grade   Patterns of Three Educational Levels: Adolescence—15
0–8
9–12
13+

               Patterns of Three Educational Levels: Age Group 16–20
0–8
9–12
13+

               Patterns of Three Educational Levels: Age Group 21–25
0–8
9–12
13+
Masturbation   Nocturnal   Petting   Intercourse   Intercourse   Homosexual
                  Emissions   with   with   Outlet
                                        Companions   Prostitutes

FIGURE 2. Patterns of sexual behavior at three educational levels, among single males, for three age groups. Each horizontal line extending across the page summarizes the pattern for one of the educational levels. Relative lengths of bars in each outlet show average mean frequencies for the group. The scales vary for different sources of outlets, but there is an approximate indication of the relative importance of each source in the total outlet.

Even a child would comprehend that the creature represented in each of these silhouettes is distinct and unlike the creatures represented in the other silhouettes.

It is, of course, of prime concern to ask why patterns of sexual behavior differ as they do in different social levels. It is of scientific importance to understand how such patterns originate, how they are passed on to each individual, and how they become standards of behavior for such a high proportion of all the individuals in each group. It is of equal importance to understand the social significances of these patterns of sexual behavior. Few of us have been aware that there were such differences in patterns in the various sub-divisions of our culture. An understanding of the facts may contribute something toward easing the tensions that arise because individuals and whole segments of the population fail to understand the sexual philosophies and the sexual behavior of groups in which they have not been raised.

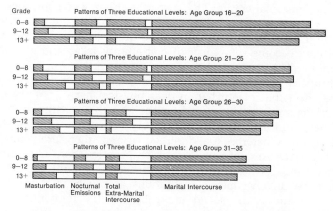

FIGURE 3. Patterns of sexual behavior at three educational levels, among married males, for four age groups. Each horizontal line extending across the page summarizes the pattern for one of the educational levels. Relative lengths of bars in each outlet show average mean frequencies for the group. The scales vary for different sources of outlet, but there is an approximate indication of the relative importance of each source in the total outlet.

We do not yet understand, to the full, the origins of these diverse sexual philosophies; but it will be possible to record what the thinking of each group is in regard to each type of activity.

Masturbation

At lower social levels, and particularly among the older generations of the lowest levels, masturbation may be looked down upon as abnormal, a perversion, and an infantile substitute for socio-sexual contacts. Although most lower level boys masturbate during their early adolescence, many of them never have more than a few experiences or, at the most, regular masturbation for a short period of months or years, after which they rarely again depend on such self-induced outlets. Among many of these lower level males, masturbation stops abruptly and immediately after the first experiences in heterosexual coitus. The lowest level boy who continues to draw any material portion of his sexual outlet from masturbation after his middle teens may be much ashamed of it, and he may become the object of community jokes and of more serious disapproval if his history becomes known. In many instances, these attitudes are bolstered by rationalizations to the effect that masturbation does physical harm; but the objections are in reality based on the idea that masturbation is either abnormal, or else an admission that one is incapable of securing heterosexual intercourse and, therefore, socially inadequate. Among some primitive peoples, there is a somewhat similar attitude toward masturbation—an attitude which does not involve moral evaluations as much as it involves amusement at the social incapacity of the individual who has to resort to self-stimulation for his sexual outlet. The better educated portion of the population which so largely depends upon masturbation for its pre-marital outlet, and which draws a not insignificant portion of its outlet from masturbation after marriage, will be surprised to learn what the less educated segments of the population think of one who masturbates instead of having intercourse.

The upper level more or less allows masturbation as not exactly desirable nor exactly commendable, but not as immoral as a socio-sexual contact. Older generations of the upper level were not so ready to accept masturbation. As many males were involved in the older generations, but the frequencies were definitely lower, and there was considerable moral conflict over the rightness or wrongness of the "habit." Upper level males have accepted masturbation more freely within the last two or three decades, and today a high proportion of the teen-age boys of the college group frankly and openly admit this form of pre-marital outlet. During their years in college about 70 per cent of these males depend upon masturbation as their chief source of outlet. They derive about 66 percent of their orgasms from this source during their college years.

The upper level's pre-marital experience leads it to include masturbation as a source of outlet after marriage. The coital adjustments of this group in marriage are frequently poor, particularly because of the low degree of erotic responsiveness which exists among many of the college-bred females. This offers some excuse for masturbation among the married males of the group; but their early acceptance of masturbation in their pre-marital histories, and their tardy acceptance of heterosexual coitus, are prime determinants in the marital patterns. There are few things in all human sexual behavior which will surprise the poorly educated groups more than this considerable utilization of masturbation by the college-bred male as an outlet after marriage.

Petting

The social levels are furthest apart in their attitudes on petting and on pre-marital intercourse. The two items are related, for petting, among males of the college level, is more or less a substitute for actual coitus.

In the upper level code of sexual morality, there is nothing so important as the preservation of the virginity of the female and, to a somewhat lesser degree, the similar preservation of the virginity of the male until the time of marriage. The utilization of pre-marital petting at this level is fortified by the emphasis which the marriage manuals place upon the importance of pre-coital techniques in married relations; and the younger generation considers that its experience before marriage may contribute something to the development of satisfactory marital relations. Compared with coitus, petting has the advantage of being accessible under conditions where coitus would be impossible; it provides a simpler means of achieving both arousal and orgasm, it makes it possible to experience orgasm while avoiding the possibility of a pregnancy, and, above all, it preserves one's "virginity." Whether consciously or unconsciously, petting is chosen by the upper level because intercourse destroys virginity and is, therefore, unacceptable. It is significant to note what different values are attached, at that level, to erotic arousal and orgasm achieved through the union of genitalia, and to erotic arousal and orgasm achieved through physical contact of other portions of the body, or even through genital contact or genital manipulation which does not involve actual copulation. There are many males in the upper level who develop a fine art of achieving orgasm by petting techniques which avoid intercourse. The youth who may have experienced orgasm scores or hundreds of times in petting, and who may have utilized every type of petting technique, including mouth-genital contacts, still has the satisfaction of knowing that he is still a virgin, as his level defines virginity. There are even cases of males who effect genital union; but because they avoid orgasm while in such union they persuade themselves that they are still virgins. The illogic of the situation emphasizes the fact that the basic issue is one of conforming with a code (the avoidance of pre-marital intercourse, the preservation of one's virginity), which is of paramount importance in the mores of this social level.

The lower educational levels see no sense in this. They have nothing like this strong taboo against pre-marital intercourse and, on the contrary, accept it as natural and inevitable and a desirable thing. Lower level taboos are more often turned against an avoidance of intercourse, and against any substitution for simple and direct coitus. Petting involves a considerable list of techniques which may be acceptable to the college group, and to some degree to the high school group, but which are quite taboo at lower levels (as discussed above). It is just because petting involves these techniques, and because it substitutes for actual intercourse, that it is considered a perversion by the lower level.

In particular cases, older persons, even at upper levels, have objected to pre-marital petting; but individual objections do not have the force of long-established mores. Pre-marital intercourse is condemned by mores which go back hundreds and thousands of years. Such taboos are very different from the criticisms which lone individuals have levied against petting within the last few decades, and for the most part the younger generation has paid little attention to such criticisms.

There is nothing in the behavior of the upper level which

is more responsible than petting is for the general opinion that college students are sexually wild. The lower level has many times as much pre-marital intercourse as the college male has, and it is not the intercourse of the college student which is the source of the lower level's criticism. It is the fact that petting may be engaged in for many hours without arriving at intercourse—it is the fact that intercourse itself is not more often accepted as a pre-marital outlet by the upper social level.

Pre-marital Intercourse

With the upper educational level, the question of pre-marital intercourse is largely one of morals. Some of the younger generation find it modern to insist that they do not avoid pre-marital intercourse because it is wrong, but because they consider intercourse too precious to have with anyone except the girl that they marry, or because they consider that marriages work out better when there has been no pre-marital intercourse. To this extent the younger generation is "emancipated"; but the change in the form of its rationalizations has not affected its overt behavior one whit.

A large portion of the 85 per cent of the population which never goes to college accepts pre-marital intercourse as normal and natural. Most of this group would insist that there is no question of right or wrong involved. Even some lower level clergymen, of the group that has never gone beyond grade school or high school, may react as the rest of the community of which they are a part preaching against profanity, smoking, drinking, gambling, and extra-marital intercourse, but considering that no moral issue is involved in pre-marital intercourse. So nearly universal is pre-marital intercourse among grade school groups that in two or three lower level communities in which we have worked we have been unable to find a solitary male who had not had sexual relations with girls by the time he was 16 or 17 years of age. In such a community, the occasional boy who has not had intercourse by that age is either physically incapacitated, mentally deficient, homosexual, or earmarked for moving out of his community and going to college.

Lower level males may have a certain respect for virginity, and this may lead them to insist (in 41 per cent of the cases) that they would not marry a girl who had had previous intercourse; but this may be more of a profession than a matter on which they will stand when it comes to the actual choice of a mate. Lower level males are likely to acquire weekly or more than weekly frequencies in intercourse soon after they start in early adolescence, or at least by the middle teens. They are often highly promiscuous in their choice of pre-marital partners, and there are many who have no interest in having intercourse with the same girl more than once. This strikingly parallels the promiscuity which is found among those homosexual males who are "oncers," as the vernacular term puts it. Some lower level males may have pre-marital intercourse with several hundred or even a thousand or more different girls before marriage, and here their behavior is most different from the behavior of the college-bred males.

Extra-marital Intercourse

In the lower social levels there is a somewhat bitter acceptance of the idea that the male is basically promiscuous and that he is going to have extra-marital intercourse, whether or not his wife or society objects. There is some continuation of the group attitude on pre-marital intercourse into the realm of extra-marital intercourse, at least in the early years of marriage. On the other hand, the upper level male who has been heterosexually restrained for 10 or 15 years before marriage does not freely let down and start extra-marital intercourse as soon as he has learned to have coitus with his wife. As a matter of fact, a male who has been so restrained often has difficulty in working out a sexual adjustment with his wife, and it is doubtful whether very many of the upper level males would have any facility in finding extra-marital intercourse, even if they were to set out deliberately after it. The lower level's extra-marital intercourse does cause trouble, but we do not yet understand all the factors which account for the fact that with advancing age there is a steady decline and finally a near disappearance of extra-marital intercourse from lower level marital histories.

The development of extra-marital intercourse in the histories of the older males of the upper level is done with a certain deliberation which in some cases may be acceded to and encouraged by the wife.

Homosexual Contacts

The considerable differences which exist in the incidences and frequencies of the homosexual in the three educational levels (Table 1) would seem to indicate basic differences in attitudes toward such activity; but we are not sure that we yet understand what these differences are.

The fewest objections to the homosexual are found in the very lowest of the social levels, in the best educated groups, and in top society. At the lowest social levels sex, whether it be heterosexual or homosexual, is more or less accepted as inevitable. The children here are the least restrained sexually and usually become involved in both heterosexual and homosexual activities at an early age. Since this is the group in which pre-adolescent behavior most often carries over into adult behavior, it is not surprising to find a fair number of the males at this level continuing both types of activity through the major portion of their lives. It is notable, however, that there are few individuals in this group who become exclusively homosexual. There are some who definitely condemn the homosexual, but there are many who accept it simply as one more form of sex. Rarely do they interfere with other persons who are involved, even though they themselves may not enter into such activities.

The acceptance of the homosexual in top educational and social levels is the product of a wider understanding of realities, some comprehension of the factors involved, and more concern over the mental qualities and social capacities of an individual than over anything in his sexual history.

The highest incidences of the homosexual, however, are in the group which most often verbalizes its disapproval of such activity. This is in the group that goes into high school but never beyond in its educational career. These are the males who most often condemn the homosexual, most often ridicule and express disgust for such activity, and most often punish

TABLE 1. Sources of Sexual Outlet for Single Males, at Three Educational Levels Showing Percentages of Total Outlet Derived by Each Group from Each Source.

Sources	Sources of Orgasm: Single Males % of Total Outlet					
	Adol.–15	16–20	21–25	26–30	31–35	36–40
Educational Level 0–8						
Masturbation	52.26	29.15	20.15	20.68	24.24	28.95
Nocturnal emissions	1.82	4.83	5.02	6.26	5.49	5.97
Petting to climax	1.06	1.66	1.23	1.96	0.68	0.05
Intercourse with companions	35.00	50.62	52.84	42.71	23.74	23.08
Intercourse with prostitutes	0.97	6.21	12.55	14.34	18.42	23.35
Homosexual outlet	8.03	6.85	8.06	14.04	27.43	18.60
Animal contacts	0.86	0.68	0.15	0.01		
Total outlet	100.00	100.00	100.00	100.00	100.00	100.00
Number of cases	712	720	361	159	61	47
Total solitary outlets	54.08	33.98	25.17	26.94	29.73	34.92
Total heterosexual outlets	37.03	58.49	66.62	59.01	42.84	46.48
Total homosexual outlet	8.03	6.85	8.06	14.04	27.43	18.60
Educational Level 9–12						
Masturbation	59.09	37.17	29.67	27.69	18.48	
Nocturnal emissions	4.44	6.33	8.10	7.48	8.21	
Petting to climax	1.46	2.37	2.77	1.82	1.35	
Intercourse with companions	24.93	39.49	38.02	29.75	42.81	
Intercourse with prostitutes	0.44	2.75	4.66	6.46	10.32	
Homosexual outlet	8.73	10.81	16.31	25.95	18.83	
Animal contacts	0.91	1.08	0.47	0.85		
Total outlet	100.00	100.00	100.00	100.00	100.00	
Number of cases	606	607	263	117	41	

Total solitary outlets	63.53	43.50	37.77	35.17	26.69
Total heterosexual outlets	26.83	44.61	45.45	38.03	54.48
Total homosexual outlet	8.73	10.81	16.31	25.95	18.83

Educational Level 13+

Masturbation	79.61	66.37	53.30	45.88	44.28
Nocturnal emissions	12.15	15.65	15.67	11.93	10.67
Petting to climax	1.54	5.26	7.50	5.17	4.98
Intercourse with companions	2.74	9.13	18.45	24.97	21.52
Intercourse with prostitutes	0.11	0.80	1.27	3.16	0.65
Homosexual outlet	3.14	2.43	3.72	8.82	17.90
Animal contacts	0.71	0.36	0.09	0.07	
Total outlet	100.00	100.00	100.00	100.00	100.00
Number of cases	2799	2861	1898	487	87
Total solitary outlets	91.76	82.02	68.97	57.81	54.95
Total heterosexual outlets	4.39	15.19	27.22	33.30	27.15
Total homosexual outlet	3.14	2.43	3.72	8.82	17.90

other males for their homosexuality. And yet, this is the group which has the largest amount of overt homosexual activity. Their involvement may be due to curiosity, to the fact that one may profit financially by accepting homosexual relations, or to the fact that one may derive a sadistic satisfaction from beating up the partner after orgasm has been achieved in the homosexual activity. In a certain segment of this group the idea is more or less accepted that one may uphold the heterosexual mores while "playing the queers," provided one punishes them after orgasm is achieved in the homosexual relation. As a group these males may strenuously deny that their sexual contacts have anything to do with homosexuality; but the full and complete record indicates that many of them have stronger psychic reactions to other males than they care to admit. When they no longer find themselves being paid for such contacts, many of them begin paying other males for the privilege of sexual relations.

If there are group attitudes in regard to the homosexual, they are not as freely discussed at most social levels. It may be that this explains why community thinking is not so well crystallized on this subject as it is in regard to other forms of sexual activity.

Illegitimacy and Patterns of
Negro Family Life

ANDREW BILLINGSLEY AND
AMY TATE BILLINGSLEY

It is appropriate that a volume on illegitimacy include a chapter on the Negro family because illegitimacy is more prevalent among Negroes than among any other ethnic group in America.[1] It is a striking fact, however, that the Negro family has largely been ignored by students of social behavior. No major study of the Negro family has been published since E. Franklin Frazier's study in 1939.[2] It is the point of view of this discussion that illegitimacy can not be understood or explained simply as psychological deviance on the part of Negroes or an historical propensity to violate social norms, or as inherent biological sexuality, and certainly not as moral decay.[3] Illegiti-

THIS IS an original article prepared for this volume.

[1] Illegitimacy is also much more "visible" among Negroes. To some extent abortion serves as an alternative to illegitimate births among white mothers. Thus 90% of the approximately one million mothers having abortions in 1960 were white. Furthermore, it is also estimated that more than 90% of babies born out-of-wedlock to white mothers are adopted. For discussion of these observations see Whitney M. Young, Jr., *To Be Equal.* New York: McGraw-Hill, p. 168.

[2] E. Franklin Frazier, *The Negro Family in the United States.* Chicago: University of Chicago Press, 1939.

[3] Each of these explanations has been seriously advanced by persons concerned about the problem and much of the effort to decrease illegitimacy is predicated on one or more of these assumptions.

macy among Negroes like other behavior patterns must be understood in the total context of Negro family life in both its historical and contemporary dimensions. This paper will examine first some major social crises in the historical development of the Negro family. Then some specific patterns of Negro family life which have emerged will be described. Throughout the paper these forces and patterns will be related to problems of social and family instability as represented by behaviors associated with illegitimacy.

SIX CRISES FOR THE NEGRO FAMILY

The family is the most basic of human institutions. Sociologically it may be considered the most intimate and influential of all the primary groups in society. From a psychological perspective it may be viewed as the basic unit for the development of the individual personality. In many respects the Negro family is similar to that of all other ethnic groups. Like all families, its primary functions are socialization and social control. It stands as a mediator between the individual and society. It teaches its members and especially its young ones how to be human, civilized, and how to make their way in society. At the same time it enforces on its members the norms of behavior generated in the larger society.

In a number of respects, however, the Negro family is unique and distinguishable from the white family in America. The Negro family has been and is in the process of being influenced by a number of historic and contemporary social forces in ways somewhat unique. These forces may be described under the rubric of six major social transitions, as follows: (1) from Africa to America, (2) from slavery to emancipation, (3) from rural to urban areas, (4) from the South to the North and West, (5) from negative to positive social status, and (6) from negative to positive self-image. Each of these transitions represents a major crisis in Negro family life.

The first two of these transitions are securely in the Negroes' past. Transitions 3 and 4 have passed the halfway mark.[4] And the latter two have barely begun. They represent both the renaissance and the future promise of the Negro family. Yet all of these transition stages are interrelated. It is one of the ironies of history that the last of these transitions is in large measure an outgrowth of the first. The rising image of the Negro in his own eyes is related, in part, to the rising status of Africa in the eyes of the world. We will examine each of these transition stages briefly, to set the stage for our analysis of the dynamics of Negro family life.

From Africa to America

Authorities are not agreed on the revelance of the African experience to Negro family life today. Anthropologist Melville J. Herskovitz has emphasized this relationship and pointed to cultural items in the behavior of Negro Americans which are traceable to African origins.[5] Sociologists such as Frazier tend to de-emphasize the African influence on Negro life today.[6]

There are, however, three factors about the Negro's transition from Africa which have profound relevance. The first is color. It must be realized that color is the most pervasive and influential characteristic of the Negro. It is being black in varying degrees, that defines a Negro in our society and heavily influences his life conditions, social behavior and psychological reactions. The Negro's color is his African heritage.

The second factor in the Negro's transition from Africa is cultural discontinuity. Nothing in the social and cultural background of the Negro in Africa prepared him for life in the Americas. This was not true of the other major waves of immigrants to the new world. The third factor related to Africa is slavery. While slavery itself was not a new institution the African slave trade is most relevant to the develop-

[4] According to the 1960 U.S. Census, two-thirds of the Negroes in this country now live in urban areas and about half now live outside the original Southern states.

[5] Melville J. Herskovitz, *The American Negro, A Study in Racial Crossing.* New York: Alfred A. Knopf, 1928.

[6] E. Franklin Frazier, *The Negro in the United States* (rev.). New York: The Macmillan Company, 1957.

ment of America. Only slaves from Africa were transported to America, and no other means of emigration to the new world were open to Africans in sgnificant numbers. Slavery had such profound influences on Negro family life that no understanding of the Negro family is possible without some reference to that peculiar institution.

Little is known about patterns of family life in Africa prior to the slaves importation to the new world. It is generally agreed, however, that the family was patriarchal, and the extended family was the meaningful social unit. In any case the manner in which Africans were captured, taken into slavery, transported to the new world and dispersed on plantations, particularly in North America, systematically cut off whatever cultural heritage the Africans might have brought with them.

The Africans were captured in intertribal warfare, marched to the West Coast of Africa often for two or three months journey from the interior, crowded and chained aboard the slave ships for the "middle passage." When they became ill or died along the route they were discarded. In the new world they were separated into small groups, sold to the highest bidder, and scattered among small plantations. Thus stripped of their heritage and their humanity, they started life anew in a situation which has its only modern parallel in the Jewish concentration camps developed by the Nazis.[7] This system lasted for more than 200 years.

Slavery in the United States was a most inhuman institution. It was very different from the institution of slavery in South America.[8] In the first place slave systems in South America did not cut off the stream of African culture as effectively as did the system in the United States in part because the plantations were larger. The cultural survivals in

[7] For an analysis of the parallels between the Nazi concentration camps and slavery and the similar effects they had on the personality of their victims, see Stanley M. Elkins, *Slavery: A Problem in American Institutional and Intellectual Life*. Chicago: University of Chicago Press, 1959.

[8] For a pioneering discussion of the differential impact of slavery in the United States and in South America, see Frank Tannenbaum, *Slave and Citizen: The Negro in the Americas*. New York: Alfred A. Knopf, 1946.

South America are so distinct that they can be identified by the African tribe from which they originated, while the major question among scholars in the United States is whether *any* African cultural survivals can be identified in Negro behavior. Secondly, slavery in the Spanish and Portuguese colonies carried little of the aura of total inferiority it did in the United States. It was therefore possible for Negroes to move from slavery to freedom without the necessity of a national holocaust.

At no time in the human experience was it a picnic to be a slave. But in Latin America and even in the Roman Empire slavery was a form of ownership of a person's labor. There were still safeguards ingrained in the society of the slave's person, of his family, and of his worth as a human being. In Latin America, there were special magistrates whose sole responsibility was to punish slave owners who mistreated and abused their slaves.[9] The killing of a slave was subject to the same laws and courts as the murder of any other person. The Catholic Church also took a special interest in the protection of the slaves from abuse and the development of viable forms of family life among them. Silberman has observed that in Latin America "Spiritually the slave was his master's equal, and intellectually, he could be his superior."[10] That was not possible in the United States.

There are several features of the slave system in the United States which left their imprint on patterns of Negro family life and particularly on the practice of illegitimacy. First, during the conquest of slaves premium was placed on young males because of their work potential. Therefore more males were imported than females. Not until 1840 was there an equal number of females. There were seldom enough females on the plantation to provide for the kind of monogamous sexual relationships demanded of the new culture and certainly not enough to provide for continuation of the polygamous pattern. It was inevitable, therefore, that if sex relations were to be possible the women must be shared. Second, marriage among the slaves interfered with their economic

[9] Elkins, *op. cit.*

[10] Charles E. Silberman, *Crisis in Black and White.* New York: Random House, 1964. See especially pp. 85–93.

productivity and was forbidden for the most part by their masters. Any offspring were by necessity illegitimate. Finally, the widespread practice of sexual exploitation of Negro slave women by their white owners and owners' sons produced a large number of illegitimate children. Even today in any large group of Negroes, a wide variation of colors may be observed ranging from black to white. These color variations are evidence of the white man's exploitation of Negro women.

Even during slavery, however, there was some social differentiation among the slaves caused principally by their relationship to the slave owners and their place in the division of labor. The three principal groups were the house slaves, the artisans, and the field slaves. The house slaves worked in and around the master's house, as cooks, nursemaids, butlers, and yardmen. The artisans were allowed to develop and practice skilled trades which were needed on the plantations. The field hands planted, cultivated, and gathered the crops. The status which accrued to the slaves was related to the proximity of their occupation to the house of the master. Even those slaves who worked inside the house had more status than those who worked in the yard. These different assignments also carried with them different privileges and opportunities. Thus the house slaves were the favorite and the elite. They were often able to bring back to the slave quarters extra quantities of food and cast-off clothing. Some were taught to read and write. Often they were left money and belongings in the wills of their masters. Because of the privileges associated with these positions, they were often assigned to the mulatto offspring of the white owner and Negro slave women. Then too, because of the proximity of the house servants to their masters, mulatto offspring developed.

In spite of frequent Negro uprisings in a vain quest for freedom, the pattern of slavery remained essentially static for over two hundred years. There were, of course, a few Negroes who were always free, and a few others who were set free by their masters, or who escaped via the underground railroad. But the bulk of Negroes remained slaves in the rural South. And the imprint of slavery has had profound effects on the patterns of Negro family life over the generations.

From Slavery to Emancipation

Throughout slavery since the Negro man was not allowed to serve as protector for his family, the Negro woman gradually emerged as the most stable, dependable, and responsible member of the family. Yet the whole Negro family existed at the pleasure of the white master. The onset of the Civil War and emancipation destroyed temporarily the authority of the master and left the Negro family adrift. The transition from slavery to emancipation thus, in addition to its positive consequences also presented a severe crisis for the Negro family. Three patterns of family life emerged from this crisis. First the majority of Negroes remained on the plantation as tenants of the former owners with little or no wages for their labor. Second, families which had been allowed to establish common residence, worked common plots of ground for extra food for the family, or where the Negro man was an artisan, or preacher, or house servant, made the transition with the least difficulty. The father became essentially the head of the family and its chief authority and support, where these roles had been fulfilled by the white master before. The third pattern was perhaps the most disruptive of family life. In those situations where only loose and informal ties had held man and woman together, in spite of the existence of numerous children, these ties were easily severed during the crisis of emancipation. These men tended to join the large bands of homeless men who wandered around the countryside in search of work and new experience. It was, indeed, this freedom to move about at will which was for them the primary reward of emancipation.

Women who were thus left behind, whether they had husbands or not during slavery became further entrenched as the only productive and dependable element in the family. Thus the crisis of emancipation accentuated the development which had begun in slavery of the female headed household.

Some attention must be given to the nearly half million Negroes who were free before the Civil War. They constituted only about 11 per cent of the total Negro population in 1860, but it is from this group that the most stable patterns of

Negro family life have emerged.[11] The reasons for this are apparent from the backgrounds of these free Negroes, their geographic concentrations, and the opportunities available to them. Free Negroes came principally from five sources: (1) children born of free Negroes and descendants from the original twenty Negroes brought in 1619 to Virginia and sold as indentured servants. (2) Mulatto children born of free Negro mothers and white men. (3) Mulatto children born of white indentured servants or free women and Negro men. (4) Children born of free Negro and Indian parentage. (5) Slaves set free by their masters or who escaped into freedom. It is impossible to tell exactly how many freedmen were produced by each of these sources, but it is easy to see from these sources why there was such a high proportion of mulattoes and light skinned Negroes among those who were free. A second feature of this group of free Negroes is that they lived in the more prosperous areas of the south and tended early toward urban and northern communities. The third factor distinguishing the free Negroes from the slaves was the opportunities they had for education and owning property including slaves, and the opportunity to enter regular and skilled occupations. Descendants of these families can be found today among the highest status, most refined, economically secure, and stable families in the Negro community.

From Rural to Urban Areas

It was only as the Negro population followed the general population to urban centers that an appreciable degree of freedom and opportunity was available, and even here such freedom and opportunity were often turned into illusions as the steady stream of Negroes into urban areas increased. But urban life had a decided impact on patterns of Negro family life. In general, two major sets of influences may be observed, one trend toward the greater disruption and the other toward the greater stabilization of family life.

The disruptive influence of the urban environment on patterns of family life for the general population have been given

[11] E. Franklin Frazier, *The Negro Family in the United States, op. cit.*

a great deal of attention. These influences were particularly detrimental to the newly developed Negro families.

The roving bands of homeless men and women who wandered around the countryside establishing temporary roots and temporary relationships around sawmills, turpentine camps, and on the roads, were the first to migrate in large numbers to the towns and cities in search of work, freedom, and adventure. These towns offered comparative freedom from the social restraints of rural communities. It is this very freedom, however, coupled with a marginal and transitory economic existence, which adversely affected family life. Often men came to town in search of work leaving their families behind. The inability of men to find work forced them to rely on the economic support of Negro women who could find domestic work. The kind of loneliness, discouragement, and sexual exploitation which developed was an outgrowth of a situation where men were thrown back on their own meagre and untutored resources without the social and economic supports which make for viable patterns of family life.

It was among this group of men and women who had not only been uprooted from the soil, but who had no deep roots in communal life in the cities, where in short, both socialization and social control were the weakest that patterns of sex behavior and family ties were most tenuous. Thus the extended family ties, rural religious norms, the demand for each person's labor on the farm, and the general binding folkways of the rural environment, were absent in the cities which were larger, impersonal, and more legalistic in their mores. These disintegrating influences affected not only those elements in the Negro group which were the least socially stable, but others as well. But in general those with stable family traditions, who brought their families with them, established other social ties in the cities, and were able to be economically independent, were better able to resist the disintegrative influences of city life. Illegitimacy then, like other forms of family disorganization, has continued to be more prevalent in the poorer sections of the Negro community which are most isolated socially and economically from the mainstream of the general society.

There were also stabilizing influences in the urban environment for Negroes which were absent in the rural communities, particularly after the turn of the century. Chief among these were some limited opportunities for stable industrial wage employment on the part of men, the gradual emergence of a middle class, and some opportunities for social integration into the larger society. These forces served to increase family stability and decrease the social problems associated with weak family life. Only during wartime mobilization, however, has the economic and the social structure of these urban communities showed more than minimal ability to absorb large numbers of Negroes moving to the cities seeking these advantages.

From Southern to Northern and Western Communities

The stream of Negro migration in this country has followed that of the general population from the southern rural communities, to northern and midwestern industrial and commercial centers, and then to the West.[12] It has often been observed that as these waves of migration accelerated, the small number of well-established Negro families in these new communities have resented the influx of the newcomers as much as the white settlers. It has often followed that racial restrictions have intensified with an increase in Negro populations and such restrictions affect the old established Negro families in these communities as they do the newcomers. The color barrier makes it difficult for privileged, established Negroes to escape the prejudice and discriminations to which their less fortunate relatives are subjected. With their intellectual, economic, and social resources, however, they are often better able to withstand the debilitating effects of these forces.

The migration of Negroes out of the deep South has undoubtedly been accompanied by expanding social and economic opportunities. But the major difference between the South and the North with respect to social, economic and edu-

---

[12] For a comprehensive analysis of Negro life in a northern city see St. Clair Drake and Horace R. Cayton, *Black Metropolis*. Vols. I and II (rev.), New York: Harper & Row, Harper Torchbooks, The Academy Library, 1962.

cational restrictions against Negroes has been a matter of form. In the South these restrictions have traditionally taken the form of explicit, formal, and codified norms, reflected in both custom and law. These formal restrictions are only grudgingly giving way now to the massive onslaught of industrialization, communications, political enlightenment, and the organized Negro protest. It is apparent that many southern communities are attempting to take a page out of the northern book by abolishing all legal restrictions and placing greater reliance on informal and extra-legal means of discrimination against Negroes.

Another major difference is that in northern communities such discrimination is not the result of deliberate efforts to deprive Negroes of opportunities as it is the inability to grasp the need for, and unwillingness to support special community efforts to overcome the pervasive poverty, social isolation, and psychological alienation in the Negro ghettos of the urban North and West.

The conditions of life for a Negro child growing up in a northern urban slum are not appreciably different from those of a child growing up in a southern city slum. And the relative absence of significant role models with which he can identify occupying major positions in the crucial institutions of socialization and social control, such as school teachers, community leaders, and policemen, present major obstacles to the efforts of families who want their children "to be somebody." In all of the 800 schools of central Harlem, for example, in 1963 there was one Negro school principal.[13] It would be hard to convince any intelligent Negro mother that this is solely because no Negroes are qualified. And even if this could be done there would remain a lingering question as to why there were no qualified Negro educators in the nation's first city. In the nation's capitol where Negroes constitute a majority, in 1963 there was not a Negro captain on the police force.

The absence of such representatives, in addition to the loss in effective teaching and police work, means that the young

[13] Kenneth B. Clark, *Youth in the Ghetto: A Study of the Consequences of Powerlessness.* Harlem Youth Opportunities Unlimited, Inc., New York, 1964, p. 223.

Negro child does not see himself in authority figures and positions of power and influence. His efforts to grapple successfully with the crisis of autonomy are severely restricted. The feeling of powerlessness is therefore pervasive in the urban Negro ghettos.

The transition from the South to the North on the part of Negroes which has now reached the halfway mark and is continuing, has by no means freed the Negro from the differential social constraints imposed by his society because of his heritage. Nor has it freed him from the psychological scars of such constraints. The stability of family life is thus continually threatened, particularly in the urban ghetto, as the incidence of illegitimacy and other social problems will attest.

From Negative to Positive Social Status

One of the most reliable indices of a rise in general social status is the rise in social class position in our society. The dominant Negro population has emerged over 100 years from a submerged group outside and below the social class structure, through a period of massive preponderance in the lower class to a period where social stratification has developed into meaningful proportions. The development of a small stable working class, the emergence of a significant middle-class element, and the solidification of a small upper class among Negroes are reflections of slowly improving economic conditions, and at the same time have had profound influence toward the stabilization of family life.[14]

The most common indices of social class position are income, education, occupation, and residence. It is a striking fact that as Negroes have risen on a combination of these indices the incidence of family disorganization has decreased. This changing social status represents not only material well-being, but a change in both opportunities and values. A rise

[14] For a discussion of Negro lower class and middle class characteristics, see Allison Davis and John Dollard, *Children of Bondage*. New York: Harper & Row, 1940, pp. 263–278; also Abram Kardiner and Lionel Ovesey, *The Mark of Oppression*. Cleveland: World Publishing Co., 1962, pp. 64–73.

in social class, is thus accompanied by more stable marital roles on the part of both parents, greater family loyalty, greater conformity to the sexual mores of the larger society, higher aspirations for their children, and in general greater striving for acceptance and respectability in the larger society. "Black Puritans" among the higher socio-economic groups are characterized by their strict codes of morals and manners. They also develop a certain amount of disdain for and efforts at disengagement from the lower classes.

The middle-class Negro experience is very different from the lower class. Here there are tendencies toward monogamy, stable residence, the ideal of economic dominance by the father, rigid discipline and sex mores, heterogeneous occupations, thrift, caution, inhibition of aggression and sex, ambition, initiative and manners. There is a tendency to emphasize individual progress regardless of race, or in spite of race. They have the goal of legal and continued marriage and sex fidelity.[15] There is powerful and continual pressure on children to study, repress aggression, attend Sunday School regularly, and avoid gambling. The goal for their children is high school education, skilled occupations and a "good" marriage. Their children are subjected to regular supervision.

The lower class is impulsive and there is a premium on physical aggressiveness. They learn that the gratification of expressing rage is greater than the pain of physical conflict. Often lower-class children are punished if they do *not* fight back. Sex mores are not rigidly enforced and children are often exposed to the sexual activity of their parents.

While two-thirds of the Negroes in the country are still in the lower levels of the socio-economic pyramid, the middle class is steadily growing. It is not expanding, however, as rapidly as the middle class in the general population. In spite of the advantages which accrue to middle-class positions among Negroes in our society, their efforts to disengage themselves from the conditions of their heritage have not been altogether successful. A Negro professional is subjected during most of his waking hours to many of the same indignities

[15] Whitney Young has observed that marital stability among middle-class Negroes is higher than among whites of similar status.

and restrictions as one who is poor and uneducated. Economic security feeds but half of man's hunger.

One explanation for the relatively active participation of middle-class Negroes in the current Negro revolt is the realization that Protestant ethic does not work completely for Negroes. For once one has worked hard, saved his money, improved his skill and refined his manners so that his conduct and values are respectably middle class, yet he is not accorded the same rewards by his society that white people take for granted. Privileged Negroes have been impressed anew with the fact, that in a very real sense, one is not truly free until all are free. The new hope is that raising the levels of opportunity for all Negroes will result in improved standards and levels of performance and equality of social rewards. Indeed, this may be the chief significance of the current Negro revolt, that Negroes and others will come to focus on the common obstacles to the many rather than be content to enjoy the limited opportunities of the talented and fortunate few. If this new hope can be sustained, it promises to have profound influences on the patterns of Negro family life. The notion of common purpose, that somebody cares, that it is possible to do something about one's conditions is already providing antidotes for the kind of apathy and alienation which is often prevalent in the Negro ghetto.

From Negative to Positive Self-Image

One of the most crippling and pervasive handicaps of the Negro experience in this country has been a deep-seated sense of inferiority. "Being a Negro," concluded Arnold Rose, "involves—everywhere in America, and independent of social class—having inferior status."[16] Du Bois put the same point more subjectively: "One ever feels his twoness—An American, a Negro; two souls, two thoughts, two unreconciled strivings."[17] In a more personal vein, James Baldwin has observed:

[16] Arnold Rose, *The Negro in America*. Boston: Beacon Press, 1948, p. 217.
[17] W. E. B. DuBois, *The Souls of Black Folk*. Greenwich, Connecticut: Fawcett Publications, Inc., 1961, p. 17.

"I was as isolated from Negroes as I was from whites, which is what happens when a Negro begins, at bottom, to believe what white people say about him."[18]

This sense of being separate and apart from the main society and yet bound by and utterly dependent on the structure of that society, has bred feelings of inferiority and doubts about self-worth among Negroes which provides one of the most difficult challenges to the Negro family. The Negro family must not only teach its members how to be human and American but also how to be Negro. Further, it must teach its members the similarities among these three roles and the differences, and more importantly, how to cope with the differences. Each Negro child, therefore, early in life must develop means of coping with the problem of being Negro in a white society. Some common modes of coping are, denial, accommodation, and protest. The stronger and more viable the family life the better it is able to approach the accomplishment of this impossible task.

This negative self-image on the part of the Negro people is now undergoing a radical change, a change which is most symbolized in the current Negro revolt. The two primary social forces stimulating this revolt are the Negroes' own increase in economic and educational achievement and the rising importance of Africa in the world.[19] Both of these developments have made the American Negro more aware of his relative deprivation in this country. The revolt is a statement of self-worth. It is an effort to disagree with the general statement of Negro inferiority. It is an expression of a newly felt sense of importance, dignity, and power. For the Negro family, the revolt provides another way of saying to its members, "you are somebody," and provides a way for persons of various talents and ages to have some part in matters which effect their lives. Martin Luther King has written:

> Watching those youngsters in Birmingham, I could not help remembering an episode in Montgomery during the bus boycott.

[18] James Baldwin, *Nobody Knows My Name*. New York: Dell Publishing Company, 1961, p. 4.

[19] For an analysis of how the rising importance of Africa has an impact on the Negro in the United States see Harold Isaacs, *The New World of Negro Americans*. New York: John Day Co., 1963.

Someone had asked an elderly woman why she was involved in our struggle. "I'm doing it for my children and for my grandchildren," she replied. Seven years later, the children and grandchildren were doing it for themselves.[20]

But the transition from negative to positive self-image is also a crisis, not without its agonizing aspects.

There is nothing more humiliating to a Negro man who cleans cuspidors and bows before white persons in an all-white barber shop than to see a nine-year-old Negro child, head high, face well scrubbed, walk through a howling mob and flying bricks to go to school. He hates himself—God how he hates himself!—and he will never forgive the white man who forced him into impotence.[21]

At the same time this crisis stimulates among Negroes renewed interest in some of the positive concomitants of the Negro experience. "I wanted to find out," says Baldwin, "in what way the *specialness* of my experience could be made to connect me with other people instead of dividing me from them."[22] Some of the special characteristics of the Negro experience are a sense of compassion, a focus on the reality of things, a sense of creative innovation in the face of changing conditions. These are contributions the Negro family can make to its members. They, and other positive attributes are being "rediscovered," or at least viewed in a new light with efforts to enhance them and perhaps, even to share them with the wider society. But the ability of the Negro family to make this contribution will depend, in great measure on its strength and vitality as a sub-cultural form.

We have described in brief, six major social influences on patterns of Negro family life. These include, the transition from Africa to America, the transition from slavery to emancipation, the transition from rural to urban environments, from southern to northern and western communities, from negative social status to positive status, and the transition from negative to positive self-image. Each of these transitions represent a crisis for the Negro family and the wider society. It remains

[20] Martin Luther King, Jr., *Why We Can't Wait*. New York: Signet, The New American Library, 1963, p. 99.
[21] Louis E. Lomax, *The Negro Revolt*. New York: Signet, The New American Library, 1962, p. 87.
[22] Baldwin, *op. cit.*, pp. 3–4.

now to specify some specific patterns of family life which have emerged from these conditions.

PATTERNS OF NEGRO FAMILY LIFE

There are essentially three distinct patterns of Negro family life which have emerged from these historical and social forces described above. These may be referred to as the matriarchal pattern, the equalitarian pattern, and the patriarchal pattern. Each of these patterns has a bearing on the problem of illegitimacy.

Matriarchal Family Pattern

The matriarchal family pattern is one in which the female head of the household is the dominant member.[23] This is most commonly the mother of the nuclear family but sometimes the grandmother. In its strict sense matriarchy implies not only dominance of the mother figure in the family constellation but that descent and kinship are traced through the mother rather than the father. In general the Negro family in America follows the basic pattern of American families which are parilineal and patrilocal. That is, not only does the kinship follow the father's line but the family generally resides in the father's house. There are some important exceptions among American Indian tribes which are matrilineal and matrilocal. There are some minor and informal exceptions among Negro families which will be discussed below.

There are, in general, three subtypes of the matriarchal family pattern. One occurs where there is no father in the home. The mother lives in her own house with her children, or sometimes in her parents' house. In these situations the family is obviously matrilocal and occasionally where the mother does not wish to reveal the name of the father, or to honor the father's lineage, the child is given the surname of

[23] This discussion is indebted to the pioneering work of E. Franklin Frazier. See especially *The Negro Family in the United States, op. cit.;* and *The Negro Family in Chicago.* The University of Chicago Press, 1932.

the mother rather than that of the father. It sometimes occurs that the mother's family informally, and on rare occasions formally, adopts the child.

The second form of matriarchal family pattern occurs where there is a temporary father, or, a series of temporary fathers to children of a single mother. A mother may have several children with different recognized fathers. This pattern is commonly matrilocal as well, though sometimes the mother will go to live for a time in the home of one of her husbands. This type of serial marriages is not uncommon among lower-class Negro families and is generally dominated by the mother who often bears the responsibility for the economic support of the children as well as the more elementary forms of mothering.

A third matriarchal form exists where there is a stable father in the family but where the mother is still the dominant authority figure. This often occurs where "weak" fathers have an unstable and precarious relationship to the labor market and are not able to either support their families or to exercise their parental authority.

Of all the family patterns where there are children the matriarchal pattern is the least stable. And of the three matriarchal subtypes, the one without a father is the least stable, and the one with the stable, weak father is the most stable. Stability, in the latter case, however, insofar as the needs of the children are concerned, is only a mixed blessing. We will return to the importance of the masculine father role below.

The matriarchal family type is not the most frequent type among Negro families, nor is it exclusive to Negro families, but it is considerably more prevalent among Negro families than among any other ethnic group in America. This is the family pattern out of which illegitimacy and other indices of unstable family life occur most frequently. These are the families most often and most commonly supported by public assistance. These are the families whose members are most deprived, economically, socially, and psychologically. These are the families whose members are most alienated from the norms and values of the larger society. In short, it is among Negro families of this matriarchal pattern whose opportunities, performance, and rewards are at such a minimal level that families in this group often come to be characterized as "multiproblem families."

In addition to the precarious economic base and the lower-class status of families in this pattern, their most pervasive and crippling charateristic is the absence of an everpresent father, with the economic security, social acceptance, and personal dignity provided by meaningful and stable work, and who exercises responsibility and authority in the family group. "Our sons need their fathers," said a Negro mother at a recent conference, "but our daughters need them more."[24] Both sociologists and psychologists have insisted that it is in the intimate family group that young people receive their basic socialization and develop internalized social controls responsive to the larger society. It is here, in short, that they learn to be human and to assume important roles in society. "A man can't be a man in society if he doesn't have a job," said the same mother. "He brings home his disgust and inferior feelings, and the children don't look up to him as the worth of a man." It is difficult for such children to look upon themselves as the worth of a man to be.

This family pattern often results in both boys and girls being closer to their mother than their father. This closeness is more continuous for girls and this helps to explain why Negro girls often show greater self-confidence, aspirations, and achievements than boys. Twice as many Negro girls as boys graduate from both high school and college, while the relationship is reversed for white youth.

These matriarchal families most often live in rural enclaves and urban ghettoes in the South and the North. They have been most victimized by their history. They are the least aided by their current society. Left so completely to their own basic resources they have developed attitudes and forms of behavior which often sets them apart from the rest of society. Sometimes this has resulted in major cultural contributions to society, most notably in athletics and the performing arts. Often, their behavior is indistinguishable from that of other

[24] Conference on The Negro Family, November 5–7, 1964, sponsored jointly by the University of California Extension Division, Special Programs and PACT, a Negro employment opportunities agency.

family types. More striking, however, have been the disproportionate representation of this family pattern among those antisocial behaviors which cause considerable pain and expense to the wider community, surpassed only by the pain and expense the wider community has inflicted on these family members.

"The culture of the matriarchy is so emphatic in its exclusion of men that a corresponding male culture . . . does exist, and its impact on a large number of men, especially in the lower class is dramatic and profound.[25] The gang is generally a street fraternity of men who set a role model for the Negro man and boy who are not integrated into the family. The gang is a hard task master. It is highly individualistic. Every man must constantly prove himself by way of physical and sexual prowess. A major goal is independence from all responsibility. There is wrath and scorn for anything effeminate. All middle-class goals and values are rejected as effeminate, including religion, occupational, and educational achievement.

Equalitarian Pattern

Perhaps the most common family pattern among Negroes as among other groups is the equalitarian pattern. This is a family type in which there are two parents who have distinctive but complementary and flexible roles and who both participate actively in the authority and decision-making structure of the family. This most often occurs where the husband has stable employment and at least operational level of education. This family pattern is common among the stable working classes and among the middle classes. Two subtypes of the equalitarian family structure may be identified, one in which the father works outside the home and the mother devotes herself primarily to homemaking, and the other type in which both parents work outside the home, and share the home and child care responsibilities among themselves, relatives, or other extra help.

It is from middle-class families of this particular type that

[25] John H. Rohrer and Munro S. Edmondson, eds., *The Eighth Generation Grows Up*. New York: Harper & Row, 1960, p. 158.

most of the Negro leaders emerge, although leading Negroes have origins in each of the family patterns. This distinction between Negro leaders and leading Negroes is very important though it is often not made. Negro leaders are distinguished by their organized social activity in efforts to change and improve the conditions under which Negroes live. Leading Negroes are distinguished, rather, by their own personal achievement. They are essentially celebrities.

Both of these groups, however, have enormous implications for Negro family life, and the recent rapid expansion of their ranks is both a cause and a consequence of increasing stabilization among Negro families. The leading Negroes serve as influential role models for achievement oriented parents and their children. The Negro leaders help to change the conditions which make achievement possible and rewarded. While a number of studies have shown that Negro leaders do not exercise a great deal of direct influence in the power structure of the general community,[26] it is equally true that "white authorities do not effect positive changes in the status of Negroes in any area of community life until professional Negro leaders have voiced long, loud, concerned protests."[27]

Families of the equalitarian type are thus both the products and the source of the kind of socio-cultural values and opportunities which contribute to stable family life and minimize the kind of behavior represented by illegitimacy and other forms of social disorganization.

While families of this basic pattern are not all middle class by any means, they are better equipped than those of the matriarchal pattern to carry out the basic functions of the family, namely socialization and social control.

The crucial roles of the father such as spending time with the children, teaching them, playing with them, and disciplining them are not only less likely in the matriarchal type family when a father is present but impossible when he is not, as is often the case. This is no doubt what the young Negro boy at the Neighborhood House in Richmond, Cali-

[26] See, for example, Floyd Hunter, *Community Power Structure: A Study of Decision Makers.* The University of North Carolina Press, 1953.
[27] Daniel C. Thompson, *The Negro Leadership Class.* Englewood Cliffs, N. J., 1963, p. 53.

fornia, had in mind when referring to a leading Negro: "Yeah man," the youth replied, "but that cat was born with a silver spoon in his mouth." When asked by his social worker what he meant, he continued, "I mean for one thing, that cat had a father; and for another, his father taught him a trade."[28] The youth, a product of a matriarchal family was immensely aware of the disadvantages which he suffers as compared with the "cat with a silver spoon."

The influence of a present and active father on the personality of young children can be appreciated by reference to the consequences of the absent father. A number of psychologists have shown through research, for example, that children growing up without a father tend to seek immediate gratification even to the point of preferring small rewards at once rather than considerably larger rewards later on. Another study showed that these children perceive less differences between men and women than children with a father in the home. Still other evidence suggests that boys growing up in these families are significantly more dependent and submissive than boys with strong father figures and it is this dependency and submissiveness which is later defended against in exaggerated forms of masculine behavior, including sexual behavior. These findings have been interpreted as suggesting that these boys have strong primary identification with their usually overprotective mothers and must later in our relatively patriarchal culture develop a conflicting secondary identification with men.[29]

These, then, are some of the strains and crippling conditions of the matriarchal family pattern from which children who grow up in the stable equalitarian family are protected to a considerable extent.

In spite of the richness of both the heritage and the potential contribution of the equalitarian family pattern, it is often vulnerable to falling into the matriarchal pattern. Remaining stable depends on a number of factors, including

[28] Silberman, *op. cit.*, p. 226.
[29] For a comprehensive discussion of research on the Negro personality see Thomas F. Pettigrew, "Negro American Personality: Why Isn't More Known," *Journal of Social Issues*. Vol. XX, No. 2 (April, 1964, pp. 4–23.

the vitality of its family tradition, employment of the father, development of a common family subculture, and the integration of the family in the life of the general community. If the father loses his job and especially becomes chronically unemployed he loses some of his functions and authority. He may even join the ranks of the deserters.

Patriarchal Family Pattern

A third general pattern of Negro family life closely approximates a patriarchy. In this family the husband and father is not only present but is dominant in an economic, social, and psychological sense. He makes most of the major decisions. Dinner is not served until he gets home, and he sits at the head of the table and guards the manners of his flock. Illegitimacy as a social problem is almost unknown among families of this type.

This patriarchal family pattern also owes its origins to the slave system but was given an impetus by the crisis of emancipation. Frazier traces this development briefly as follows:

The more stable elements among the free men who had been in a position to assimilate the sentiments and ideas of their former masters soon undertook to buy land. This gave the husband and father an interest in his wife and children that no preaching on the part of white missionaries or Negro preachers could give. But it would be a serious mistake to overlook the manner in which the new economic position of the man was consolidated by the moral support of the Negro church.[30]

The Negro minister is only one source of the patriarchal family pattern. Essentially this pattern of male dominance in the family is a concomitant of all the forces in the wider community which makes for dominance. For Negroes these have resulted in a history of freedom even before emancipation, mulatto origin, and the privileges, economic and social stability associated with these backgrounds. Upper-class Negroes are consequently, heavily represented in this pattern of family life, though the distinctions between upper class and middle class among Negroes are not as great as for

[30] E. Franklin Frazier, *The Negro Church in America*. New York: Schocken Books, 1963, pp. 32–33.

whites. These families whether upper or middle class are considered the elite of the Negro community. They are "the Black Puritans." They often have inherited wealth and a genteel tradition. They commonly intermarry among themselves, and react to Negroes of lesser station as outsiders.

Dorothy West presents a vivid description of a patriarchal family headed by "Mr. Benny" a prosperous Negro business man in Boston. Living in an all white neighborhood he warned his two children not to associate with the lower-class Negroes who were beginning to move to the edge of the neighborhood. After his son got into a fight with one of the newcomers, Mr. Benny gave him the following lecture:

> It is time you learned a hard and fast rule, Simeon. A colored man can never afford to forget himself, no matter what the provocation. He must always be superior to a white man if he wants to be that white man's equal. We are better fixed financially than any family on this street. You and Thea attend private schools. The other children go to public school. Your manners are superior. Your mother has more help. We set a finer table. If our manner of living was exactly like theirs, we would not be considered good enough to live on this street.[31]

The dilemma for the "Black Puritans" is that being isolated from the Negro masses, they must be even more virtuous than their white models, and even then the rewards for such behavior are not nearly equal to the effort.

The most noteworthy feature of this particular pattern of family life for our purposes is its stability and strict patterns of socialization and social control according to the values shared by the dominant group in our society. They are the ultra-conformists. Illegitimacy as a social problem among this group is almost totally absent.

CONCLUSION

We have described six major social transitions affecting the Negro and traced the influence of these forces on three gen-

[31] Dorothy West, "The Living is Easy," in Herbert Hill, *Soon One Morning: New Writing by American Negroes, 1940–1962*. New York: Alfred A. Knopf, pp. 481–502.

eral patterns of Negro family life including varieties of the matriarchal, equalitarian, and patriarchal families. Of the transitions, it has been suggested that the least stable and most vulnerable pattern is the matriarchal pattern. And it is from families of this type where most of the social disruption occurs as represented by illegitimacy. Efforts to decrease illegitimacy among Negroes might well take these patterns into account.

It may be that the illegitimacy rate would be more effectively attacked by policies designed to build two-parent families involving men who exercise status, authority, and influence equal to that of other men outside the home, and equal to that of their wives inside the home. Thus concerted efforts to raise the levels of education, employment, and adequate housing conditions, would seem to have more effect than public exhortations to stamp out illegitimacy, moral crusades, or birth control clinics, or psychotherapy for mothers of illegitimate children. It may also be that those social welfare policies designed to attack the problem by keeping men away from the homes of unwed mothers might have a more desirable effect if they were completely reversed.

Illegitimacy, Anomie,
and Cultural Penetration

WILLIAM J. GOODE

Since the family is a prime instrumental agency through which the needs of various institutional needs are met, and legitimacy is the keystone of the family system, an examination of family systems with high illegitimacy rates should yield useful data on the integration of societies. Analysis of high illegitimacy rates indeed suggests that some modifications may be profitably made in several segments of sociological theory: (1) the cultural and social conditions under which high illegitimacy rates occur; (2) the classical theory of the assimilation of both native rural and foreign-born immigrants in the United States; (3) effective procedures for destroying cultural and social systems; and (4) the relation between social and cultural integration.

Illegitimacy rates are, or have been, relatively high in three major areas: Northwestern Europe, industrializing sub-Saharan Africa, and the New World, from Tierra del Fuego to the non-white Southern population of the U. S. To consider these in turn, let us note that Iceland and particular regions in Sweden, Germany, and Austria have had rates of about twenty to thirty per cent in recent years.[1] In special studies

REPRINTED FROM *The American Sociological Review*, Vol. XXVI, No. 6 (December, 1961), pp. 910–925, by permission of the author and the publisher. (Copyright, 1961, by The American Sociological Association.)

[1] Iceland's rate was 27.9% in 1950 (Meyer F. Nimkoff, "Illegitimacy," in *Encyclopaedia Britannica,* 1954. The Swedish illegitimacy rate has been dropping over the past generation. The highest rates have been found in

of native urbanizing areas in sub-Saharan Africa, rates of forty per cent or more have been reported.[2] In the New World, particular provinces may have rates over eighty per cent, a handful of mainland countries have rates over seventy per cent, and a majority of all the political units have rates over thirty per cent. The non-white populations of the Southern states in the United States had rates of twenty to thirty per cent in 1957.[3]

Stockholm (1841–1860, 43% illegitimate; 1901–1910, 34%; 1921–1925, 28%), but presumably these include many rural mothers. However, the regions of Gävleborglän and Jamtland län have continued to be relatively high (23% and 21% in 1921–1925; 17.6% and 18.5% in 1956). In Steiermark in Austria, the rate was 19% in 1956 (*Stat. J. Oesterreichs,* 1956). Oberbayern in Germany had a rate of 18.5% in 1954 (*Stat. J. Für Bayern,* 1955). I have recently found that certain regions of Portugal (Lisboa, Beja, Evora, and Setubal) have rates of 20%–30%, but I have found no special reports on them.

[2] The best surveys of recent changes may be found in *Social Implications of Industrialization and Urbanization South of the Sahara,* Paris, UNESCO, 1956, and Survey of African Marriage and *Survey of African Marriage and Family Life,* edited by Arthur Phillips, London: Oxford University, 1953. Twenty-three per cent of all unmarried women in certain Kxatla groups had borne children, 19% among the Ngwato and 17% among the Kwena (I. Schapera, *Migrant Labour and Tribal Life,* New York: Oxford, 1947, p. 173). An analysis of Bantu attitudes toward illegitimacy may be found in I. Shapera, "Pre-marital Pregnancy and Public Opinion," *Africa,* 6 (January, 1933), esp. pp. 83–89. Krige reported an illegitimacy rate of 59% in three locations in Pretoria (Eileen J. Krige, "Changing Conditions in Marital Relations and Parental Duties Among Urbanized Natives," *Africa,* 9 [No. 1, 1936], p. 4.) Janisch found that some half of the couples in a Johannesburg native township were "merely living together." (Miriam Janisch, "Some Administrative Aspects of Native Marriage Problems in an Urban Area," *Bantu Studies,* 15 [1941], p. 9.) In Capetown, illegitimacy rates of 26%–41% were reported in the period 1939–1944 (Ruth Levin, "Marriage in Langa Native Location," *Communications From the School of African Studies,* Capetown: University of Capetown, 1947, p. 41.) The rate was 30% in Capetown in 1958. For Leopoldville, S. Comhaire-Sylvain reports almost half of the couples in certain native wards were living in concubinage, "Food and Leisure Among the African Youth in Leopoldville," *Communications From the School of African Studies,* N.S., No. 25, December 1950, p. 23. Similar processes of "living together" have been described in the urbanizing area of Kampala (A. W. Southall and P. C. W. Gutkind, *Townsmen in the Making, East African Studies No. 9,* Kampala: East African Institute of Social Research, 1956, pp. 72, 74, 79, 174–8.)

[3] Data courtesy of U. S. National Office of Vital Statistics.

Why did the New World rates become so high? They cannot be "survivals of native customs," since neither the native Indian groups nor the New World immigrants, whether White or African, had especially high rates of illegitimacy.[4] Moreover, they had many *different* family patterns—patriliny and matriliny, low and high divorce rates, polygyny and monogamy—but the rates are *generally* high.

Another common explanation is that the consensual union, out of which such high rates grow, is part of the "development of a new sub-culture." That is, the union without benefit of wedlock is the "native," normatively supported equivalent of a legalized union. Consequently, Malinowski's Principle of Legitimacy, according to which every society has a rule condemning illegitimacy, is to be discarded. This explanation is not satisfactory, either. For at least the Caribbean, where this explanation has been widespread, it has been shown that both mother and child have a lower status outside the legal union, that women prefer to be married, and there is general agreement that the ideal family relationship is that of marriage. Moreover, a majority eventually do marry in the Caribbean. The Principle of Legitimacy is, then, roughly correct. But we did correct Malinowski's Principle in certain respects and described the bargaining process of consensual courtship outside parental or peer group controls, by which the young girl, unprotected by a kin network, must risk an unstable union and childbirth in order to have a chance at eventually entering a legal union.[5]

That analysis seems to be generally applicable, with only minor and obvious modifications, to the New World south of

[4] There are, of course, numerous monographs on the African societies that furnished the slaves. Because the Indian groups were, for the most part, destroyed before the anthropologists arrived, New World societies are less well known than the African, but an excellent summary of the known South American (including the Circum-Caribbean) societies may be found in *Handbook of South American Indians,* edited by Julian H. Steward, Washington, D.C.: Smithsonian Institution, Bureau of American Ethnology, Bulletin No. 143, 6 vols., 1946–1950.

[5] For details of this process, see William J. Goode, "Illegitimacy in the Caribbean Social Structure," *American Sociological Review,* 25 (February, 1960), pp. 21–30. The best analysis of this process in Jamaica is by Judith Blake, *Family Structure in Jamaica,* Glencoe, Ill.: The Free Press, forthcoming.

the Mason-Dixon Line: the consensual union is not the normative equivalent of marriage. Let us now consider the larger structural conditions under which such rates *develop,* to complement our previous analysis of the processes of individual social interaction which *maintain* these rates. From such a view, Northwestern Europe, urbanizing sub-Saharan Africa, and the New World exhibit very different patterns.

NORTHWESTERN EUROPE: A RURAL SUB-CULTURE

The relatively high rates in Northwestern Europe were the product of a courtship system which permitted considerable sex freedom to the young, under indirect but effective adult and peer group supervision. The choice of sex partners and of eventual spouse was restricted to a pool of eligibles, who were children of farmers. When premarital conception or even birth occurred, the young man was likely to be known as the girl's partner, and both were likely to be acceptable to both sets of parents.[6] Illegitimacy was likely to occur mainly when there was some reason for delaying marriage (e.g., unavailability of farm or housing), rather than because either partner or set of parents had rejected the marriage.[7] Childbirth outside of marriage was not approved. Rather, the exact *timing* of the marriage, whether before or slightly after the birth of the first child, was not a focus of intense moral concern.

This pattern was a "native," rural custom, upheld within an integrated social and cultural system of norms which was *not* integrated with those of the dominant national society.

[6] The most complete description of this pattern, and of its temporal and geographical distribution, is to be found in K. Rob. V. Wikman, *Einleitung Der Ehe,* Abo, *Acta Academiae Aboensis; Humaniora,* 1937. He asserts, however, that the pattern was not found in Iceland.

[7] And consequently, the rate of divorce for such marriages would be lower than for "forced" marriages in the United States. See Harold T. Christensen, "Cultural Relativism and Premarital Sex Norms," *American Sociological Review,* 25 (February, 1960), pp. 31–39. See also Sidney H. Croog, "Aspects of the Cultural Background of Premarital Pregnancy in Denmark," *Social Forces,* 39 (December, 1951), pp. 215–219.

Both the national state and Church opposed this pattern for centuries. It is not, then, a recent development, an index of "disorganization" in an urbanizing epoch. It is a subcultural difference, which has gradually been disappearing as isolated rural cultural and social systems have become more closely integrated with national cultural and social systems.

CLASSICAL ASSIMILATION THEORY

Studies of United States rural-urban migrants and of immigrant populations in the period 1910–1935 outlined a theory of assimilation and theory of cultural destruction which fit both these cases of migration but which must be modified to fit the other two great cases of culture contact being analyzed in this paper, Africa and the New World south of the Mason-Dixon Line.

These migrants entered as *individuals* and families, so that their initial social systems were undermined. Thus, their cultural patterns could not be maintained by those social systems and were dissolved by an open-class, individualistic, secular culture which gave substantial rewards to those who assimilated. The in-migrating populations were culturally absorbed by the dominant, numerically larger group. In the transitional period, they also became somewhat anomic: they lost their allegiance to their native cultural patterns but for a while felt no great commitment to the norms of the dominant group. To some extent, in various cities[8] they developed new social sub-systems and kept some of their cultural integration by living in ghettos, from which individuals moved out as they became acculturated into the larger society. Younger and older generations were in conflict, since each was oriented to different cultures. Some people lived as "marginal men," being accepted by and accepting neither culture and neither social system fully.

These in-migrants typically entered society in the United

[8] Mr. John Western has pointed out to me that there may be considerable difference in the assimilation patterns of those who "just landed" in the cities and stayed there and those who deliberately chose to migrate to the city.

States at the bottom of the class structure, where they were somewhat freed from both the older social controls and the controls of the new country. Some customs were difficult to obey under urban conditions and lost their force. Younger people could use either set of norms as a justification for any desired course of action. Generally, the native-born generation became acculturated, and the grandchild generation was *both* socially and culturally integrated in the larger society.

The cultural and social systems of the in-migrating peoples were undermined by these factors: (1) the dispersion of the immigrating social systems, (2) the political power and prestige standards of the receiving populations, which judged the migrants as belonging at the bottom of the class system, (3) the economic and social opportunities in the new system, which gave rewards to those who became acculturated and punished those who refused to do so, (4) the sheer numerical superiority of the receiving populations, and (5) the irrelevance of older customs to the new social situation.

Transitional populations exhibited, of course, relatively high rates of deviation in such areas as juvenile delinquency, adult criminality, desertion, illegitimacy, and so on. Unfortunately, the studies of that time did not make independent measures of "anomie," or "social disorganization," and correlate them with the usual rates of deviation in various areas of action. However, their findings do add corroboration to the modifications of Malinowski's Principle, offered in the paper on the Caribbean: (1) its foundation is not primarily the protection which the male gives the child, but the social importance which a kin or family line enjoys; i.e., it focuses on status placement, and (2) the strength of the norm commitment will vary with the importance of the kin line and thus will be higher toward the upper strata where the proportion of important kin lines is greater and where as a consequence illegitimacy rates will be lower.[9]

[9] William J. Goode, *op. cit.*, pp. 27 ff.

AFRICAN ILLEGITIMACY: BREAKDOWN OF THE CULTURAL AND SOCIAL SYSTEMS

Classical assimilation theory was, then, an outline of the processes by which a given "native" system moves from (a) being internally integrated both socially and culturally to (b) being internally non-integrated or anomic *both* socially and culturally and then (c) eventually absorbed. *Individuals* moved from state (a), their original situation in their native region, to (b), losing their position in their native social system, but gaining one in the new United States social system and, for a considerable time, being part of the older cultural system but not part of the new one. Ultimately, of course, they became integrated in the new social and cultural system. That set of phases must be modified somewhat to fit urbanizing or industrializing sub-Saharan Africa and still more to fit the New World. On the other hand, both the suggested modification of Malinowski's Principle and the anonymous "bargaining" pattern of Caribbean courtship may be applied to the African situation.

The African anomie is like the older United States rural and foreign immigration in these respects: (a) African individuals have been greatly dispersed in the urban locations, (b) native customs are often irrelevant and inconvenient in urbanizating areas, and (c) white standards and customs have higher prestige. It differs chiefly in these respects: (a) the original dominance of the white group was achieved by force, (b) those being assimilated outnumber the dominant group, (c) the African cultures were much more different from that of the dominant group than were the cultures of the United States in-migrants from that of the United States, and (d) because the Africans face caste barriers, they often cannot obtain substantial rewards for accepting European ways.

Important political consequences flow from these differences—for example, the inevitable creation of independent

African nations throughout the continent—but here we shall confine ourselves to the matter of illegitimacy.

The natives in the African urban or industrialized locations have come from tribes in which elders were once powerful, marriages were arranged, and illegitimacy was rare. The skills and knowledge of the elders are not greatly respected in the urban areas, because they are no longer effective. Social control is therefore likely to be reduced to the formal controls of the outside, white society. Although there is some tendency for people from the same tribe to cluster together, as happened in urban ghettos in the United States, such groupings achieve less social control over the individual than do the economic and political imperatives of urban life, and at every turn the native is reminded that both his parental culture and community have no prestige and can be ignored. The kin lines that his family was once at pains to preserve need not be taken seriously. A young man need not worry that a girl's elders or male siblings will bring him to account for a pregnancy outside marriage. A girl need not wait until her sweetheart has saved enough for the bride price; nor is she, unprotected by a kin network, in any position to force him to wait. White governments in Africa, like those in the United States *ante-bellum* South, are little interested in maintaining legitimacy, since by caste definition African legitimacy has no relevance for white legitimacy. By contrast, U. S. white rural or foreign in-migrants could marry native whites so that public agencies were concerned about their legitimacy patterns.

The African couple need not bother with marriage. Indeed, marriage can no longer achieve its former manifest objectives: (1) it cannot maintain a respected lineage for yet another generation, since the kin line itself has lost its importance and because in an urban agglomeration the young man and woman may well be from different tribes, (2) it does not integrate a tribe by joining two lineages within it, since the tribe itself is disappearing and the tie may not be known to either lineage, and (3) it does not give a fully respected adult status to the young male, since under the Western caste pattern his rank will remain a lowly one, and whatever rank he does achieve will be based on his occupation and not his tribal position or the marriages he enters. Since, finally, both kin and elders have lost the authority on which social control once rested, both the young man and woman can and must make whatever individual role bargain with one another their circumstances permit.

In short, the political and economic dominance of the new urban world has begun to undermine that self-evident rightness of older family values which once guaranteed a legitimate position for the newborn child. The younger urban African generation has begun to feel a less intense commitment to those values, has acquired some opposing values, and in any event does not possess the means with which to achieve the older goals. The anomie of native African urban life in some centers surpasses anything observed in United States immigrant life, because the original culture of the African was more different from the Western culture, to which he must adjust, and his present deprivation is greater than that of the United States immigrant. The latter was already part of Western Culture, so that the cultural destruction he experienced was minor by comparison. The native is at the bottom of a caste system and is no longer part of an integrated social group or cultural system which would permit him to assert his own worth or the worth of the family. Thus, the stigma of illegitimacy becomes minor.

In the urbanizing African areas, the native patterns are neither (1) socially or culturally integrated internally nor are they (2) integrated socially or culturally with the dominant societies. In this transitional period, when the social importance of kin lines has become minimal, illegitimacy is high because of casual liaisons, promiscuity, and delayed marriage. On the other hand, the consensual union has perhaps not become the *usual* pattern of marital unions. The numerical preponderance of the native population has prevented its being absorbed into white cultural patterns, but modern industrial and economic expansion has prevented the whites from "keeping them in their place," either in the tribes or in the stratification system.[10] As a consequence, the phases

[10] The dominance of European nations is also weakened by important changes in the political philosophy of Europeans. They no longer accept colonialism as morally right.

of destruction have proceeded rapidly, and perhaps re-integration will occur more swiftly than in the New World.

THE NEW WORLD

The conquest of the New World seems at first to exhibit a very different pattern. First, no case of cultural penetration on so huge a scale can be found since Rome, unless the Islamic conquest be excepted. From Alaska to Tierra del Fuego, aside from a few tribal pockets, the hemisphere is Western in culture. The native cultural systems have been penetrated, undermined, and destroyed, though of course some elements of the older cultures do survive.

Next, two different forms of destruction may be distinguished. One of these, shared by the Southern United States and the Caribbean, was primarily a physical destruction and overwhelming of the native population, together with the substitution of alien slaves, who were so mixed geographically that their social systems were destroyed, and thus they could not maintain their African cultural heritage. These slaves, emancipated for the most part late in the nineteenth century, became Western in culture. Their descendants generally occupy the bottom social strata in the countries in which they were introduced, but in a few countries some occupy higher strata as well.

The second major pattern of destruction, socially more complex, was found on the Latin American mainland, from Mexico southwards. The main attacks were first concentrated on the three great population centers, the Aztec, Mayan, and Inca civilizations. Intent on political conquest and economic exploitation, the Iberians nearly undermined their own aims in the Conquest period by wiping out from one third to one half of their subjects, through disease, overwork, and underfeeding. At first, they ruled in part through native leaders, but by 1600 they had also removed this top stratum from power. Although the Church often opposed those actions, its own efforts at destroying native religions were backed by political leaders, so that even when the Church attempted to save native bodies, it persisted successfully in its goal of undermining native cults and substituting some form of Catholicism. The Iberians, like the whites in Africa, were greatly outnumbered by native Indians until relatively late in the Colonial period, but within a hundred years after the first conquests most of the cultural destruction had already taken place.[11] The Iberians imposed their cultural patterns on the natives, unlike the Manchus in China, the Spanish in the Philippines, the Dutch in Indonesia, or the English in India.

Both the assimilation and destruction processes differed somewhat from those in Africa. The U.S. and the Caribbean masters dispersed the (forced, slave) immigrants, but the whites outnumbered them in the United States and did not in the Caribbean. On the mainland, the Indians outnumbered the Iberians, but their social systems were in part undermined by death and partly by forced dispersion and relocation in villages. There was no industrial expansion, and little economic expansion, so that there was little need (in contrast to modern Africa) to use the natives in higher level jobs. Native African customs are essentially irrelevant to the problems faced in urban and industrial situations, but since in the New World the natives or slaves were used primarily in an agricultural setting, their customs might have been maintained had the whites not opposed them. In all these cases, the rule of the whites was based to a considerable degree on face-to-face interaction rather than indirect rule.[12]

The destruction pattern in these major cases are summarized in the following table.

Before analyzing the consequences of these different patterns, let us comment further on the situation of the mainland natives. Although the Iberian rulers attempted to hold the Indians in economic and therefore political subjection and thus sought to keep a rigid caste line between the two groups,[13] the emergence of two new classes in the stratifica-

---

[11] See the estimates of the proportion of destruction by certain dates, in Sol Tax, *et al., Heritage of Conquest,* Glencoe, Ill.: The Free Press, 1952, p. 264. Most of these groups are among the less acculturated peoples in the New World.

[12] Of course, the whites first ruled indirectly in Africa through native chiefs, but this becomes impossible in industrial and urban locations.

[13] The Creoles faced similar restrictions also: only four viceroys in Spanish America up to 1813 were American born, and these were sons of

TABLE 1. Comparison of Cultural and Social Destruction and Assimilation Patterns: Modern U.S. Cities, Modern Industrializing Sub-Saharan Africa, and the Past New World

| Patterns | Immigration to U.S. Cities, Rural or Foreign | Africa, Modern | New World: Pre-1900 | | |
			Ante-Bellum U.S. South	Caribbean	Mainland Iberian Countries
1. Physical destruction of acculturating population	No	Some	Little or none	Some	Considerable at first
2. Dispersal of social groupings	Yes	Yes	Yes	Yes	Yes
3. Numerical preponderance of population being acculturated	No	Yes	No	Yes	Yes
4. Prestige dominance of absorbing population	Yes	Yes	Yes	Yes	Yes
5. Caste system	No	Yes	Yes	Yes	Yes
6. Industrial expansion	Yes	Yes	Yes	No	No
7. Economic expansion	Yes	Yes	Yes	No	No
8. Relevance of native customs to new situation	No	No	Yes	Yes	Yes
9. Situation of culture contact	Urban	Urban	Rural	Rural	Village and Urban

tion system had considerable effect on the subsequent development of the family system. One new class, eventually to become the top stratum, was the Creoles, those born in the New World as legitimate offspring of Iberian families. As in the colonial United States, these rulers gradually loosened their ties with the Old World and led the revolutions which, in one country after another, freed all these possessions, except Puerto Rico and Cuba, from Mexico southwards, during the first quarter of the 19th century. The second class, which began at first from illegitimate unions between Iberians and Indians, were the mestizos, who gradually came to be a majority of the population in most Latin American countries. Likely to be intermediate in both appearance and culture between the rulers of pure descent and the Indians, this class reduced the strength of barriers against mobility.

More important for our understanding of cultural penetration, the mainland caste patterns permitted mainly only one form of mobility, what is called "passing" in United States white-Negro relations. This pattern is still found in the so-called caste relations between Ladinos and Indios in Guatemala and in the Andean Highlands of Bolivia, Ecuador, and Peru. That is, the individual could enter the Iberian world, for the most part in urban areas, only by becoming Iberian in all observable cultural characteristics, by ceasing to be Indian. He might starve as easily being all Iberian as being Indian, but without becoming Iberian the way upward was entirely closed. This structural pattern permitted some upward mobility without softening the low evaluation of Indian culture and without eroding the social barrier between Indian and Iberian.

In the New World, then, the native social and cultural systems were undermined by the steady economic and politi-

---

Spanish officials; 601 of the 706 bishops and archbishops came from Spain. Moreover, the restrictions had become more severe in the eighteenth century (C. H. Haring, *The Spanish Empire in America*, New York: Oxford University, 1957, p. 209). It can be argued that the first *social* revolution in Latin America was the 1910 Mexican Revolution (Robin A. Humphreys, *The Evolution of Modern Latin America*, New York: Oxford University, 1946, pp. 119–122).

[14] Melvin M. Tumin, *Caste in a Peasant Society*, Princeton: Princeton University Press, 1952.

cal pressures of a *closed*-class system, rather than by the open-class, expanding industrializing system of the modern world. The destruction was greatest among the slaves of the ante-bellum South, less in the Caribbean, and least on the Iberian mainland. Southern slaves were "seasoned" in the Caribbean first and were further dispersed on arrival in the U.S. Indians were able, especially in areas of less economic and political interest to the Iberians, to maintain some part of their social and cultural integration for many decades, and a few tribes still exist in remote regions, such as the upper Amazon. An index of the disorganization of Caribbean slaves is their failure to reproduce,[15] so that slave-running continued to be profitable almost until the end of the slavery period. In general, the illegitimacy rates of former slave areas are still higher than the non-slave areas; and on the mainland countries rimming the Caribbean, the coastal provinces where Negro slaves were introduced have higher rates than the interior.

The caste barriers were most severe in the ante-bellum South, somewhat less severe in the Caribbean non-Iberian islands, and least severe on the Iberian mainland. As Tannenbaum has shown, the Iberian treatment of even Negroes was less rigid than the treatment by any of the other New World settlers.[16]

The Iberians also made the most conscious effort to indoctrinate their subject peoples, the Indians, in Western norms, especially those relating to religion. However, in all these cases the inculcation of the new, Western values proceeded slowly and inconsistently. It is difficult to socialize an individual unless he is assured of acceptance as a full member of the social system, but the Iberians refused to accept the Indian anywhere until recently. *Village* controls were weak, because norm commitment to either native or Iberian values was weak and because the local social system was truncated: the locus of economic and political power was in the Iberian world, and the religious system accepted the Indian as parishioner, not as priest. Rewards for becoming

[15] For an analysis of one attempt to solve this problem, see "The Problems of Slave Labor Supply at the Codrington Plantations," by J. Harry Barnett, *Journal of Negro History*, 37 (April, 1952), pp. 115–141.
[16] Frank Tannenbaum, *Slave and Citizen*, New York: Knopf, 1947.

Iberian were low or non-existent. For example, the Indian might be exhorted to work hard, but he would be subjected to economic exploitation if he acquired any wealth. Learning to read would help little, since there were few positions open to him if he became literate. The Iberian pressures were directed toward keeping the Indians docile, not toward transforming them into Iberians.

In the slave areas, primarily the United States, Brazil, and the Circum-Caribbean, neither master nor slave had any concern about illegitimacy, since the slave kin line had no social importance: slavery undermines the status of the male as family head, more than that of the female,[17] and it is precisely the male elders who would be (in an independent society) the guardians of the family honor. It was to the interest of the conquerors or masters to prevent the development of native systems of social control, whether family or community, for therein lay a potential threat to their dominance. Even in the twentieth-century United States South, whites have opposed the "pretensions" of Negroes in seeking certificates of marriage and divorce. Slavery was abolished only late in the nineteenth century, and we could expect that where the caste barriers against Negroes were stronger, especially outside the Iberian regions, concern about Negro legitimacy among both whites and Negroes would develop only slowly.

ILLEGITIMACY AND THE STRUCTURE OF COMMUNITY INTEGRATION

Our review to this point suggests that it is the *community*, not the individual or the family, that maintains conformity to or deviation from the norm of legitimacy. The community defines and confers legitimacy. The individual decision, his or her role bargain, determines whether illegitimacy will be risked, and both family and individual may lose standing if illegitimacy results, but there is little stigma if the com-

[17] Ruth Landes, "Negro Slavery and Female Status," in *Les Afro-Américains, Institut Français d'Afrique Noire* (Dakar), 1952, pp. 265–266.

munity itself gives almost as much respect for conformity as for non-conformity. Lacking integration, the community cannot easily punish the deviant. In any population, the maintenance of a high individual or family commitment to a given norm or conformity to the norm, is dependent on *both* the commitment of the community to the *cultural* norm and the strength of its *social* controls. In the New World during the Colonial Period and the nineteenth century, as in contemporary industrializing sub-Saharan Africa, both native community controls and the commitment to the norm of legitimacy were weak. Correlatively, neither conquerors nor masters were concerned, since such deviations had little effect on their primary interests, power and economic exploitation.

The failure of community social integration means, then, a high rate of illegitimacy, since (a) it is likely to occur along with a weakening of norm commitment and (b) even if norms are not greatly weakened, controls are weak. However, the nature of this community integration or non-integration must be *specified*. We cannot fall back on the frequent alternative term, "anomie." The classical definition of "anomie," *normlessness,* is not adequate because such a state is so extreme: almost no cases of it, perhaps none at all unless we accept the examples of Nazi concentration camps and of United States prisoners of the Chinese during the Korean War, have been described by modern investigators. Here we can more usefully think of anomie or non-integration as a matter of. *degree.* However, sociological theory has not agreed on a clear meaning for "non-integration." Moreover, most analysts have viewed New World villages as "communities," i.e., as integrated. Thus, it is fruitful to specify the *several* structural points where "integration" may or may not exist.

We are asserting that for a period of about two centuries most of the slave and peasant populations of the New World lived in relatively stable, *non*-integrated settlements, kept from integration by United States, Iberian, and other European rulers. They were kept from either being integrated into the Western cultural and social systems *or* establishing independent, *internally* integrated cultural and social systems of their own. Here, of course, we necessarily go beyond the available data, but some of the specific descriptions can eventually be tested.

The points of non-integration can be outlined as follows:

I. These villages were not internally *culturally* integrated. This statement also holds, of course, for the U.S. Southern Negro population, only a few of whom ever lived in separate communities. Without even a geographical basis, cultural integration is most difficult to achieve. This general assertion means:

    A. There was a commitment, though relatively weak, to a wide range of norms from *both* cultures: religious elements from both cultures, allegiance to both languages, songs and music, or local and "national" loyalties.

    B. There was relatively low norm commitment to various *instrumental* norms, such as literacy, Western languages, skills in economic activities, etc., which might have been useful in fulfilling *other* Western norms to which there was some commitment.

    C. Conditions for the achievement of norms in the villages were difficult (contradictions of norms and conditions).

       1. Costs of church marriage were high.

       2. Masters or conquerors were little interested in facilitating formal marriage.

       3. Costs of the *fiesta*, or reception, after marriage were high.

       4. There were few means for economic expansion, literacy, and even learning Church beliefs precisely.

       5. Conquerors and masters opposed native or slave efforts to pretend to the status honor enjoyed by rulers.

       6. European goods were urged on them, but prices were high.

       7. Responsibility for debts or labor was encouraged, but caste prohibitions against mobility were strong.[18]

II. These villages were not internally *socially* integrated. Of course, where there is very low norm commitment, social integration may be low: there is little to be integrated *about*. Again, the Southern Negro population obviously fits this description, which means:

    A. White rulers prevented the development of local leadership or self-rule, thus hindering community controls.

    B. Natives were not generally permitted to participate in Church activities as priests or officials (the cofradías may be viewed

[18] See an examination of these contradictions by George Kubler, "The Quechua in the Colonial World," in *Handbook of South American Indians, op. cit.*, Vol. 2, pp. 374–375 *passim*. Indians in Peru were not even allowed to own horses, though there were many of them: Bernard Mishkin, "The Contemporary Quechua," *Ibid.*, p. 427.

as a partial exception, but they were organized to ensure proper contributions to the Church).

C. Any local community pressures, decisions, or rules were subject to being overridden by the whites.

III. The village *cultural* patterns were not integrated with "national," white patterns. This means:

A. The two patterns were differently oriented toward various important norms: the value of working and owning agricultural land, the value of living in the city, nationalism-patriotism, or belief in the details of Church doctrine.

B. Whites viewed the native or Negro patterns as alien, rather than as merely lower class or a variant of the dominant culture.

C. Whites viewed the native or Negro people as requiring acculturation or training (even when they wasted little energy on the task), not as having a different culture of equal validity.

IV. The villages were not *socially* integrated with the dominant social system of the whites or the larger social system of the nation.

A. Natives did not generally feel part of the nation and had little interest in the changing political fortunes of the elite.

B. Relatively few inter-community relations existed.[19]

C. The native was not viewed as a "citizen" everywhere in the nation, and many barriers to free movement existed.

D. The economic system was locally oriented, for the most part.

E. The wishes of the local villages were little taken into account in national planning or action.

All four structural connections have been specified, in order to avoid needless debate as to whether these populations were "anomic," or "non-integrated." The outline is thus partly a summary of the preceding analysis but emphasizes the special character of the non-integration of these populations, which also applies *mutatis mutandi* to the Negro population of the Old South in the United States. The caste pattern of India is different in that the local village is *internally* both socially and culturally integrated; and it is culturally integrated with the larger Indian cultural pattern, in that the local caste norms and patterns are viewed as a legitimate part of the national moral fabric. It seems doubtful,

[19] Mishkin (*ibid.*, p. 448) reports this of the Quechua today. The "isolation" of New World villages south of the Rio Grande has been commented on by most observers.

however, that until recently such local village castes were *socially* integrated with the national social system except through a lengthy series of intermediate steps. Under such circumstances, social control remains strong locally and so does the commitment to the norm of legitimacy.

Consequently, in the New World from the Old South in the United States to Cape Horn, the non-whites assimilated only slowly into the social and cultural patterns of the West. They accepted the superiority of these patterns or at least did not assert the contrary. However, the barriers to integration into the national dominant patterns and the forces arrayed against local social or cultural integration failed to yield the rewards which are necessary for effective acculturation, so that the process did not accelerate in most countries until the twentieth century.[20] Consequently, both low norm commitment to legitimacy and weak community controls maintained relatively high illegitimacy rates.

PHASES OF ASSIMILATION: RURAL-URBAN ILLEGITIMACY DIFFERENTIALS

Although the foregoing outline of non-integration in the New World seems both theoretically and descriptively correct, it goes far beyond available data from individual community studies, which would test whether any large proportion of existing or historical villages were in fact non-integrated. However, some further conclusions can be derived and tested in this analysis, so that we are not left merely with speculations.

The first of these concerns the *phases* of non-integration. If the line of theory pursued so far is correct, then in the conquest period in the Iberian world the illegitimacy rates first began to increase in the urban centers where contact was first made and the primary undermining of the Indian patterns began. Thereafter, however, because urban centers

[20] It is worth noting that Alexander von Humboldt also commented on the relation between the Indian's anomie and lack of motivation (see Haring, *op. cit.*, pp. 201-202).

were the source of Westernizing forces and the urban Indians were more likely to assimilate, the norm of formal marriage was more likely to be followed. In addition, of course, the cities contained Iberians who would usually follow this norm. Thus, while the rural areas were kept in a relatively non-integrated state or forced gradually into it as Iberian dominance spread, the urban regions moved toward Western norms.

We should, therefore, suppose that in most cases the urban illegitimacy rates would now be *lower* than the rural rates, even though the modern rapid urbanization of Latin America may be creating all those disruptions of social and cultural patterns which have elsewhere been recorded when rural peoples enter an urban milieu.[21] In the following table, the rural and urban rates are presented.

As can be seen, the conclusion is validated, except for Paraguay. If our theory of phases in disintegration and reintegration is correct, this means that Paraguay, the socioeconomically least developed of independent Latin American

[21] I am, of course, aware of the difficulties in interpreting illegitimacy rates in countries where recording procedures are undeveloped: (1) Official urban rates might be higher than rural rates, because recording procedures are more thorough. (2) In some rural areas, those classed as "Indios" may be generally ignored by officials. (3) Where social services are available in the city, as in San Juan, Puerto Rico, some illegitimacies may be recorded there, although the mothers come from rural villages. (4) The disorganization of urban slums may lead to much promiscuity and thus *override* any of the factors presented in my analysis (e.g., Caracas, Venezuela). (5) It is difficult to obtain true "rural-urban" breakdowns, because the political sub-units (provinces, departments, sections) of Latin American nations typically contain both an urban center and a surrounding rural countryside and the data are recorded for the sub-unit as a whole. Nevertheless, all of these except the last (whose effect is unknown) would bias the official rates *against* my hypothesis. Consequently it seems safe to use the data. Many analysts have claimed that consensual unions, and therefore illegitimacy, are more common in rural areas. As we shall see, however, that assertion is correct only for mainland, independent Latin America. (See, for example, Kingsley Davis and Ana Casís, *Urbanization in Latin America,* New York: Milbank Memorial Fund, 1946, pp. 39–40.)

Included under "illegitimate" are those born of a consensual union, whether or not the offspring are "recognized," as well as those born outside of any continuing marital relationship. These are official rates.

TABLE 2. Differences in Illegitimacy Rates Between Capitals and Remainder of Country, Mainland Independent Countries South of the Rio Grande

Political Unit	Year	Federal Capital Major Urban Province	Per Cent (23.8% for Whole)	Remainder of Country (Per Cent)	Highest Rate in Any Department or Province Per Cent
Argentina	(1957)[a]	Federal Capital	10.4	27.0	60.3 (Formosa)
Brazil	(1952)[b]	Capital Territory	12.4	15.0	
				(total for country as a whole)	
Chile	(1958)[c]	Valparaiso Province	16.3	25.2	30.2 (Coquimbo)
Uruguay	(1943)[d]	Montevideo	18.4	27.5	66.7 (Florida)
Paraguay	(1946)[e]	Capital	62.4	56.5	(no figure obtainable)
Colombia	(1956)[f]	Cundinamarca Section	20.2	30.1	69.1 (Córdoba)
Ecuador	(1947)[g]	Pichincha Province	22.3	34.7	84.9 (Los Ríos)
Peru	(1953)[h]	Callao Department Lima & Callao	30.9	43.9	59.6 (Loreto)
Venezuela	(1954)[i]	Departments	46.4	43.0	54.7 (Lambayeque)
Nicaragua	(1947)[j]	Federal District	47.2	58.3	74.9 (Yaracuy)
Honduras	(1957)[k]	Managua Department	57.5	62.3	70.4 (Chinandega)
Costa Rica	(1957)[l]	Francisco Morazán	68.4	69.3	80.3 (Colón)
Mexico	(1956)[m]	Province San José	14.2	28.1	49.1 (Limón)
El Salvador	(1955)[n]	Distrito Federal	12.9	23.9	27.9 (Sinaloa)
Guatemala	(1956–57)[o]	San Salvador Urban Area	30.8	59.3	67.6 (Santa Ana)
		Urban Areas	64.5	76.1 (Rural Areas)	
Panama	(1958)[p]	Urban Areas	64.5	79.6 (Rural Areas)	

[a] Dirección Nacional de Estadística y Censos, Argentina, 1959 (Personal Communication).

[b] Anuario Estadístico de Distrito Federal 1949–53 Rio de Janeiro, Departmento de Geografía e Estatística, 1955, p. 46. Also Demographic Yearbook Questionnaire, 1952, Statistical Office of the United Nations, New York.

[c] Comité Nacional de Estadísticas Vitales y Sanitarias de Chile, 1959 (Personal Communication).

[d] Anuario Estadístico de la República Oriental del Uruguay, Año 1943, Volumen I, Montevideo, Imprenta Nacional, 1943, p. 8. The Boletín de Estadística, Intendencia Municipal de Montevideo, Dirección de Censo y Estadística, Año 41, 1943, gives figures which yield a rate of 24.4% for Montevideo. I do not know whence the discrepancy.

[e] Anuario Estadístico de la República del Paraguay 1946–47. Asunción, Imprenta Nacional, 1948, pp. 39–40.

[f] Anuario General de Estadística 1956. Colombia, Departamento Administrativo Nacional de Estadística, 1957, pp. 33–34.

[g] El Trimestre Estadístico del Ecuador. Dirección General de Estadística y Censos del Ecuador 1947, p. 30.

[h] Anuario Estadístico del Perú, 1953. Lima, Ministerio de Hacienda y Comercio, 1956, pp. 76–77.

[i] Anuario Estadístico de Venezuela, 1954. Caracas, Ministerio de Fomento, 1957, pp. 82–83, 108–109.

[j] Anuario Estadístico de la República de Nicaragua, Año 1947. Managua, Publicaciones del Ministerio de Hacienda y Crédito Público, 1953, p. 61

[k] Figures obtained from Dirección General de Estadística y Censos, República de Honduras, C. A., 1959 (Personal Communication).

[l] Anuario Estadístico de Costa Rica, 1957. San José, Impreso en la Sección de Publicaciones, 1958, p. 25.

[m] Dirección General de Estadística, 1959, México (Personal Communication).

[n] Anuario Estadístico 1955. Volumen 1. San Salvador, Dirección General de Estadística y Censos, 1956, p. 37. El Salvador, although in the predicted direction, may be changing: the Anuario Estadístico for 1949 yields different figures: San Salvador 72.2% illegitimate, remainder of country 65.1% illegitimate. (Anuario Estadístico de la República de El Salvador, Tomo 1, San Salvador, Dirección General de Estadística y Censos, 1953, p. 81.) In 1955, all the urban areas had a rate of 57.5, the rural, 56.5.

[o] Figures obtained from Dirección General de Estadística y Censos, República de Guatemala, C. A.

[p] Excludes Indians in purely Indian territories. Personal communication from Dirección de Estadística y Censos of Panama.

countries, has not yet entered the phase in which urban rates have begun to drop below rural ones. It should do so in the future. Correspondingly, of the seven independent Iberian countries with very high rates (over 50%) all are little developed, and still show very low differentials between urban and rural rates.[22] Finally, in the more advanced countries, such as Uruguay and Mexico, the differences should *diminish* in the future.

The mainland *dependent* countries do not fit this phase pattern (British and Dutch Guiana, British Honduras), nor do the Caribbean island countries. Of the three Caribbean countries that have been independent for more than half a century, Haiti, Cuba, and the Dominican Republic, we have been able to obtain rural-urban breakdowns for only one, the Dominican Republic, where the rural rate *is* slightly higher but has become so only recently (65.1%–63.9%, 1958).[23]

In the Caribbean political units, the rural rates are almost the same as the urban and are very slightly *lower* in over half of them. This region differs from the mainland Iberian lands primarily in these characteristics: (1) almost all their population is descendant from slaves. Caste restrictions were more severe against Negroes than on the mainland against the Indios; (2) almost all of them have been dependencies until this century, so that there has been little basis for national integration; (3) most important, the phases which apply to the mainland Iberian countries do not apply here, since the initial disorganization *was as intense in rural as in urban regions*. The Indians were everywhere destroyed. The slaves who replaced them were no longer members of a community, and the bulk of them was used in agriculture. We should not expect the Caribbean, then, to follow all the phases of the mainland development, though we predict that the urban rates will become lower than the rural. Several of the differentials are given in the following table. The United States Southern Negro rates are also included, as following the Caribbean pattern.

[22] The apparent exception, El Salvador, had a rural-urban differential in 1955 of only 1% (42.5%–43.5%). The table compares the extreme of *urban* San Salvador with the rest of the country.

[23] Figures supplied by Dirección Nacional de Estadística.

TABLE 3. New World Rural-Urban Differentials in Illegitimacy Rates, Selected Mainland Dependencies and Caribbean Countries[a]

	Illegitimacy Rates	
	Urban	Rural
U.S. South, Non-White (1957)	18.6–32.7%	18.6–32.1%
Puerto Rico (1956)	34.6 (San Juan)	27.4 (rest of country)
British Guiana (1955)	43.8	33.6
Trinidad and Tobago (1956)	47.3	47.4
Dominican Republic (1958)	63.9	65.1
Surinam (Dutch Guiana) (1951)	43.0 (Paramaribo)	38.0 (rest of country)
Jamaica (1954)	73.1 (Capital)	71.5 (rest of country)
British Honduras (1956)	52.9 (Capital District)	49.8 (rest of country)
Barbados (1955)	65.2 (Capital Parish)	59.3 (rest of country)

[a] Rates calculated from figures furnished by Caribbean Commission, and from U. S. National Office of Vital Statistics.

ILLEGITIMACY AND DEGREE OF NATIONAL INTEGRATION

A second conclusion may be drawn from our earlier analysis. The New World countries have succeeded in varying degrees in integrating their formerly Indian or slave populations into the national cultural and social systems. Since their illegitimacy rates are in part a function of this variable, countries which have moved *further* toward such an integration should have *lower* rates. The degree of this type of integration is greatly dependent on the extent of industrialization and urbanization, since these variables require more interconnections between different parts of a nation and offer rewards to the individual for entering the cultural systems. Thus, it becomes both easier and more desirable to conform to the norm of legitimacy. However, the rank order of the illegitimacy rates has a Spearman-Brown coefficient of correlation of only .50 with the rank order of urbanization as measured by the percentage of the national population living in the major metropolitan areas.

In the following table, most of the New World political units are ranked by the degree to which their formerly slave

TABLE 4. New World Political Units According to Their Degree of National Integration and Illegitimacy Rates[a]

Degree of National Integration	Illegitimacy Rates (Percentages)	Date
A. Higher integration		
Brazil	15	1952
Chile	16	1958
Uruguay	20	1954
Mexico	22.5	1956
Costa Rico	25	1957
B. Medium integration		
Argentina	28	1957
Colombia	28	1957
Cuba	30	1939
Puerto Rico	28.5	1955
U. S. Old South, Negro	19–32	1957
C. Lower integration		
Ecuador	36	1956
Peru	43	1955
British Guiana	34	1957
Paraguay	48	1955
Surinam	34	1953
French Guiana	65	1956
Venezuela	57	1955
Guatemala	70	1957
Panama	71	1956
Jamaica	72	1954
Martinique	48	1956
British Honduras	48	1957
D. Not classified		
Dominican Republic	55	1956
El Salvador	59	1953
Honduras	65	1957
Nicaragua	62	1945

[a] All rates were obtained from the *United Nations Demographic Year Book Questionnaire* for the respective dates, except the figure for Puerto Rico, which was obtained from the Caribbean Commission. It was not possible to obtain recent Cuban data and many smaller political units have been omitted.

or Indian populations have been brought into the dominant cultural and social systems. As can be seen, with few exceptions the conclusion holds: in general, where the formerly slave or Indian populations have been more fully integrated into the national cultural and social systems, the national illegitimacy rates are lower.

ILLEGITIMACY AND THE INTERNAL
INTEGRATION OF COMMUNITIES

A third deduction from our earlier analysis can be tested: because of the wide variety of geographical and sociological factors in New World history, some communities have either continued to be *internally* integrated both socially and cul-

---

Bolivia has been eliminated because any birth is recorded as legitimate if the couple has been living together for two years (personal communication from Dirección Nacional de Estadística). As noted later, in Guatemala many births are classified as illegitimate because no civil ceremony preceded them, though other types of marriage ceremonies may have occurred, so that its real rate is lower than its official rate.

With respect to the independent variable, there is reason to believe that this classification would for the most part be conceded by New World specialists. Several such specialists have already accepted it.

The bases for the classification are these: (1) The maintenance of caste barriers, which remain strong in Guatemala and the Andean Highlands and are weak in Brazil and Mexico. (2) Extent of ethnic hemogeneity. Uruguay and Costa Rica, for example, are very "Spanish" or "European," and in Mexico, Cuba, Chile, and Puerto Rico a thorough-going mixing has occurred, in contrast to Guatemala. (3) The status of political dependency. (4) The existence of national programs for education, literacy, economic development (Puerto Rico, United States, Argentina). (5) The existence of large pockets of geographically and socially isolated populations (Bolivia, Ecuador, Peru). (6) Comparison of comments by New World experts, with respect to how much the natives care about or take part in national political affairs or how long various forms of labor exploitation have continued (e.g., indentured labor was abolished in Jamaica in 1917). Too much weight may have been given to the relatively unintegrated Andean populations of Bolivia, Peru, and Ecuador. If so, they would move to "medium" integration, and their reported illegitimacy rates would "fit" better. For relevant material on the degree to which the populations of these countries are integrated into the national life, see: Harold Osborne, *Bolivia*, London: 1954, Royal Institute of International Affairs, 1954, pp. 93–99; W. Stanley Rycroft, *Indians of the High Andes*, London: Routledge and Kegan-Paul, 1952, pp. 211–219, 231–236; Mary Patricia Holleran, *Church and State in Guatemala*, New York: Oxford University Press, 1949, pp. 244–245; Melvin Tumin, *Caste in a Peasant Society*, Princeton: Princeton University Press, 1952; James Preston, *Latin America*, New York: Odyssey, revised edition, 1950, pp. 44, 46, 69, 71, 76, 120, 124–125, 193–195, 212, 213, 221, 316, 352, 531, 619, 644, 662, 708, 710; Olen E. Leonard, *Bolivia*, Washington: Scarecrow, 1952, pp. 90–101; Thomas R. Ford, *Man and Land in Peru*, Gainesville, Florida: University of Florida, 1955, pp. 111–116.

Doubtless, many observers would classify *all* those in D as "lower integration" units. I have no objection but simply have been unable to obtain sufficient data on them to be certain.

turally (but *not* integrated culturally or socially with the *national* systems) or else reachieved such an integration after the initial dissolution. Such communities would then be the main source of individual or family honor and rank, and would be able and willing to ensure conformity to the norm of legitimacy. Thus, their illegitimacy rates would be low. Their *formal* official rates might be *high,* since the national registration system will recognize only the legal, civil ceremony; but their social rates would be low, since few people will enter a union without a public marriage ceremony of some kind in which both family lines participate. Such communities might be found, for example, in the Andean Highlands of Peru, Bolivia, and Ecuador, or the north-western highland region of Guatemala and even here and there in the Caribbean. We should find low real rates of illegitimacy in such villages and high rates in villages where such integration seems weak. In the following table, various

TABLE 5.   Illegitimacy and Integration in Selected New World Communities[a]

	High Rate of Illegitimacy	Low Rate of Illegitimacy[b]
High Integration:		Tzintzuntzán (Mexico)
		Cherán (Mexico)
		Cruz das Almas (Brazil)
		Tusik and Quintana Roo (Mayans of Mexico)
		Orange Grove (Jamaica)
		Nyame (British Guiana)
		SDoució (Colombia)
		Santa Eulalia (Guatemala)
		Peguche (Ecuador)
		Otóvalo (Ecuador)
Low Integration:	Rocky Roads (Jamaica)	Chichicastenango (Guatemala)
	Sugartown (Jamaica)	
	Moche (Peru)	
	Tobatí (Paraguay)	

[a] The relativly highly integrated communities here outnumber the less well integrated, because anthropologists seek out the "unspoiled," the "culturally unified" village.

In the citations which follow I have quoted the pages which are most relevant for the classification presented. To classify a village as *non*integrated appears to be places which have been the object of community studies are classified by illegitimacy rates and by the degree of integration, i.e., the extent to which the village forms a self-validating social and cultural system.

As can be seen, we find relatively low rates of illegitimacy

---

more difficult than to show its integration, possibly because there are many different ways in which a village may *not* be internally integrated. Indices such as these seem relevant: (1) how many of the young adults are attracted to city life and ways, (2) how well the elders still control the young, (3) how important is a "good name in the village," (4) how effectively nonlegal, informal relationships may decide local issues, (5) how large a portion of the village participates in ceremonies and how much of village life centers around such ceremonies. Tzintzuntzán: *Empire's Children,* Smithsonian Institution Institute of Social Anthropology, Publ. No. 6, Mexico: Nuevo Mundo, 1948, pp. 1, 2, 11 ff., 23, 33, 247 ff.; Cherán: *Cherán: A Sierra Tarascan Village,* Smithsonian Institution Institute of Social Anthropology, Publ. No. 2, Washington: 1946, pp. 1–2, 12, 176 ff.; *Cruz das Almas,* Smithsonian Institution Institute of Social Anthropology, Publ. No. 12, 1948, pp. 1–13, 127–143, 197 ff.; Tusik and Quintana Roo: Robert Redfield, *The Folk Culture of Yucatan,* Chicago: University of Chicago, 1941, Chaps. III and VIII; Orange Grove and Sugartown: Edith Clarke, *My Mother Who Fathered Me,* London: Allen and Unwin, 1957, pp. 78–79, 82–84, 90–102, 127; Nyame: Raymond T. Smith, *The Negro Family in British Guiana,* New York: Grove, 1956, pp. 181–182. Saucío: Orlando Fals-Borda, *Peasant Society in the Colombian Andes,* Gainesville, Florida: University of Florida, pp. 37, 204–207, 211; Oliver LaFarge, *Santa Eulalia,* Chicago: University of Chicago, 1947, pp. 21–44; Else Clews Parsons, *Peguche,* Chicago: University of Chicago, 1945, Chap. 1, pp. 54–60; Otóvalo: John Collier and Aníbal Buitrón, *The Awakening Valley,* Chicago: University of Chicago, 1949, pp. 31–32, chap. on "Marriage"; Rocky Roads: Yehudi A. Cohen, "The Social Organization of a Selected Community in Jamaica," *Social and Economic Studies,* 2 (1954), pp. 104–33, and "Four Categories of Interpersonal Relationships in the Family and Community in a Jamaican Village,"*Anthropological Quarterly,* 28 (October, 1955), pp. 121–147; John Gillin, *Moche,* Smithsonian Institution Institute of Social Anthropology, Publ. No. 3, Washington: n.d., pp. 30, 93 ff.; *Tobatí:* Elman R. Service and Helen S. Service, Chicago: University of Chicago, 1954, pp. xix–xxiii, 206–9, Chaps. 9 and 10; *Chichicastenango:* Ruth Bunzel, New York: Augustin, second edition, 1952, pp. 1–14, 25–30, 109–117.

A number of communities have not been classified with respect to their integration, because each might require a separate analysis and debate: Marbial (Remy Bastien, *La Familia Rural Haitiana,* México: Libra, 1951); Mocca (Clarke, *op. cit.*); August Town, Perseverance, Better Hope (Raymond T. Smith, *op. cit.*); Quiroga (Donald D. Brand, *Quiroga,* Smithsonian Institution Institute of Social Anthropology Publ. No. 11, Washington: 1951); Capesterre (Mariam Kreiselman, *The Caribbean Family: A Case Study in Martinique,* Columbia University, unpublished Ph.D. thesis, 1958); Tepotzlán (Oscar Lewis, *Life in a Mexican Village: Tepotzlán Restudied,* Urbana, Ill.: University of Illinois, 1951) and the several areas in Puerto Rico which are described in Julian Steward, *op. cit.* Commonly, authors refer to their village as a "community" and treat it generally as a coherent unit, while giving explicit details which would deny any such integration. Considering the island Caribbean studies, I would at present view only Morne-Paysan (M. M. Horowitz, *Morne-Paysan,* unpublished Ph.D. dissertation, Columbia University, 1959), Orange Grove and San José as "relatively integrated" (Eric R. Wolf, "San José: Subcultures of a 'Traditional' Coffee Municipality," in *The People of Puerto Rico,* Julian Steward, *et al.,* Urbana, Ill.: University of Illinois, pp. 171–264. Quiroga and Tepotzlán may not have high illegitimacy rates because they are now somewhat integrated into the Mexican national social and cultural systems.

[b] Low illegitimacy means, of course, relative to the level prevailing in the respective countries. Specific rates cannot be calculated from the descriptions.

in specific communities which have achieved, or re-achieved, an internal social and cultural coherence, an acceptance of themselves as the source of prestige.[24] Individuals in such communities are participants in their social systems and presumably also committed to their cultural norms. If prestige is earned within the system, then a family line or the community as whole will insist on conformity with the norm of legitimacy. The communities which form a self-validating social system have low rates, and the communities which are less integrated have higher rates.

CONCLUSION

The present paper has attempted to relate cultural penetration, cultural and social anomie, and illegitimacy rates, by considering the main areas of high rates: Northwestern Europe, urbanizing Africa south of the Sahara, and the New World south of the Mason-Dixon Line. In the first case, the community retains control, and though some children are born outside of wedlock, they are likely to be only technically and temporarily illegitimate, not socially illegitimate. In urbanizing Africa, by contrast, Western culture has undermined the native cultural and social systems, and the Western community has not created conditions which permit the native to become a full member of the Western social and cultural system.

This situation is also observable in the history of the Western Hemisphere among both United States rural and foreign immigrants, where however the later phases in such a massive process of penetration have also taken place. The parallels among the United States and Latin American mainland, the Caribbean, and urbanizing Africa are striking, if we

---

[24] Various observers have remarked on the lesser ease, openness, and friendliness of the Andean peasants who work on a *finca* or *hacienda* compared with those who have continued to live on communal lands; Rycroft, *op. cit.*, p. 82; Harry Tschopik, "The Aymara," *Handbook of South American Indians, op. cit.*, vol. 2, p. 501; Osborne, *op. cit.*, pp. 211–12.

allow for the differences which the twentieth century political situation has imposed on Africa. At the same time, apparent differences suggest theoretical reformulations of the assimilation process. We see a conquering people who first rule indirectly through native leaders, and then directly, in Africa and the New World south of the Rio Grande; considerable destruction of native populations and forced migrations; destruction of the native cultures, but the erection of quasi-caste barriers to prevent the full achievement or even complete acceptance of Western norms by the native; the undermining of the *local* community as the source of prestige; bars to entrance into the conquering Western community; and the dissolution of native family systems, without granting the rewards for conformity to the new Western family norms. We have also outlined the differences among these cases.

Behind the New World, however, are four hundred years of assimilation, so that it has been possible to see what happens after the initial period of cultural penetration. It is in the cities that full assimilation of the peasant is possible, and under the later industrialization that assimilation is even useful to the upper strata. Thus, it is in the city that the Indian peasant may become not only culturally but also socially assimilated, while in the rural areas, the encomiendas, and villages he has taken over Western *culture* with less commitment, because he has been denied a part in the Western *social* community, with its concomitant rewards and punishments. Thus, it is in the urban areas that the rule of legitimacy begins to be imposed more stringently by the community, and the mestizo becomes willing to pay the price of marriage, such as the wedding feast which serves as both a community blessing and a ritual of passage.

In a parallel fashion, those countries in which strides have been taken toward integrating their populations into the national community will have lower illegitimacy rates.

And, finally, where the village becomes the cosmos, usually in isolated or mountainous areas, so that the individual in it is participating in both the cultural system and the social system of a genuine community, there again we find a stronger commitment to the norm of legitimacy, and greater community and family concern about marriage. The dominant value system does not set norms which the individuals cannot achieve; there is less contradiction between norms, so that there is a stronger commitment to them; and the coherence of the community permits more effective sanctions to enforce conformity to the norm of legitimacy.

PART V

Alternate Solutions Available to the Unwed Mother

Illegal Abortion in
the United States

ALFRED C. KINSEY

INCIDENCE

CHAIRMAN GUTTMACHER: I think we have all been penalized in our thinking by lack of actual knowledge about illegal abortion.

In the first place, there are no good figures that I know of that in any way depict the incidence. . . .

Furthermore, we talk a lot about the practice of illegal abortion and how it is carried on—again without any factual data. Therefore the Steering Committee sought to bring before you two men who, through their work, can give us naked facts. The first is Dr. Kinsey.

DR. KINSEY: I think it is necessary to begin with a discussion of the way in which we secure data on the incidence and frequency of abortion. As long as any activity is illicit and

THIS PAPER was originally given at a conference on abortion sponsored by the Planned Parenthood Federation of America, Inc. at Harden House and the New York Academy of Medicine in April 1955, with comments by Alan F. Guttmacher, M.D. (Chairman of the Conference), Mary S. Calderone, M.D., Louis M. Hellman, M.D., and Abraham Stone, M.D. Quotations from "Illegal Abortion in the United States," by Alfred C. Kinsey in *Abortion in the United United States* edited by Mary Steichen Calderone, M.D. Copyright © 1958 by Paul B. Hoeber, Inc. Medical Book Department of Harper & Brothers. Reprinted with the permission of Harper & Row, Publishers.

punishable by heavy penalty, it is not going to be possible to get persons freely to tell anyone—much less anyone in an official position—what has actually happened in their own lives. This has been true of a great many aspects of our whole study of human sexual behavior, and it has been equally true of abortion. The persons who confide in us are taking their lives in their hands in a very literal sense when they tell us things that could send them to the state penitentiary if their confidences were betrayed.

I should point out that I know of no more untrustworthy fashion of securing statistics on the incidence of any illicit activity than to take the official figures that are obtained either through police departments or through reports that are required by state law in any other fashion. The number of premarital copulations occurring in a city such as New York is not to be determined by calculating the number of arrests that are made in any year for premarital intercourse. In no type of sexual activity can you begin to get, through official statistics, any approximation of the incidence of behavior—if it is illicit behavior.

So we have had to develop a rapport with the groups with which we have worked, and sometimes it has taken months—even years—to develop such rapport.

We worked with one lower-level Negro community in a large Midwestern city for two full years before we felt that we had won the confidence of that community, and for six more years before we had the sort of sample that we wanted from it. The sample at that point was not the statistician's ideal. The statistician would have started by making a census of the entire population in the area that we were studying, and would then have sent the workers back into that population to take records from persons selected on a random basis.

In our own research we have used a group sampling method, often getting 100 per cent of the persons making up a particular group. Hence we are minimizing the possibility of selecting an undue portion of persons who would be more likely to have abortions.

I have been amused at the suggestion that only abnormal women who would not have families are the ones who engage in all the premarital and extra-marital activities that we reported in our volume on the female, and some persons have actually stated that no decent lady would have given us a history! I have been approached time and again through the years by sociologists and statisticians in other areas who have wanted to know what sorts of families these women had. We had not then calculated this for our volume on the female, and because we have been unable to tell them, many of them have jumped to the conclusion that we must have gotten the histories of women who would rather have abortions than families.

I can now report to you that the parity rate on our particular sample is only about 10 per cent lower than that which is reported for a comparable segment of the urban, white population in the U. S. Census. We find our sample to be over-represented in the Northeast and underrepresented in the South. The fact that the Northeast is lowest and the South highest in fertility may account for some of the differences in the two parity rates. Differences in religion and in the number of women employed in the labor force between our sample and the U. S. Census also account in part for differences in the parity rate.

Our abortion data were gathered as part of the total records of sexual activity of women with whom we worked. In our total sample we have a record of 6,300 pregnancies experienced among nearly 8,000 women. Today I am reporting on 4,248 pregnancies that occurred among 5,293 white, non-prison females in our sample.

PREGNANCIES AMONG SINGLE WOMEN

One item of interest is that the incidences of pregnancies—not of live births, but of pregnancies—reported for our total group of *single* women, who had premarital coitus and who were born in the decades 1890–1900, 1900–10, 1910–20, and 1920–30—the incidences in these four groups are very close to each other after age twenty. We have thus no evidence that incidences of premarital pregnancy have been modified a great deal in the last forty years. This is in spite of the fact that there has undoubtedly been an increase in the use of more effective contraceptives; but it is, again, a medical mistake to believe that contraceptives were totally inadequate forty years ago. As a matter of fact, there are very few women in our histories who have not at some time used contraceptives of one form or another.

Selecting from the total group of single white females only those who have had coitus, we find that by fifteen years of age 6 per cent of them have become pregnant, and by forty years of age, of those who remained single, approximately 25 per cent have become pregnant.

I have the record for live births, the record for spontaneous, and the record for induced abortions of these pregnancies. Time will not allow me to give you any but the last figures. We have not attempted to make any distinction here between so-called therapeutic abortions and criminal or illegal abortions. Our reason is that we have talked to a considerable number of persons in the medical profession, and find that it is very nebulous in their own minds exactly under what circumstances an abortion may be performed therapeutically. There appears to be little agreement in the medical profession on this point.

In the present day, abortions are being recommended by some psychiatrists for a variety of situations that very closely match the indications written into the Scandinavian laws. In consequence, a physician who is ready to follow such a recommendation for abortion exerts a different effect on the total abortion picture from the one who says, with religious conviction, that even if it costs the life of the mother, one is never justified in performing an abortion. I do not believe, therefore, that statistically you can compare the data on so-called therapeutic abortions in one hospital or in one physician's practice with those from another hospital or another physician's practice.

We are also well aware of the fact that we have had to depend upon the subject's judgment of whether she was ever pregnant or whether she ever aborted. We are as conscious as any of you of all the errors that may be involved there, . . . but I think it is just as extreme an error on the other side to believe that all reports of self-induced abortion are groundless.

I am also cognizant of the fact that induced abortions, even when an operation has been performed and money has been paid, may also not represent a pregnancy, for it is perfectly clear from the accounts that we have of abortionists—we have the histories of several of them—that they will operate if the woman believes that she is pregnant. In many cases, if they find that she is not pregnant, they do not report it to her, so it goes down in her mind as an induced abortion. There are these errors, and I know of no way of securing data on a large scale that will overcome them.

To compensate for all this, there is no doubt that the number of induced abortions that have been reported to us is minimal. Persons have not laid themselves open to possible legal difficulty by telling us that they have had abortions performed by physicians or other persons, when, in actuality, they have not; quite the contrary. If there is any disparity either in their recall or in their admission to us, it will be in the direction of covering up the fact. I will add that about 87 per cent of all the induced abortions that we have in our records were performed by physicians. It is only about 8 per cent that were self-induced, and if you were to throw out all those, it would not materially change the over-all picture of induced abortions.

Going back to the records of the single white females, I say that the incidence of pregnancies after age twenty that have occurred in the last forty years among women having premarital coitus has not been materially modified. As we and others have already reported, there is a much higher percentage of girls in the United States who are having premarital intercourse today than was true forty years ago. That is the chief product of the concerted attack on prostitution. The *number* of males ever having gone to prostitutes has not been reduced in these forty years. But, because of all the legal and social objections to prostitution, the *frequency* with which these males go to the prostitutes *has* been materially reduced, and there has been a compensatory increase in the frequency with which males have premarital coitus with girls who are not prostitutes.

For the rest of my time I shall confine my discussion to our record of induced abortions.

ABORTIONS AMONG UNMARRIED WOMEN

The proportion of premarital conceptions resolved before marriage by induced abortions ranges from 88 to 95 per cent in the present sample. Whether it is desirable that this percentage be decreased and the number of live births from unmarried mothers be increased are among the problems that I think a conference like this one should face.

ABORTIONS AMONG MARRIED WHITE WOMEN

Among married white females, the pregnancy rate for the generation born between 1890 and 1900 was higher than it has been since. The pregnancy rates in each of the succeeding generations have dropped, until the recent upswing following World War II. The outcomes of the pregnancies have also varied. At older ages among married white females, abortion, either spontaneous or induced, becomes an increasing factor in reducing the pregnancies that come to term.

A record on the number of induced abortions among these married women born in the various decades shows an interesting trend. It would indicate that the smallest number of induced abortions was in the generation born before 1890, and that the prevalence of such abortion increased among the women born in successive decades up to 1909, but among women born in the decades 1910–19 and 1920–29, induced abortion decreased. It is possible that the public concern over abortion, the apparent increasing use of contraceptives, the shift in mores toward larger families, and the periodic drives in enforcing the law have all played a part in this decrease.

At all events, among all women in our sample ever married, 10 per cent of them had induced abortions by twenty years of age. By forty-five years of age, approximately 22 per cent of them had had at least one induced abortion. . . .

EDUCATION AND ABORTION FREQUENCY

There are differences between different educational levels. Among the whole group of single white females the largest incidence of premarital pregnancies, about 12 per cent, occurs among those women who did not go beyond high school. For the single women who go into college or beyond, about 10 per cent utimately become premaritally pregnant, but this usually occurs at later ages. My explanation for the smaller percentage of premarital pregnancies at younger ages in the upper educated groups relates to the comparatively lower frequency of premarital intercourse among the better educated segment of the population.

If you consider only those females in the group who have had coitus, 26–30 per cent of these having only high school education become pregnant before marriage, and between 20–22 per cent of the college educated. Inasmuch as both these categories reported an induced abortion incidence of about 20 per cent, it follows that nearly 95 per cent of all the premarital—as a scientific recorder I never use the term "illegitimate"—pregnancies for college-educated women resolved before marriage in induced abortion, as against a somewhat smaller percentage in those women who never went beyond high school. The agreement of the following two figures is worth thinking about: Among all the women in the sample ever married, 22 per cent have had abortions in marriage by the age of forty-five. Among all the single white females who have had coitus, 20 per cent have had abortions.

RACE AND ABORTION FREQUENCY

If we had time I would show you the Negro data, in which the figures are considerably lower. The Negro is securing induced abortion less often in comparison to the white female. This is partly a mattter of sociology. The birth of a child prior to marriage is not the social disgrace among the socially lower-level Negroes that it is among college girls, and this is something that touches upon a reality we must always take into account. . . .

RELIGION AND ABORTION FREQUENCY

We have made breakdowns by religion. It is true among both Protestant and Jewish groups that there is some correlation between the frequency of marital pregnancy and the infrequency of abortion, which means a higher proportion of live births in relation to pregnancies. The highest frequency of marital pregnancy in both the Protestant and Jewish groups comes among the more devout members of those two groups. The highest frequency of abortion occurs in the least devout. Hence the live birth rate is considerably higher among the devout.

DR. CALDERONE: Will you tell us how you measure devoutness?

DR. KINSEY: We have laid down a definition which satisfies nobody, but is the best we have been able to arrive at.

In Protestant groups it depends partly upon the frequency with which they attend church and the frequency with which they engage in other church activities.

Among Jewish groups it less often depends upon the frequency of attendance at the synagogue, but depends primarily upon the extent to which they observe orthodox Jewish custom. There are more details that you will find in print, but, roughly, those are the criteria that we have used.

In Catholic groups it is measured partly by the frequency with which they attend church services and particularly by the frequency with which they go to confession. However, the Catholic group in our sample is too small to yield reliable data on abortion.

DR. HELLMAN: I am much interested in your earlier statement that there was a small and insignificant group of self-induced abortions—8 per cent, I believe you said. I wonder if you had included the colored population, and particularly if you had included the colored population north of the Mason and Dixon's line, and whether this would have changed it? I am of the impression that self-induced abortion in this group is rather high, particularly in the New York area.

DR. KINSEY: I think all these figures may change considerably with particular communities. It so happens that the Negro groups with which we have worked lie mostly north of the Mason and Dixon line, and we have a minimum of material out of New York, so I cannot answer you specifically there. Our Negro material has come from Philadelphia, from Chicago, from St. Louis, from the Pacific Coast; a large sample from Chicago and Indianapolis.

We find in our Negro sample that the number of induced abortions of any sort, particularly in premarital histories, and also in marriage, is consistently lower for each breakdown— educational, age groups, and so on—consistently lower among the Negroes than it is among whites and it is most markedly low among the Negro females who have never been married. In consequence, while many of them attempt to make some gesture toward induced abortion, and have told us that they have attempted it, we have really a much smaller percentage reporting the accomplishment of abortion through self-induction.

The records of the most experienced abortionist whom we have known indicated that about 80 per cent of the women who came to him for consummation of an abortion had previously attempted some sort of self-induction. Now the cases that have run into complications would be the cases that you would get in the hospital or in court, but they do not begin to cover the whole body of cases.

DR. STONE: Do you have any data about the influence of midwives in abortions? If I understand correctly, in New York City the midwife does play an important role in certain areas of the population.

DR. KINSEY: Our record is that the midwife played a much more important role in older generations, and that nearly 90 per cent of the operative abortions that are being performed today are being performed by physicians, most of whom are not recognized abortionists. . . .

There is no question that there is increasing difficulty in finding a physician who will perform an abortion. In our earlier histories, before there was as much restraint as we have right now on induced abortion, we could rather quickly find out the persons who were chiefly involved in induced abortions in particular communities. But inasmuch as there are still a very considerable number of abortions being performed, I should like to know who are the persons—(and they are primarily physicians; don't forget that)—who are the persons providing the induced abortions today?

Social and Psychological Factors in Status Decisions of Unmarried Mothers

WYATT C. JONES

HENRY J. MEYER

EDGAR F. BORGATTA

In prior studies the association of background characteristics —such as race, religion and education—to the decisions of agency samples of unmarried mothers to surrender or keep their babies has been examined.[1] Some findings were sufficiently striking to suggest that further study might establish empirical relationships that would make it possible to identify persons in terms of their likelihood of making a particular decision. This might alert practitioners serving such clients to differential problems, especially where decisions appear to differ from those predicted. The first purpose of this paper is to examine another set of cases and to suggest in more gen-

REPRINTED FROM *Journal of Marriage and the Family* (formerly *Marriage and Family Living*), Vol. 25, August, 1962, pp. 224–230, by permission of the authors and the National Council on Family Relations.

[1] H. J. Meyer, W. Jones, and E. F. Borgatta, "The Decision by Unmarried Mothers to Keep or Surrender Their Babies," *Social Work*, 1 (April, 1956), pp. 103–09. H. J. Meyer, E. F. Borgatta, and David Fanshel, "Unwed Mothers' Decisions About Their Babies: An Interim Replication Study," *Child Welfare*, 38 (February, 1959), pp. 1–6.

eral terms the implications of the empirical relationships that now appear to be reasonably stable.

A second purpose is to report associations between a series of personality and attitude measures and the decision to keep or surrender the baby. In the prior studies certain personal characteristics rated by caseworkers appeared to have some association with the decision. Here we report relationships based on test response data obtained before the birth of the baby. Such information, not usually available, has intrinsic interest and adds as well to knowledge about the unmarried mother's decision.[2]

As a third purpose, this paper presents changes reflected in these same measures before and after delivery of the unmarried mother's baby. Without a comparison of unmarried mothers and other mothers, it is not possible to determine whether giving birth out of wedlock is accompanied by psychological effects different from those accompanying legitimatized motherhood. Nevertheless, information about any changes accompanying the experience is of interest to those concerned with management of psychological problems of the unmarried mother.

BACKGROUND CHARACTERISTICS AND THE UNMARRIED MOTHER'S DECISION

The empirical relationships found in the series of studies can be interpreted briefly by reference to general theories about American society. In broadest terms, the relationships can be viewed as reflecting a conflict between the dominant values and mores of American society, on the one hand, and opposing values of relatively unassimilated subgroups or subcultures and of deviant individuals, on the other hand. The dominant values of American society, phrased simply, include

[2] Unmarried mothers who kept and surrendered their babies were compared on the California Personality Inventory in C. W. Vincent, "Unwed Mothers and the Adoption Market: Psychological and Familial Factors," *Marriage and Family Living*, 22 (May, 1960), pp. 112–18, and C. W. Vincent, *Unmarried Mothers*, New York: The Free Press, 1961, Chapter VII.

a negative view of births outside of wedlock. To illustrate from one subgroup, Negroes in America can be assumed to support the ideal of having children within the legally constituted family unit, but this ideal is apparently not so strongly held as it is within the society as a whole. Such an assertion is not totally circular (i.e., Negroes hold the ideals less strongly because there is more illegitimacy) since it rests on evidence of historical tradition and also on analysis indicating that, even when such important factors as education and socio-economic class are controlled, some aspects of behavior are left unexplained and must be attributed to the "culture" or common behavior of the group. Raising economic and educational levels of any group may constitute an important change, but it does not automatically change the values of the group in regard to such things as orientations of pleasure, friendship, dating, courtship, and marriage. However, as the subculture becomes more integrated, its values may be expected to approximate the dominant values of the general society. This explanation would fit the experience at one social agency[3] in respect to decisions of its Negro clients. In 1954, 83 per cent of the Negro clients kept their babies. In 1956, the proportion was 76 per cent. In the 1957–1959 sample, the percentage had fallen to 62. During the same period, the proportion of white clients who kept their babies fell from 38 per cent in 1954 to 21 per cent in the current sample. Over a five-year period, the differential between Negro and white clients was reduced by three per cent. Other explanations, such as changes in agency policies and increases in adoption outlets, are also possible, of course.

As decreasing association between subgroup membership and deviance occurs, predictions for the general society may be expected to apply equally for Negroes. Such is not the case at present, and we therefore consistently find that Negro unmarried mothers, in comparison to white mothers, keep

[3] Youth Consultation Service, New York City, from which the present data are obtained as well as data for earlier years. We gratefully acknowledge the cooperation of the director and staff in this research. It was conducted while more extended research on adolescent girls was in progress, supported by a grant from Russell Sage Foundation.

their babies rather than surrender them. The explanation for this difference need not assume any innate peculiarities of these Negro mothers. The status of the Negro in the total society produces a number of compelling social pressures. Thus, even if a Negro girl wishes to surrender her baby for adoption, in addition to subcultural norms imposed on her or internalized by her, social, economic, or legal barriers may make it impossible for her to do so. Our only assertion is that it is efficient, at this point in history, to predict that Negro unmarried mothers will keep their babies to a greater extent than white unmarried mothers.

Our earlier studies found four background variables most useful for predicting the disposition decision of white unmarried mothers: age, education, and religion of the mother, and marital status of the putative father—the male involved in the relationship. Agency clients who were young, more highly educated, and of non-Catholic religion tended to surrender the baby for adoption. It also appeared in these earlier studies that when the putative fathers of the babies were unmarried, the mothers tended to surrender, but this appears to be a less relevant variable for predictive purposes than the other background characteristics.

Consideration of the marital status of the putative father was suggested by the theory that when a girl has relationships with a man who is unavailable for marriage, she will, upon becoming pregnant, perpetuate her deviance for the same psychological reasons that led to her situation by tending to keep rather than surrender the baby. In the absence of consistent evidence for this theory, however, we prefer to give attention to more direct social and psychological variables.

Although by no means invariant, there is a consistent relationship between the Catholic religion of an unmarried mother and the tendency to keep the baby. Our data are insufficient to explore why this is so. Like Negro girls, Roman Catholic girls might be considered to come from a cultural subgroup of American society. We might speculate that girls from Catholic backgrounds have accepted obligations of natural motherhood as more compelling than restoration of single status. Perhaps this reflects strong religious beliefs associated with sex, marriage, and motherhood, or with retribution and responsibility. Perhaps it reflects differential ethnic values deriving from national origin because Catholics are more likely to be of recent immigration than Protestants. Our previous studies do not, however, support the interpretation that the association between professed Catholic religion and keeping the baby is a reflection of socio-economic status because it occurs even when social class is held constant. Whatever the explanation, the empirical relationship has persisted throughout the series of studies and constitutes a predictor, even though not a determiner, of the decision about the baby.

Education, particularly at the college level, is associated with surrendering the baby. A direct and obvious interpretation of this relationship might suggest that keeping the baby constitutes a handicap to continuation of a normal educational, occupational, and marital career. Surrender of the baby represents the only means by which a girl, socialized through years of education, can remain consistent with general American values of marriage and motherhood.

Younger ages are associated with surrender of the baby. At the youngest ages, subadult status minimizes individual choices and subjects the unmarried mother to the imposition of adult control more likely to conform to the general value system. The older the unmarried mother, the more free she is to express subcultural or personal values by keeping the baby. Similarly, the younger the unmarried mother, the less likely that the attributions of adult independence will occur to inhibit a return to the more normal non-mother status.

In the historical sense, these predictive variables are almost certainly transitory. With secularization of knowledge, any subcultural values that may exist for Catholics with respect to unmarried motherhood are likely to change in the direction of the more general value system. A similar change can be expected for Negroes. If values become more homogeneous, it appears that in the long run most unmarried mothers will return to their non-mother status by surrendering their babies. If this is the trend, race, religion, age, and education will eventually have but trivial potency as predictors of the decision. It may simply be predicted that unmarried mothers will seek to surrender the baby.

It may be further suggested that reduced insulation of sub-
cultures will lessen whatever satisfactions might be obtained
from conformity to subcultural values. If the basic proposition
is accepted that, in general, conforming behavior yields more
total satisfaction—social as well as psychological—than non-
conformity, the general societal norm will be more widely
accepted. When norms conflict, in the absence of subcultural
isolation, it is more likely that the general norm will be accepted. If surrendering their babies becomes recognized by
the unmarried mothers as a general norm, keeping the baby
can be expected to become less and less satisfying.

We postulate surrender of the baby as a general norm for
a number of reasons. In the first place, there is little evidence
that the status of unmarried motherhood is more acceptable
now than formerly. Further, widespread acceptance of contraception may be expected to reduce further any tolerance for
"accidental pregnancy" among the unmarried. We would
presume also that other means—such as abortion—of returning to non-mother status would become more widely acceptable. The trend toward secularization, as already mentioned,
would point in the same direction with respect to surrender of
the baby as the general norm. Accompanying this, emphasis
on individual careers, rather than on continuity and maintenance of family and communal traditions, would discourage
unmarried mothers from keeping their babies. Finally, there
appears to be sufficient infertility among married couples to
provide a ready market for adoption of babies surrendered by
unmarried mothers.

Although we postulate the general norm of surrender, we
do not imply that subcultural, family, and individual factors
may not result in some deviant behavior in respect to the unmarried mother's decision. What we insist is that until there
is, in actuality, such a general norm, background factors
now associated with the decision are likely to predict better
than more individual or psychological variables. As a consequence, studies of psychological factors associated with the
decision should be interpreted with caution unless background factors—especially race, education, religion, and age
—are taken into account. Put another way, psychological
factors may more appropriately be interpreted for the light

they throw on general and subcultural norms than as psychological explanations for the decision.

THE PRESENT SAMPLE

Over a three-year period, the unmarried mothers who were clients at a non-sectarian, private social agency in New York City were studied. The agency offers casework services to adolescent and young adult female clients. Most of them were known to the agency for one to four months prior to delivery of the baby. Information was obtained for a large proportion of these clients, as well as from caseworkers, through tests administered both before and after delivery. The clients for whom information is lacking appear not to differ from the usual clientele of the agency. The sample, obviously not representative of all unmarried mothers, is composed of persons from a wide range of socio-economic levels and a variety of geographical and subcultural backgrounds.[4]

PREDICTION FOR BACKGROUND CRITERIA

Of the total sample studied (113 clients), 20 per cent were Negro and 80 per cent were white. The proportion of Negro unmarried mothers keeping their babies was 62 per cent, smaller than our earlier studies found but nevertheless significantly greater than the 21 per cent of whites who kept their babies.[5] Thus, in accord with prior experience, we may conclude that the prediction that Negro girls will keep their babies can be made with some confidence.[6] The smaller number of cases here precludes detailed examination of other characteristics of the Negro unmarried mothers in our sample,

[4] The sample will be described in detail by Wyatt C. Jones in his doctoral dissertation submitted to the Department of Sociology, New York University.

[5] Statistical significance in this paper corresponds to satisfaction of the .05 level with a symmetric hypothesis test.

[6] See footnote 1, above.

and hence our subsequent analyses will be confined to whites only. Furthermore, the prior studies have not yielded factors that would improve the prediction for Negro unmarried mothers.

Using the 90 white clients who constituted our sample for this analysis, we have made a "test" that includes the variables of age, education, and religion. For this purpose, young age (under 17 years of age), non-Catholic religion (rather than Catholic), and some college education (rather than less education) are taken as predictors that the unmarried mother will surrender her baby. While the fact of being white is a substantial predictor in itself, since 71 of the total 90 in the sample surrendered, a more efficient prediction can be made for such groups of the sample using these additional variables. Thus, if two or three of these criterion variables are present, 23 out of 24 unmarried mothers surrendered their babies. If none of these variables is present the probability is 40 per cent (8 out of 20) that the baby will be kept. If only one of the criterion variables is present, the results are more ambiguous, 36 surrendered and 10 kept their babies. These results are consistent with our previous studies.

PERSONALITY CHARACTERISTICS AND THE DECISION TO KEEP OR SURRENDER

Unlike information about background characteristics, prior quantitative data based on personality or other psychological variables have been scarce. Only recently, for example, has Vincent published some data using the C. P. I.[7] We therefore examined such variables in our study to see which differentiate unmarried mothers, prior to the birth of their baby, with respect to the decision. For the 90 white clients, responses to a sentence completion test (MAST),[8] the Cattell 16 Per-

[7] Vincent, op. cit.

[8] The MAST (Make a Sentence Test) items, scoring and cross-validation are described in E. F. Borgatta, (in collaboration with H. J. Meyer), "Make a Sentence Test: An Approach to Objective Scoring of Sentence Completions," Genetic Psychology Monographs, 1961, 63, pp. 3–65.

sonality Factor Test,[9] and a checklist of items about feelings and problems have been analyzed for this purpose.

Personality Characteristics Measured Through the MAST

Of the 11 MAST scoring categories, only one discriminated between the mothers who surrendered and those who kept their babies. This was the scale indicating paranoid responses (MAST 1). Significantly more mothers who kept their babies had scores above the median cutting point for the variable. With scores of 0–3, 41 of 71 mothers surrendered; with scores of four or more, 14 of 19 mothers kept their babies.

Several other scoring categories seemed to indicate differences, but none achieved the significance level.[10] The largest additional difference is an association of MAST 8, Anxious, with keeping the baby.

The Cattell 16 Personality Factor Test

Five of the personality factors were significantly associated with the decision to keep or surrender the baby. Scores for girls who kept their babies would characterize them as: "insecure, anxious" (0 score), "tense, excitable" (Q_4 score), "emotional, unstable" (C score), "dull, low capacity" (B score), and "submissive, mild" (E score). In contrast, those who surrendered their babies could be described as: "con-

[9] R. B. Cattell, D. R. Saunders, and G. Stice, *Handbook for the Sixteen Personality Factor Questionnaire* (1957 Edition), Institute for Personality and Ability Testing, 1602 Coronado Drive, Champaign, Illinois, 1957.

[10] The scoring categories for the MAST sentence completion test are listed as follows: 1. Paranoid, 2. Hostile, 3. Assertive, 4. Annoyed, 5. Conventional, 6. Avoidant, 7. Depressive, 8. Anxious, 9. Self-Analytic, 10. Hypochondriac, and 11. Optimistic.
The data analysis follows several arbitrary decisions that tend to minimize the possibility of interpreting spurious findings. For example, in the MAST analysis, the variables were dichotomized prior to analysis to give two most nearly equal halves. The 16 PFT variables were trichotomized with the two central scores comprising the "moderate" category, and then were further dichotomized on the same principle as the MAST. An example of a dichotomy in the form of L vs. MH is the Low group versus the Middle and High groups.

fident, unshakeable," "phlegmatic, poised," "mature, calm," "bright, intelligent," and "dominant, aggressive." Thus, unmarried mothers who kept their babies, in comparison with those who surrendered them, tended to be: (a) lower in intelligence, (b) lower in ego strength or emotional stability, and (c) more submissive.[11]

Discussion of Personality Characteristics

The constellation of personality characteristics describing the unmarried mother who keeps her baby implies general immaturity and this is the same conclusion suggested by earlier examination of caseworker ratings of unmarried mother clients in another social agency.[12] Those who ultimately surrender the baby can be described as exhibiting greater intelligence, independence and emotional stability, less anxiety and tension, and less feeling that others make things difficult. These are characteristics that might be associated with greater competence than the contrasting characteristics of those who kept their babies.

These findings are in general agreement with those of Vincent who compared 71 unmarried mothers who surrendered their babies with 34 who did not.[13] These unmarried mothers were clients of two social agencies in California. Using the California Personality Inventory, Vincent found that those who released their babies for adoption had significantly higher scores than those who kept them on subscales grouped as measures of poise, ascendency, and self-assurance; measures of socialization, maturity, and responsibility; and measures of achievement, potential and intellectual efficiency. They did not differ significantly on measures of intellectual and interest modes (psychological-mindedness, flexibility,

[11] The scoring categories of the Cattell 16-PFT are as follows: A. Warm, sociable, B. General intelligence, C. Emotional stability, E. Dominant, aggressive, F. Talkative, enthusiastic, G. Conscientious, persistent, H. Adventurous, I. Sensitive, L. Suspecting, M. Eccentric, unconcerned, N. Sophisticated, polished, O. Anxious, insecure, Q_1. Experimenting, critical, Q_2. Self-sufficient, resourceful, Q_3. Controlled, and Q_4. Tense, excitable.

[12] Meyer, Borgatta, Fanshel, *op. cit.*, p. 3.

[13] Vincent, *op. cit.*

femininity). Vincent interpreted these findings and some questionnaire responses as suggesting that unmarried mothers who keep their babies have minimum positive identification with individuals or social groups from whom traditional sex norms and the stigma of an out-of-wedlock child could be meaningfully communicated. Stating impressions from the data about the mothers who surrendered, Vincent says: "They had a positive identity with and acceptance by parents, adults, peers or social groups which served to communicate and maintain a meaningful awareness of the stigma attached to illegitimacy."[14] This is in essence similar to our suggestion of subcultural deviance as an explanation of the relationship of background characteristics to the decision about the baby.

Such an interpretation is suggested for several reasons. One might expect that young women with less social maturity are either less aware of the norms of the general society, or less able to resolve subcultural conflicts of values in accordance with such norms. It might be, however, that these are individual traits associated with prior deviance, and, hence, with continued deviance in the decision to keep the baby. It should be noted that, with regard to the disposition of the baby, most of the girls in this sample are known (from other data) to have followed the intention they indicated at the time of testing. Therefore, personal indications of anxiety, tension, and similar feelings might be a consequence of, rather than an anticipation of, the decision to keep. In this sense, a decision to surrender (in keeping with a more normal future for single women) might be reflected in our measures as less disturbing and as producing less anxiety and tension.

The idea that those who surrendered were, on the whole, somewhat better adjusted or felt more competent in the face of their situation is supported by responses to a short checklist of attitudes toward problems and other circumstances. When asked the simple and direct question: "How do you feel?", 46 of the 90 clients answered "very well" or "excellent," but among those who eventually surrendered their babies, the proportion giving these responses was slightly higher (although not statistically significant) compared to those who

[14] *Ibid.*, p. 117.

eventually kept their babies. Similarly, those who surrendered gave somewhat more favorable responses when asked if they felt better at present than two months earlier, but, again, the difference did not achieve statistical significance. Likewise, those who ultimately surrendered were slightly more likely than the other category to say that they were getting along very well with family and friends.

TABLE 1. Relations of Disposition Decision to Responses on Selected Cattell Scores and Self-Assessed Problem Status, White Only

Responses	Scores	Surrender	Keep	Totals
Emotional stability	LM	42	17	59
(C)	H	29	2	31
Anxiety	LM	48	7	55
(O)	H	23	12	35
Tension	LM	50	7	57
(Q₄)	H	21	12	33
Intelligence	L	27	13	40
(B)	MH	44	6	50
Dominance	L	39	17	56
(E)	MH	32	2	34
Number of prob-	Many	28	11	39
lems indicated	Few	43	8	51
Ability to take	Well	52	5	57
care of problems	Trouble	19	14	33
Totals		71	19	90

Table 1 may be interpreted in keeping with the idea that surrender of the baby is associated with maturity and competence, and that this in turn related to conformance with the general norm of surrendering the baby so that legitimate non-mother status is restored. The proportion of those who indicated that they had many problems was smaller for those who surrendered than for those who kept their babies. A higher proportion (statistically significant) of the group who surrendered also expressed confidence in their ability to take care of their problems in the future. These findings suggest more secure and confident attitudes on the part of those who surrendered than of those who kept. Realistically, those who surrender have fewer problems to face in the future precisely because keeping the baby constitutes continued and visible deviance as well as increased economic and other responsibilities. The more mature may be expected to recognize this.

When we ask whether variables associated with the disposition decision are those to be expected from the general theory of subcultural deviance, we conclude that this is a plausible interpretation. Because of the small size of our sample, we cannot examine personality and attitudinal variables holding constant the social background characteristics found to be predictive of the decision. But we would surmise that the differences in personality measures would reflect the background characteristics we consider indicators of subcultural variation.

COMPARISON OF PERSONALITY MEASURES BEFORE AND AFTER BIRTH OF BABY

It is of further interest to examine the data about personality and general feelings of the 67 white unmarried mothers who completed tests both before and after the birth of their babies. Without comparative data for married mothers, we must interpret the findings with caution because they may simply reflect changes associated with having a baby. However, since there is relatively little systematic information yet available on this subject, the findings for unmarried mothers may be suggestive.

On the sentence completion test, only the measure of optimism (MAST 11) discriminated with statistical significance the before and after scores (Table 2). Mothers were higher on this score after the birth of their babies.

It should be remarked that if surrender and keep groups are held separate, this shift in the score persists. Indeed it

seems to persist even when the following caseworker ratings
are held constant: satisfaction with the decision, degree of
adequacy in resolution of the problem, attribution of responsibility for the problem, or rating of emotional health after
the delivery. In other words, from a general point of view,
unmarried mothers tend to be more optimistic once the baby
is born and this appears to be independent of other considerations.

TABLE 2.   Relationship of Pregnancy Termination to Responses on
Selected MAST Scores and Cattell Scores, White Only

Responses	Scores	Before Delivery	After Delivery
Optimistic	0–8	42	27
(MAST 11)	9 or more	25	40
Withdrawn	0–1	24	30
(MAST 6)	2 or more	43	37
Talkative	LM	61	47
(F)	H	6	20
Sensitive	LM	19	34
(I)	H	48	33
Critical	L	44	31
(Q₁)	MH	23	36
Sophisticated	L	39	26
(N)	MH	28	41
Total		67	67

With regard to a comparison of pre- and post-test data on
the MAST 6 (withdrawn) score, there is not quite a significant
difference (Table 2). The direction of the shift, however, was
interesting and led to more intensive analysis. In particular,
it was found that among 34 persons who were *satisfied with
the decision* in their disposition of the child, according to the
rating of the caseworker, there was a significant shift towards
less withdrawn responses on the post-test. Two or more withdrawn responses were made by 23 mothers before delivery
but by only 15 after delivery. This shift seemed to be em-

phasized in persons rated favorably in terms of: constructive resolution of the problem, emotional health, and adequate psychological functioning. For pesons not satisfied with the decision, there was a slight (but not statistically significant) trend in the opposite direction.

Four of the Cattell 16 Personality Factor Test scores appear to indicate shifts in the period from before to after delivery (Table 2). On their first tests, the unmarried mothers were characterized on these scores as "glum, silent" (F), "sensitive, effeminate" (I), "conservative, accepting" (Q_1). Significant increases were recorded in the following scores: "enthusiastic, talkative," "tough, realistic," "experimenting, critical." The Cattell N score, which measures the naiveté-sophistication dimension, also showed a significant shift towards the sophisticated pole of the continuum. It was noticed, however, that the shifts are in two directions from the pre- to the post-period. Those who are high and those who are low on this score tend to move toward the center. On the "before delivery" tests, 15 were moderate and 52 were high or low; on the "after delivery" tests, 37 were moderate and only 30 were at the extreme. In other words, persons who are characterized as simple or awkward and persons who are characterized as sophisticated and polished tend after delivery to become less extreme.

When the unmarried mothers were compared in before and after testing on the checklist about feelings, significant differences occurred on the general questions: "How do you feel?" and "Do you feel better than about two months ago?" As might be expected, the mothers indicated "feeling better" after they had their babies. For the first question, the shift was from 32 favorable out of 67 before delivery to 47 favorable after delivery. On the second question, the change was even more pronounced, 14 favorable responses before to 37 after delivery.

A similar trend toward more confident, optimistic outlook is reflected in before and after responses to questions asking whether the girl had many or few problems and whether she felt these problems could be adequately met. Statistically significant shifts occurred on both these items. Before delivery 28 out of 67 indicated having many problems and 24 thought they would have some trouble later. After delivery, only 18 indicated many problems and only 15 thought they would have trouble later.

Discussion of Before and After Findings

The general impression from our data of changes occurring within the few months that include birth of the unmarried mother's baby is one of relief of anxiety, increased sense of confidence and optimism, and a tendency toward more interest in things other than herself. There appears to be a reduction of exaggerated reactions, a subsiding, as it were, from extremes. These shifts in responses are what one might well expect to accompany termination of the long months of pregnancy and the restoration, in the sheer sense of physical capacity, of opportunities to pursue normal activities.

Since our sample consists of clients receiving the services of caseworkers, it is tempting to believe that some of the shift toward positive responses might be a consequence of casework treatment. The finding that the girls who were rated as satisfied with their decision about the baby exhibit less withdrawn responses encourages such as interpretation because resolution of conflicts about this question is often a central objective of casework effort. As previously noted, however, we must reserve conclusion until a comparison can be made between married and unmarried mothers. One would reasonably expect the special circumstances of illegitimate pregnancy to intensify the normal feelings of anxiety, sensitivity, withdrawal, and pessimism before the birth of the baby, followed by a sense of relief after the baby is born. This explanation would be in keeping with the hypothesis that elimination of deviant status and restored conformity with the value system of American society would be more satisfying.

CONCLUSION

This paper has briefly reviewed current research about social and psychological factors in status decisions of unmarried mothers. Cumulative evidence appears to show considerable consistency in findings on background factors such as race, religion, education, and age and some consistency also for psychological variables. The findings lead to the tentative conclusion that the phenomenon of unmarried motherhood may be appropriately interpreted, at this stage of available research knowledge, through analysis of subcultural values. Such values may be exhibited in differential intrafamily relationships, in differential peer relationships especially those involving dating and other heterosexual activities, and in differential cognitive orientations, attitudes, and self-images internalized during the socialization of girls who have babies before they are married. However, until subcultural variations can be taken into account, it would seem premature to interpret status decisions of the unmarried mother, such as the decision to keep or surrender the baby, primarily as manifestations of individual, psychological dynamics.

Studies available to the present time have been based on relatively small samples of agency clients. The selective bias of agency samples limits generalization and the small sample sizes limit the detail of analysis that is now possible. Replication of the gross findings lends support to a subcultural hypothesis and suggests that it is timely now to develop comprehensive research on the factors affecting the status decisions of unmarried mothers.

Illegitimacy and the AFDC Program

KERMIT T. WILTSE AND
ROBERT W. ROBERTS

Concern about illegitimacy among women receiving or likely to apply for financial assistance under the Aid to Families with Dependent Children program runs in many different directions. At the most obvious level is the public or "taxpayer" concern with what is perceived as a rising tide of illegitimate children born to promiscuous women and irresponsible men; children who become dependent upon the public for support during all of their childhood years. The extent of public concern with the AFDC program is a matter of conjecture. The evidence of such concern can only be a reference to articles in popular magazines and daily newspapers. It is the evidence from which we infer a crescendo of national concern about this problem.

We need hardly document the long standing interest of social welfare and public health professionals with the unmarried mother and her child as objects of special concern. There have been few national or local conferences of health or welfare personnel but that some part of the program deals with the question of out-of-wedlock childbearing. So much professional activity attests to the persistence and vitality of the issues connected with this social problem in both fields. Health people are concerned about the obstacles faced by many unmarried pregnant girls in obtaining adequate pre-

THIS IS an original article prepared for this volume.

natal and natal care; [1] welfare people with the current and future adjustment of the girl and the protection of her child. These concerns cut across questions of financial need, although lack of financial resources often adds to the difficulties faced by these girls.

When the concern about unmarried mothers is shifted to a focus upon illegitimate childbearing within or as related to the AFDC program, it acquires an additional dimension. It is the spectre of an increasing number of dependent children, supported by the persistent fear that the operation of the program somehow contributes to the incidence of repetitive out-of-wedlock childbearing, or the feeling that the people administering the program ought to be able to do something to halt the process. It is extremely difficult to document an assertion about what the public believes, but we suggest that the public belief that illegitimacy is fostered by the AFDC program will not be put down by the efforts of professional health and welfare people to change this public concern into a concern for the disadvantaged mother and her children. Better answers must be sought to questions regarding the extent and the nature of out-of-wedlock childbearing with specific reference to the AFDC program. Parenthetically, there must be no implicit promise that increased services might reduce the extent of illegitimate childbearing among AFDC recipients while the program itself remains essentially undescribed.

This article endeavors to carry the description of out-of-wedlock childbearing in relation to the AFDC program beyond the level of census data into some of the more definitive characteristics. Data on the characteristics of the AFDC unmarried mother population within one geographic area are presented and compared whenever possible to similar data from studies in two other cities. The type of data presented in this article does little to explain out-of-wedlock childbearing as related to the AFDC program; but efforts such as

[1] For example, a recent study in New York City entitled "Deterrents to Early Prenatal Care and Social Services Among Women Pregnant Out-of-Wedlock," authored by Blanche Bernstein and Mignon Sauber, (New York State Department of Social Welfare, Albany, 1960) sprang from a concern expressed by the New York City Department of Health over the high prenatal mortality rate of children borne out-of-wedlock.

this to describe the nature of the problem may give pause to those who would seek oversimplified explanations of and solutions to so complex a social phenomenon. By putting the problem of illegitimacy in the AFDC program into perspective, we not only suggest directions for studies that reach to deeper levels of insight and explanation but also to some extent illuminate certain general assumptions about this part of the AFDC caseload.

These data, concerning the AFDC population in a district of Contra Costa County, California, come from the early stages of a project which attempts to explore the nature of repetitive out-of-wedlock childbearing within the AFDC program. A later stage of the project will examine a sample of this population in depth in an effort to develop more refined insights and suggestive hypotheses.

The metropolitan area from which the data were drawn is in the western end of Contra Costa County, California, and includes the cities of Richmond, El Cerrito, and San Pablo plus other smaller incorporated and unincorporated towns. Richmond is the largest city, with a population of approximately 80,000 people in 1960, and is a major industrial center and seaport. During World War II Richmond was a major site of the famed Kaiser shipyards, and it jumped in population from a city of 23,000 to about 100,000 in the early years of the war. The majority of this influx of workers were housed in temporary war housing units. These temporary units were finally demolished by the mid-1950s, and the former occupants spread out to the suburbs or found permanent housing within the Richmond area. The villages and plantations of the South were a major source of this flood of immigrants, and the war years irretrievably changed the racial composition of the area. Today approximately 20 percent of the area's residents are non-white, but only a fraction of this non-white population is Oriental.

In common with other northern metropolitan areas to which there was an influx of new migrants from the South during the war, the welfare caseloads typically exaggerate the changed racial composition of the population. For example, according to the Greenleigh Associates study of Cook County, Illinois, between 1942 and 1960 the population of non-white families receiving AFDC (then ADC) in Illinois shifted from 57.7 to 90.0 percent.[2] In this section of Contra Costa County under study it has not reached these proportions. As of the time of our study approximately 63 percent of the AFDC families were non-whites.

Since the focus of our study was illegitimacy within the AFDC population, and particularly the phenomenon of repetitive out-of-wedlock childbearing, we first broke the total caseload down into those mothers who had, as against those who had not, ever borne a child out-of-wedlock. On this breakdown slightly over 47 percent of the AFDC mothers had borne one or more illegitimate children. Those who had borne out-of-wedlock children were in turn broken down into four groups and labeled Groups I, II, III and IV. Group I were those who had borne one child out-of-wedlock; Group II, two out-of-wedlock children; Group III, three out-of-wedlock children; and Group IV had borne four or more children who were illegitimate. This process yielded the following simple table.

TABLE 1.   AFDC Unmarried Mother Population by Number of Illegitimate Children

No. of Illegitimate Children	No. of Mothers	Percent of All Unmarried Mothers[a]
1 illegitimate child	498	49.9
2 illegitimate children	225	22.7
3 illegitimate children	135	12.7
4 or more illegitimate children	139	14.7
Total	997	100.0

[a] Can be partially compared with the New York findings where 26% of all mothers studied had three or more out-of-wedlock children. However, their data, on a sample of mothers coming to hospitals for delivery, were not specific to AFDC. (Berstein, *op. cit.*, p. 30)

From this total count of AFDC mothers in the district who had borne children out-of-wedlock (and very often legitimate children also) we read samples of their case records in the

[2] Greenleigh Associates, Inc., "Facts, Fallacies, and Future: A Study of the ADC Program of Cook County, Illinois," 437 Fifth Aveue, NYC, p. 21.

Social Service Department. Of Group I, 123 (25%) case records were read, 113 (50%) of Group II, 73 (50%) of Group III, and 139 (100%) of Group IV. All cases in Group IV were read because of our special interest in this extreme group of out-of-wedlock childbearing mothers.

A pre-coded schedule was used to draw off information on the age of the mother, race, education, state of birth, year she came to California, age at time of first child, age at first marriage (if any), year she first received assistance, employment history, ages of each of her children (legitimate and illegitimate), and an estimate of the type of relationship to the father of each child. This list of items represents most of the "hard data" items of social characteristics of the AFDC families consistently available in the case records.

The highlights of the data are described below, with comparisons where appropriate to the data from Cook County[3] and to the New York study which obtained data in a few similar areas.[4] Since the AFDC population of the district studied included so few whose race was other than Negro or Caucasian, we will use only a Negro-white dichotomy for this analysis, dropping other ethnic groups from the sample.

RACE

The proportionate representation of Negroes in the sample increases as the number of illegitimate children born to the mother increases. Hence Negroes constitute 68% of the Group I (one out-of-wedlock child), 80% of Group II, 81% of Group III, and 88% of Group IV (those with four or more out-of-wedlock children).[5]

[3] Greenleigh, op. cit.

[4] Bernstein, op. cit.

[5] Greenleigh also found that the proportion of non-whites increased as the number of illegitimate children increased. However, the proportion of whites in his total sample was so much smaller and differences in sample selection make more refined comparisons dangerous. The New York study also found the same type of progression, with Negroes being overrepresented among the repeaters, and conversely, whites underrepresented. Again differences in sample selection make refined comparisons difficult.

Oriental mothers and those listed by the worker as Mexican were tabulated separately. However, there were no Orientals found among the unmarried mother groups, and so few Mexicans as to be unworthy of retaining them in the remainder of the analysis.

AGE

As might be expected there was a progression in average age of the mother, as one moved from Group I to IV; the average ages being 27, 28, 31 and 33 years respectively. However, it is to be noted that Group I and II mothers are mature in terms of years and do not, therefore, appear to be young girls on their way to a career of repeated out-of-wedlock childbearing.

Negro mothers tended to average a year younger than white mothers for all groups except for Group IV, where Negroes averaged a year older.

YEARS OF SCHOOL COMPLETED

It is noteworthy that the educational achievements of the AFDC unmarried mothers studied were reasonably high and did not show a large variation according to race. On the average the women who had borne illegitimate children had achieved a tenth grade level of education, and if anything, Negroes were slightly better educated than whites. With reference to education as related to the number of children borne out-of-wedlock, there was great similarity between most groups except for the extreme group, those with four or more illegitimate children, who averaged about a year less of education than the others. Certainly no case can be made for a theory that illegitimate childbearing is related to extremely low education attainment.[6]

[6] Bernstein found that the unmarried mother in New York City was less well educated than the City's female population 25-44 generally, but their data, although again not strictly comparable, do not show the unmarried mother population as a conspicuously uneducated group. The modal group had had some high school.

TABLE 2.   Number of Years of Education of AFDC Mothers
by Number of Illegitimate Children

No. of Illegitimate Children	White		Negro		Both Races	
	No. of Mothers	Average Education in Years	No. of Mothers	Average Education in Years	No. of Mothers	Average Education in Years
1	36	9.94	84	10.82	120	10.56
2	19	10.47	90	10.49	109	10.49
3	8	10.75	59	10.02	67	10.11
4 or more	8	8.87	122	9.20	130	9.18

Averages, of course, disguise a wide range of differences;
there were a few with one or two years of college, but also a
few who had not achieved a first grade level. Also, grade level
reached is only a rough measure of actual educational
achievement.

STATE OF BIRTH

The majority of AFDC mothers of both races who have
illegitimate children were born outside of California, hence
have migrated to California at some point in their lives. Of
the total, 88.2% were born in other states. The birthplaces of
the white mothers were roughly divided into one-third California, one-third born in the South, and one-third distributed
among all other states. With Negroes, a small percentage were
born in California, an overwhelming proportion in the South,
and a small percentage distributed among other states.

The percentage of out-of-state births increases with an increase in the number of illegitimate children born to the
mother. This is primarily due to the fact that, as noted above,
multiple out-of-wedlock births become so overwhelmingly a
phenomenon related to race as one moves from Group I to
Group IV, and Negroes are more likely to have been born
outside California, and more specifically, in the Southern
states.

The data with reference to year the unwed mother came to California is consistent for all four groups and both races, that is, there was a rapid rise during the early years of World War II, with 1943–1944 as peak years, then tapering off to a steady flow in the years since.

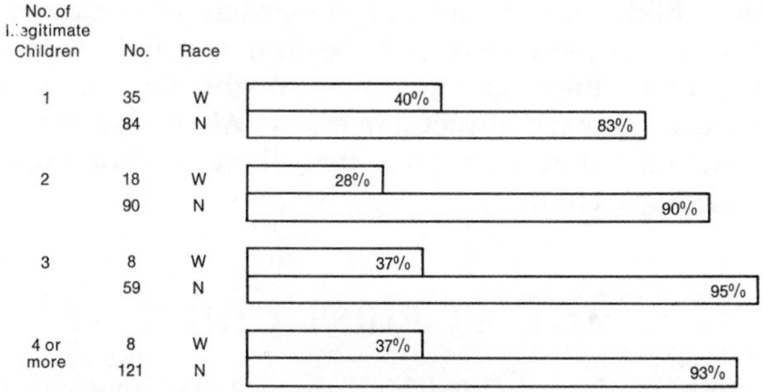

No. of illegitimate Children	No.	Race	
1	35	W	40%
	84	N	83%
2	18	W	28%
	90	N	90%
3	8	W	37%
	59	N	95%
4 or more	8	W	37%
	121	N	93%

FIGURE 4. Percentage of AFDC mothers born in the South by race and number of illegitimate children. Census definition of the South includes 16 states: Alabama, Arkansas, Delaware, Florida, Georgia, Kentucky, Louisiana, Maryland, Mississippi, North Carolina, South Carolina, Oklahoma, Tennessee, Texas, West Virginia, Virginia, and Washington, D.C.

NUMBER OF YEARS IN CALIFORNIA BEFORE RECEIVING AID

A most interesting finding was that unwed mothers, on the average, resided at least five years in California before receiving aid. This finding supports the statement that people do not typically migrate in order to qualify for public assistance. Negroes tended to go on aid sooner than whites and those with multiple out-of-wedlock births sooner than those with just one out-of-wedlock child. As a group, Negro mothers with four or more illegitimate children had the lowest number of years of residence before coming on aid (5 years), and white mothers with one illegitimate child the longest residence (11 years).

It was not possible to obtain data from the records as to

whether or not these mothers tended to be either second-generation on aid or whether they themselves might or might not have been illegitimate children. Such data are not consistently available in AFDC records. The records did reveal the age of the mothers when they first received assistance and the data showed that the mothers who had only one out-of-wedlock child came on aid at a somewhat younger age than those who had more than one illegitimate child. This would suggest that those mothers who might be perceived as the "career" unmarried mothers on the AFDC program, actually came on aid at a later age than those who had only one out-of-wedlock child.

AGE AT FIRST CHILD

A study of the ages at which these AFDC mothers began their childbearing careers showed very little difference between groups and between races. Again there is no indication of a type of mother who starts having children at an early age and goes on to be the one who has multiple out-of-wedlock children on AFDC. All four groups were about 19 years of age, on the average, when they began having children, though in all four groups Negro mothers tended to have their first child one-half year earlier than the white mothers. The assumption that Negro girls generally begin childbearing and receiving public assistance very early was not borne out by our data.

LEGITIMATE AND ILLEGITIMATE CHILDREN

Over half of these AFDC mothers (57%) had legitimate as well as illegitimate children, and differences between races on this score were too small to be significant. Greenleigh mentioned the same finding with reference to the AFDC study in Chicago.[7] However, it still means that 43% of the cases had only illegitimate children in this California sample.

[7] Greenleigh, *op. cit.*, p. 15.

On the question of fertility, our findings are suggestive. There was a progression in average family size as we moved from Group I to Group IV from an average of 2.8 children per mother to 5.7. It must be remembered that the Group IV mothers were an average of six years older than the Group I, but this cannot explain the striking difference in fertility. Differences between white and Negroes in childbearing were again not significant. If anything, Negro mothers tended to have slightly smaller families. However, the greater over-all fertility that goes along with the tendency to have more out-of-wedlock children is suggestive. We might hypothesize that a difference in physiological fertility is a factor, in the greater production of both legitimate and illegitimate children by the AFDC mothers with multiple out-of-wedlock children, and exposure, or opportunities to become pregnant, is more or less a constant factor.

Of all the AFDC mothers who had borne illegitimate children nearly two-thirds had been married at some time in their lives, and whether or not they have been married at some time is not closely related to race or to number of out-of-wedlock children they may have borne. The important point to emphasize is that the bearers of illegitimate children are not set apart as a group who never marry.

EMPLOYMENT HISTORY

A noteworthy fact with reference to employment from our study was that 37% of all AFDC mothers with illegitimate children had never been employed, and of those who had been employed only a handful had been employed at work considered skilled. Negro mothers were less likely to have ever been employed, but of those who had been employed, domestic employment was a major type, while domestic employment was negligible among whites.

This is a lower percentage of employment history than reported by Greenleigh in Chicago;[8] also the proportion in our sample who had had special vocational training of some

[8] *Ibid.,* p. 11.

type was negligible, while he reported a much higher percentage. This difference may be partly due to varied methods of obtaining the data, but it can be said that very few of these AFDC mothers who had borne out-of-wedlock children had received special job preparation or had significant work experience that would be a means of earning a livelihood.

MOTHER'S RELATIONSHIP TO THE FATHERS OF HER CHILDREN

An attempt was made to classify the mother's relationship to the father of each of her children into one of four categories. If she was married to the father, the child was, of course, counted as legitimate. If they were not married, but the relationship was a long-term stable one with cohabitation (often erroneously referred to as "common-law" marriage), the relationship was placed in the second category. The third category was made up of those cases where there was an emotional involvement with the father, often of a long-term nature, but without cohabitation. The fourth, or "casual," category was defined as a very short-lived relationship in which there was no indication of any quality of feeling in the relationship. This is a definition as close as possible to the real meaning of the word casual. On the basis of this narrow definition, the number of children resulting from casual relationships was very small.

Distributed among 448 cases (mothers) in our sample were a total of 1976 children, both legitimate and illegitimate. Although there is an unavoidable subjective element in the determination of the difference between categories, the consistent impression one obtained from the case records is that these mothers typically invested themselves in each relationship and that truly casual relationships were rare. The impression was borne out by the data, in that only 2.6 percent of all relationships that resulted in children were rated as "casual." Conversely, nearly half (48.8%) were rated as long-term stable without cohabitation, one-seventh (13.9%) as stable with cohabitation (common-law), and over one-third

(34.7%) of these 1976 children were conceived in legitimate unions.

Racial differences on these dimensions were generally too small to draw conclusions. With reference to children born from casual relationships, the data, if anything, favored the Negro mothers. That is, white mothers were more likely to have borne children from this type of relationship so generally condemned in our society.

Stable type relationships with cohabitation, often referred to as common-law, generally showed an increase in the expected direction. That is, among mothers with only one child borne out-of-wedlock this type of relationship with the father was negligible, while among those with four or more this type accounted for nearly one child out of four. However, it is to be noted that among this latter group, the Group IV mothers, 32 percent of the children born to white mothers were from this type of relationship; among Negroes the figure was 24 percent. Although this is contrary to a frequently expressed assumption that "common-law" type marriages are much more common among Negro families, it must be remembered that most of the Group IV mothers were Negro, hence this 32 percent represents only 16 white children born from a "common-law" type relationship, while 24 percent of the Negro mothers actually represents 190 children.

In order to classify the mother's relationship to the father of each of her children we had to somewhat arbitrarily decide to use these four broad categories and define them sharply so that each case could be fitted into one or the other without any overlap. Since there is almost an infinite variety in the kind and quality of relationship between two human beings, a classification system can soon become hopelessly elaborate if it attempts to capture all the variations. For example, a relationship of very brief duration that results in illegitimate children will usually be counted as "casual," but only by knowing each case thoroughly would it be possible to judge whether or not the quality of feeling of involvement, the other major dimension of human relationships, could appropriately be termed casual. We attempted to take both brevity and quality into account, and in so doing found very few instances resulting in out-of-wedlock children that met the root meaning of the word "casual."

CONCLUSION

In this article we have reported the major findings of a survey of the AFDC records within one California county of cases in which the mother has borne one or more children out-of-wedlock. As in previous studies in Chicago and New York, our findings showed an overwhelming proportion of the AFDC mothers with multiple out-of-wedlock children to be Negro, Southern born, and themselves migrants to the area under study. Refined comparisons were not possible because of differences in samples and methods of data collection, but these major observations hold. More detailed aspects of the data are interesting in themselves and suggestive of directions for research aimed at a deeper level of understanding. Far from "explaining" illegitimacy, data such as have been presented may demonstrate the folly of pat explanations, and give us a glimpse at the distance we must travel before we can speak of understanding so complex a social phenomenon. Explanations that rely vaguely on differences in education, economic status, in culture (particularly as related to the assumption of a Negro sub-culture), to Southern birth, lack of preparation for urban living, and various unspecified combinations of these factors are premature and may be just as dangerous as the more patently superficial ones.

PART VI

Research Perspectives on the Unwed Mother

An Assessment of Research Knowledge Concerning the Unmarried Mother

JANE COLLIER KRONICK

This paper is restricted to a consideration of research concerning the unmarried mother, and consequently, consideration of the unmarried father and the illegitmate child has been rather arbitrarily omitted. In preparing this paper, I have reviewed approximately 120 articles and books selected from the extensive Bryn Mawr bibliography on illegitimacy as representative of the thinking and research in this general area. The paper is divided into four sections: first, a general discussion of illegitimacy as a research problem and the difficulties common to the research in this area; second, consideration of the incidence of unmarried motherhood; third, motivational aspects of pregnancy out of wedlock in terms of subcultural variation in dating and mating patterns and of psychological variables; and fourth, systematic differences among groups of unmarried mothers in the method of coping with the problems inherent in pregnancy and birth out of wedlock.

REPRINTED FROM *Research Perspectives on the Unmarried Mother,* edited by The Child Welfare League of America, New York, 1962, pp. 17–31, by permission of the author and the publisher. (Copyright, 1962, by The Child Welfare League of America, Inc.)

ILLEGITIMACY AS A RESEARCH PROBLEM

The years from 1900 to the present have been characterized by an increasing flow of written material concerning the problem of pregnancy and birth out of wedlock. Yet, despite the attention that has been given to this subject, relatively little of the writing is based on knowledge derived from research. Most of the writers discuss the problem from the point of view of popular concern and offer a single explanation for the existence of illegitimacy. As the period of writing changes, so do the explanations. The early twentieth century reflects the impact of evolutionary theory, with mental retardation and genetic inheritance viewed as the primary variables explaining illegitimacy.[1] In the depression years, environmental conditions become the chief explanation;[2] in the forties, the emphasis shifts to subculture;[3] and in the fifties, psychological variables seem dominant.[4]

Today, despite the time that has passed, we can pose the same questions that Ruth Reed framed in 1926 in *Negro Illegitimacy in New York City*:[5] What is the true incidence of illegitimacy as compared with the reported incidence? What are the circumstances surrounding the conception of children out of wedlock? What background experiences are critical in the lives of the unmarried mothers? How do un-

[1] See, for instance: W. E. McClure and B. Goldberg, "Intelligence of Unmarried Mothers," *Psychological Clinic*, XVIII (1929) 119–127; and Percy Kammerer, *The Unmarried Mother* (Boston: Little Brown & Co., 1918).

[2] See, for instance: Ruth Reed, *The Illegitimate Family in New York City* (New York: Columbia University Press, 1934).

[3] See, for instance: E. Franklin Frazier, *The Negro Family in the United States* (Chicago: University of Chicago Press, 1939); and William F. Whyte, *Street Corner Society* (Chicago: University of Chicago Press, 1943).

[4] See, for instance: Jeanne Caughlan, "Psychic Hazards of Unwed Paternity," *Social Work*, V. No. 3 (1960), 29–35; and Leontine Young, *Out of Wedlock* (New York: McGraw-Hill, 1954).

[5] Ruth Reed, *Negro Illegitimacy in New York City* (New York: Columbia University Press, 1926).

married mothers differ systematically from other mothers? What differences, if any, exist within the group of unmarried mothers, particularly in relation to the variables of race and of social class? And what problems and difficulties following birth are unique to the mother and her illegitimate child?

Unquestionably, part of the explanation for the lack of research knowledge about the unwed mother derives from the nature of the problem. It is unlike many other social problems in that the central figure, the unwed mother herself, does not necessarily represent the problem. Her behavior is not generally aggressive or destructive to others. She is not *necessarily* a seriously disturbed individual, although she may be. Pregnancy and motherhood per se are essential to society, not anathema. What the unwed mother does represent is a violation of the behavioral norms essential for the maintenance of a basic social institution, the family. This violation is defined legally with reference to the child, and as the law varies from state to state and country to country, so does the interpretation of her behavior. For those whose motherhood has occurred outside the legally defined institutional boundaries of marriage, no ready solution for child rearing is open. Thus, society is confronted with the necessity of providing for children whose conception threatens the effectiveness of societal mechanisms for the preservation of an institution. To paraphrase Kingsley Davis, the existence of institutional norms without completely effective enforcement insures deviant behavior. Yet when society is confronted with the product of the deviancy, the child, some provision for its welfare seems essential in the context of western European values.[6]

If the preceding discussion is correct, then consideration of the general problem of the unwed mother with reference to individual case studies but without reference to the social structure will yield a relatively meager return. As the position of the unwed mother in relation to the social structure changes, so should the nature of her problems and the meaning of her behavior. In this sense, there may be many different populations of unwed mothers, not one population. Few

[6] Kingsley Davis, "Illegitimacy and the Social Structure," *American Journal of Sociology*, XLV (1939), 215–233.

writers on illegitimacy, however, have identified the unique characteristics of the population that they have studied.

Another difficulty with much of the thinking about this problem is the failure to distinguish between the behavior itself, or sexual intercourse, and the product of the behavior, or the illegitimate child. It is conceivable that the problems of pregnancy, birth, and adoption or retention of the child represent a series of problems that do not necessarily constitute a single research problem, although they may share common elements. Thus, in considering the general problem of the unmarried mother, *both* the population and the specific problem must be defined clearly and objectively and with as much freedom as possible from moral concern and emotional interpretation, which, as we know from studies of experimenter bias,[7] may affect the outcome of the research.

Another inadequacy in many studies stems from the difficulty of obtaining a randomly selected sample of unmarried mothers and the relative ease of studying the residents of a given agency or maternity home. Thus, most studies are sharply limited in generalization to a very specific subgroup of unmarried mothers. If Sarah Edlin's book[8] can be taken as illustrative of changes in the population of most maternity homes during the twentieth century—from the independent, relatively stable, immigrant, working-class girl to the psychologically maladjusted, dependent girl—the validity of generalization from these studies to the total agency population may be sharply curtailed by change in the characteristics of the clients over a period of time. A further difficulty is the generally small sample size and, even when the sample has been selected to insure representativeness, a large standard error, implying a general lack of reproducibility in the data. When the research problem has been clearly defined and logically developed, a small sample may be adequate to demonstrate the validity of the argument. When a poorly

[7] See, for instance, the mimeographed reports by R. Rosenthal, K. Fode, C. Friedman, and L. Vikan entitled "Subjects' Perception of Their Experimenter under Conditions of Experimenter Bias" (University of North Dakota).

[8] Sarah Edlin, *The Unmarried Mother in Our Society* (New York: Farrar, Straus and Young, 1954).

developed, unclear problem is combined with small-sample error, however, the end product adds little to our knowledge.

Many studies suffer also from the handicap of researcher bias or interpretive bias. This bias is effective in limiting the range of variables studied (which also contributes to a lack of comparability between studies) and can result in the selective documentation of a hypothesis rather than a more rigorous and impartial testing with the data. Individual studies suffer as well from unsophisticated methods of measurement, as illustrated by Clark Vincent's measure of ego involvement,[9] which I shall discuss later. Few studies move beyond the identification of relevant variables to utilize statistical techniques in order to determine the relative importance of the isolated variables. As indicated earlier, the studies also fail to relate the behavior under consideration to other forms of social behavior or to integrate findings about unmarried mothers with other theoretically relevant knowledge in the social sciences. Therefore, it would appear that research knowledge about the unwed mother is rather limited, having suffered from the nature of the questions asked (or not asked), the population from which the data were collected, the selection of variables, and the analysis to which the data have been subjected.

The actual reported data on the unmarried mother can be grouped into three categories: first are the studies without a thesis or a problem that simply attempt to describe a given group of unmarried mothers. Included in this category, for instance, are recent studies of Aid to Dependent Children recipients in Chicago,[10] Delaware,[11] and other areas. Second and equally numerous are the studies that begin with an explanation of one or more unmarried mother problems and proceed to document the assumed explanation with selected case material. I would include in this group studies like the

[9] Clark E. Vincent, "Ego Involvement in Sexual Relations, Implications for Research of Illegitimacy," *American Journal of Sociology*, LXV, (1959), 287–295.

[10] Charles O'Reilly and Margaret Pembroke, *Chicago's ADC Families* (Chicago: Loyola University School of Social Work, 1960).

[11] Committee on Unmarried Mothers, *Unmarried Mothers in Delaware* (Wilmington, Del.: Welfare Council of Delaware, Inc., 1954).

recent paper by Marcel Heiman[12] and even the insightful book by Leontine Young.[13] These studies frame hypotheses that need to be tested in future studies. Finally, there are the very few studies concerned specifically with the unmarried mother that have defined a research problem and proceeded in accordance with standard research methods to collect the data necessary for acceptance or rejection of the hypotheses. One of the most notable recent studies in this category is the work of Clark Vincent.[14]

INCIDENCE OF UNMARRIED MOTHERHOOD

If we examine the specific questions contained in these studies, we find that one of the first is the question of the incidence of unmarried motherhood and the change in the rates of incidence over a period of time. Analysis of data reported by the National Office of Vital Statistics indicates that illegitimate births in the United States increased from 88,000 in 1938 to 194,000 in 1956, an increase of 106,000.[15] Since 1945, however, the total number of births has risen at an unprecedented rate. It is therefore misleading to talk about the numerical increase in illegitimate births unless one is speaking simply of the absolute magnitude of the problem. As the number of all births increases, so does the number of illegitimate births. When the numerical incidence of illegiti-

[12] Marcel Heiman, "The Significance of Out-of-Wedlock Pregnancy in Adolescence," paper read at 10th Annual Conference of Florence Crittenton Homes Association, Atlantic City, June 7, 1960.

[13] Young, op. cit.

[14] Vincent, op. cit.; "The Adoption Market and the Unwed Mother's Baby," Marriage and Family Living, XVIII (1956), 124–127; "The Unwed Mother and Sampling Bias," American Sociological Review, XIX (1954), 562–567; and "Unwed Mothers and the Adoption Market: Psychological and Familial Factors," Marriage and Family Living, XXII (1960), 112–118; see also William J. Goode, "Illegitimacy in the Caribbean Social Structure," American Sociological Review, XXV (1960), 21–30.

[15] Taken from Howard Stanton, "Working Paper on Illegitimacy," Bryn Mawr Graduate School of Social Work and Social Research, 1959, mimeographed.

mate births is considered in relation to total births per year, an increase is still apparent, although it is much smaller than might have been assumed from the numerical increase. In 1940, 3.4 percent of all children born were illegitimate; in 1958, the figure was 4.9 percent, an increase of 1.5 percentage points.[16]

In drawing upon data reported by the National Office of Vital Statistics, it is necessary to remember that illegitimacy is determined by state law and therefore differs in definition from state to state. In addition, not all states report births by legitimacy status. Given a geographically stable population, we might assume that the effect of this might be constant over time. The twentieth century, however, has been witness to major population redistribution within the United States, of which the most notable movements have been northward and westward, from country to city, and from center city to suburb.[17] Therefore, the effect of lack of comparability from state to state in the statistics has most likely *not* been constant over time; thus, if the effect were determined, reported trends in illegitimacy might be modified considerably.

From studies like the Kinsey reports,[18] the Freedman-Whelpton-Campbell study of abortion,[19] and the Christensen studies on premarital pregnancy,[20] it is clear that the incidence of unwed pregnancy in the higher social classes is underreported, in large part because of their greater ability to manipulate the social structure to their own advantage. Studies of other problems, however, indicate that there may have been in the past a substantial underreporting of illegitimate births among the lower classes also, particularly among

[16] United States Department of Commerce, *Statistical Abstract of the United States, 1960*, pp. 55–56.

[17] See "A Crowding Hemisphere: Population Change in the Americas," *The Annals*, Vol. 316, March 1958.

[18] Alfred Kinsey, *et al.*, *Sexual Behavior in the Human Female* (Philadelphia: W. B. Saunders and Co., 1953).

[19] Ronald Freedman, Pascal Whelpton, and Arthur Campbell, *Family Planning, Sterility and Population Growth* (New York: McGraw-Hill, 1959).

[20] Harold Christensen, "Premarital Pregnancy as Measured by the Spacing of the First Birth from Marriage," *American Sociological Review*, XVIII (1953), 53–59.

the rural southern nonwhite. A recent article by Mongeau, Smith, and Maney[21] indicates that prior to the 1940's in approximately 67 percent of all nonwhite births in North Carolina the babies were delivered by untrained midwives, many of whom were illiterate. Frazier's work[22] indicates a higher incidence of illegitimate births among the Negro than among the urban white; therefore, we may assume that many of these births may have been illegitimate and, since the babies were delivered by illiterate individuals, that they were not recorded in the Vital Statistics. We can deduce that more and more of them have been reported as rural southern nonwhites have moved north into urban areas and as the proportion of midwife deliveries has dropped in rural areas of the South. If this has occurred, then the apparently increased *rate* of illegitimacy among nonwhite (from 1.9 percent of all births in 1940 to 3.1 percent in 1958)[23] may reflect a change in the reporting of births rather than a true increase in the current rate of illegitimacy among Negroes of lower socioeconomic status.

The problem of changes in incidence of illegitimate births becomes even more acute when a city is the unit for analysis and the area is defined in terms of the legal city limits. It is almost always true in the United States that the center city, as defined by the legal city limits, has been abandoned to the lower social classes and particularly to the nonwhite. This is a consequence of the move of the higher economic groups to the suburbs as the urban area expands. Since the incidence of illegitimacy consistently appears to be higher among those who have least to lose, least access to knowledge, and least power to control their own destinies, this redistribution of the population within the metropolitan area would automatically increase the rate of illegitimacy for the center city but not necessarily for the total metropolitan area.

One final note about the incidence of illegitimacy. It seems

[21] Beatrice, Mongeau, Harvey L. Smith, and Ann C. Maney, "The Granny Mid-wife: Changing Roles and Functions of a Folk Practitioner," *American Journal of Sociology*, LXVI (1961), 497–505.

[22] E. Franklin Frazier, "An Analysis of Statistics on Negro Illegitimacy in the U.S.," *Social Forces*, XI, No. 2 (1932), 249–257.

[23] *Statistical Abstract of the United States, 1960.*

to be a rather common assumption in the literature that unmarried mothers are getting younger. Since legally, at least, it is difficult for a married woman to have an illegitimate child, one would expect the incidence of illegitimacy in the total population of women to be highest at those ages, excluding the years of physical immaturity, when most females are unmarried. As the numerical incidence of illegitimacy increases, so will the numerical incidence of illegitimacy among ten-, eleven-, and twelve-year-olds, even though the proportion in these age groups remains the same. Yet since the youngest unmarried mothers are most visible, the situation being more unusual and the girls being less able to cope with it, three eleven-year-old mothers in four months will seem much greater than one. This, it appears, is the source of the phrase "the mothers are getting younger." Data from one large metropolitan area indicate that this is apparently what has occurred, since, statistically, teenage mothers are no younger now than were teenage mothers eighteen years ago, the mean age and the variance remaining the same.

To summarize the preceding discussion, analysis of the incidence of illegitimacy is a relatively complex problem. The variables affecting incidence depend upon the definition of the research problem. If we consider all the variables that may affect the reported rate of illegitimacy—in particular, population redistribution and its implications—the apparent increase in the rate over the past two decades might disappear.

MOTIVATIONAL ASPECTS OF UNWED PREGNANCY

Let us now consider the motivational aspects of unwed motherhood. Among the most important *research* articles concerning the motivational aspects of sexual intercourse that results in pregnancy is Clark Vincent's article on ego involvement.[24] Vincent drew his sample of 1062 unwed mothers from four sources in Alameda County, California—

[24] Vincent, "Ego Involvement in Sexual Relations, Implications for Research on Illegitimacy."

physicians' private practice, hospital reports, and residents in two maternity homes—and his data were collected through a mailed questionnaire. Unfortunately, his data appear limited in terms of the number of variables studied. In addition, his measure of ego involvement is somewhat crude; rather than *ego involvement,* perhaps it should be called simply *involvement.*

Vincent's measure consists of each respondent's characterization of her relationship with the father of her child as either a deep love relationship, a friendly relationship, or a casual relationship. Even with this simple measure, he has established three important relations. First, for all but adolescents, the nature of the relationship with the man varies with social class position, the higher social classes characterizing their relationship with the father as a deep love relationship more frequently than the lower social classes do. Second, the adolescents do not exhibit the same pattern of relationship as the older women, but universally characterize their relationships as "casual." Hence, the relationship with the father varies by age and by social class. Vincent also examined the relation between race and involvement with the father. Although, at first analysis, a relation appears to exist between these two variables, in a partial analysis including social class, the relation with race disappears. Thus, the difference between white and Negro women in their relationship with the putative fathers is a function of the concentration of Negro women in the lower social classes. Vincent has in this work established several different populations of unwed mothers. He has shown a difference between the adolescent mother and the older woman, and also a difference between the higher and lower social classes. Finally he has cast doubt upon the utility of race as an explanatory variable.

For a full understanding of the implications of Vincent's study, it is necessary to turn to more general research in related areas. A partial explanation of his data exists in the studies of mating and dating patterns. Studies such as Ehrmann's on premarital dating behavior[25] have shown the importance of a romantic ideal for middle-class college popula-

[25] Winston W. Ehrmann, *Premarital Dating Behavior* (New York: Henry Holt Co., 1959).

tions and the difficult role of the unmarried girl in protecting herself from pregnancy while engaging in what Waller and Hill call the "bargaining" and exploitative period of courtship.[26] As innumerable students of the family have indicated, the older the woman, the less favorable her chances in a marriage market where the initiative is defined as the prerogative of the male, and perhaps the more desperately she may gamble, and occasionally lose, in her search for a marital partner.

For the lower social classes, the romantic ideal appears to have somewhat less importance. August Hollingshead's studies of social classes in New Haven,[27] William F. Whyte's article "A Slum Sex Code,"[28] and the work of Ruth Cavan[29] all indicate that marriage is more frequently accompanied by pregnancy before the ceremony in the lower social classes than in the upper. The norm that "You've got to try out a woman before you marry her," however, is accompanied by the norm of male independence and of the loss of status for the female who forces a man to marry her. With cognizance of these norms, both the findings of Vincent and the higher incidence of illegitimacy among the lower social classes are understandable. If the woman must sleep with the man in order to marry him and yet has little power to enforce the marriage, some women inevitably will bear children that are illegitimate.

Combined with differences in mating patterns among the social classes are differences in knowledge and attitudes about contraception. In a recent book, Rainwater and Weinstein[30] describe the limited knowledge of contraception on the part of the lower social classes, together with the prevalence of beliefs that their use can cause potential physical harm.

Parenthetically, in the casework literature there seems to

[26] Willard Waller, *The Family,* revised by Reuben Hill (New York: Dryden Press, 1951).

[27] August B. Hollingshead and Frederick Redlich, *Social Class and Mental Illness* (New York: John Wiley and Sons, 1958).

[28] William F. Whyte, "A Slum Sex Code," *American Journal of Sociology,* XLIX (1943), 24–31.

[29] Ruth Cavan, *The American Family* (New York: Thomas Y. Crowell, 1956), pp. 119–187.

[30] Lee Rainwater and Karol Weinstein, *And the Poor Get Children* (Chicago: Quadrangle Books, 1960).

be a rather common assumption that the promiscuous girl uses contraception effectively and thus is not the unwed mother. This does not appear to have been established. On the contrary, it seems likely that at least some of the women who are repetitive mothers of illegitimate children are promiscuous (as, indeed, the article by Dorothy Levy[31] and the ADC articles[32] would indicate).

The importance of race as an explanatory variable is problematic. Frazier, in his history of the Negro family in the United States,[33] has provided a historical base for a Negro subculture involving a matriarchal family structure with minimal value placed on legal marriage. I do not wish to quarrel with the historical accuracy of Frazier's account for the rural Negro. The research data, however, appear to be somewhat inconsistent with this theory. In addition to Vincent's research, the data on the ADC families of Eastern cities, which are predominantly Negro, indicate that illegitimacy occurs only in one-half to two-thirds of the families, about the same proportion as among the white ADC population, with a higher incidence among locally born Negroes than among those born in the Southern states. Frazier himself, in his book *Black Bourgeoisie*,[34] demonstrates the acculturation of middle-class Negro families to white middle-class values. It is possible that the same process has occurred or is occurring among the lower-class urban Negro despite residential segregation. If so, it may be more profitable to think in terms of lower-class subculture rather than racial subculture.

PSYCHOLOGICAL ASPECTS

Having established the existence of different patterns of behavior among subgroups of unmarried mothers according

[31] Dorothy Levy, "A Follow-up Study of Unmarried Mothers," *Social Casework*, XXXVI (1955), 27–33.

[32] O'Reilly and Pembrmoke, *op. cit.;* and Jane Kronick, Dolores Norton, and Elizabeth Sabesta, "The Legitimacy Status of Children Receiving AFDC," *Child Welfare*, XLII, No. 7 (July, 1963), 339–344.

[33] Frazier, *The Negro Family in the United States*.

[34] E. Franklin Frazier, *Black Bourgeoisie* (Glencoe, Ill.: Free Press, 1957).

to their age and social class, we are left with the problem of why some girls in all of these groups move safely into marriage before bearing children and why others become pregnant out of wedlock. The fact that the unwed mother has in a sense been defeated by the rules of the game may indicate that she has been among the less well equipped for the game in the first place. While sociologically oriented research may explain the systematic variation in rates of behavior among groups within society, the explanation for behavioral variation among individuals within these groups rests in psychological research. Studies of the psychology of the unwed mother cover a number of issues and show a wide range in quality. Among the substantive areas that have been investigated are the importance of mental retardation; the unwed mother's vocational capacity and motivation; her interests and attitudes; broken versus intact homes; family dynamics, including the mother's relationship with her parents and siblings; and her emotional maturity.

Studies of mental retardation, the majority of them completed in the earlier part of the twentieth century, are generally inconsistent in their conclusions. For instance, McClure, in his studies contained in *Psychological Clinic* for 1929, reports 27.4 percent of his cases as feebleminded and 23.8 percent as borderline.[35] Nottingham,[36] in her study in the 1937 volume of *Genetic Psychology Monographs*, reports only 12.5 percent mentally retarded and a generally normal distribution of scores. Part of the variation in the data may be attributed to the methods of testing and to known variation in intelligence scores among culturally and geographically diverse groups within the population; part may be due to variation among the studies in the selection of unwed mothers for testing. Nottingham studied residents of a Florence Crittenton Home; McClure studied eighty-seven referrals for mental examination from a juvenile adjustment agency. Unfortunately, in social science, the variables that attract researchers

[35] W. E. McClure and B. Goldberg, "Intelligence of Unmarried Mothers," *Psychological Clinic*, XVIII (1929), 119–127. See also W. E. McClure, "Intelligence of Unmarried Mothers," *Psychological Clinic*, XX (1931), 154–157.

[36] Ruth Nottingham, "A Psychological Study of Forty Unmarried Mothers," *Genetic Psychology Monographs*, XIX (1937), 155–228.

change with time. More recent research on the unwed mother tends either to treat IQ very peripherally or to eliminate the mentally retarded mother from the group under study. On the basis of the discrepancy in the existing data, however, the only possible conclusion we can draw is that some unwed mothers are mentally retarded but that many, perhaps the majority, are of normal intelligence.

Related to the variable of mental retardation are the variables of educational attainment and vocational aptitude. Again the data appear somewhat inconsistent. Nottingham, in her study of forty residents of a Florence Crittenton Home, reports data on IQ, educational achievement, interest and personality, and vocational aptitude and socioeconomic tests. Kasanin and Handshin,[37] in a clinical study of sixteen agency-referred unwed mothers, include information on educational attainment. Nottingham's data indicate a general consistence between IQ and educational placement as measured by a series of achievement and literacy tests, with the average grade placement equal to tenth grade. By contrast, Kasanin and Handshin report for their subjects inferior education as compared with IQ. As one would anticipate, Aid to Dependent Children studies uniformly report low educational attainment among the unmarried ADC mothers. Perhaps the data are reflecting the different selection processes used in obtaining the cases. A difference in the socioeconomic status of the subjects might well explain the variation.

With regard to data on broken homes, Kasanin and Handshin report 19 percent of the mothers coming from broken homes, and Nottingham reports over 50 percent from broken homes. Similar variation exists in the data from other studies.

Many writers and caseworkers considering the unwed mother assume the existence of personality disturbance in these women. Thus, Louise Trout writes in *Child Welfare* "We recognize unmarried motherhood as a symptom of a more pervading personality disturbance."[38] Marcel Heiman has

[37] J. Kasanin and Sieglinde Handshin, "Psychodynamic Factors in Illegitimacy," *American Journal of Orthopsychiatry*, XI (1941), 66–84.
[38] Louise K. Trout, "Services to Unmarried Mothers," *Child Welfare* XXXV, No. 2 (1956), 21.

stated, "Out-of-wedlock pregnancy is an expression of a neurotic and/or psychotic disturbance of a female—the expression of an intra-psychic conflict."[39] Leontine Young, in her book *Out of Wedlock,* identifies the girl's relationship with both or either of her parents as the critical source of motivation toward pregnancy out of wedlock, hypothesizing that the unmarried mother, to a greater degree than other women, is dominated (and/or rejected) by her mother and, similarly, that she may be alienated from her father. If we turn to the research that has attempted to investigate this area, we see that few of the studies have clearly specified the problem under investigation. Many of them, and in particular the studies by caseworkers, have proceeded very naïvely, relying upon the accounts the girl offered of her familial relationships. Little recognition is given to the possible distortion in the accounts of these girls as they face the disturbing problems accompanying their pregnancy.

The two studies we have considered in relation to other variables, the one by Nottingham and the other by Kasanin and Handshin, are representative of the research attempting to document the existing hypotheses on personality disturbance. They use two radically different research methods. Nottingham relies upon psychological testing, Kasanin and Handshin on clinical diagnosis. Neither provides clear support for the hypotheses. Nottingham found no significant deviation in her group from a normal population. Kasanin and Handshin report no trends in the women's relationship with their mothers, but some indication of ambivalence toward their fathers. They conclude by offering another hypothesis: ". . . that these pregnancies represent hysterical dissociation states in which the girls act out their incest phantasies as an expression of the Oedipus situation."[40]

It is probable that all the psychological explanations in the literature are true of some unwed mothers. We need much more research to determine to what extent, and of whom, any of these explanations is correct. Such research should include studies to develop more sensitive measurement instruments, as well as development of a logical conceptualization

[39] Heiman, *op. cit.*
[40] Kasanin and Handshin, *op. cit.*, p. 84.

of the research problem and recognition of sampling variation and its implications. Clinical studies should also include a control group with which the unmarried mothers can be compared. If psychological variables are critically important in predicting who will become an unwed mother, then pregnancy out of wedlock should be one among a series of functional alternatives through which the problems might be manifested. Thus, pregnancy should be studied in relation to alcoholism, drug addiction, crime, and other forms of deviant behavior. The functional relationship among these forms of behavior has not, to my knowledge, been investigated, except tangentially in such studies as Albert Reiss's "Sex Offenses: The Marginal Status of the Adolescent."[41]

PATTERNS IN SOLUTIONS TO PROBLEMS ACCOMPANYING PREGNANCY OUT OF WEDLOCK

Pregnancy out of wedlock presents problems both in terms of the immediate necessity for adequate medical care and, particularly for the middle classes, in terms of the maintenance of secrecy. It is clearly established that different groups of people deal with these problems in different ways. The flight to the anonymity of the metropolis is employed (together with adoption of the child, or abortion, or compulsory marriage) by the higher social classes.[42] Furthermore, these same techniques have been employed by generations of upper- and middle-class women. These women are occasionally residents of private maternity homes, or they maintain independent residence under the care of a private physician. If not married, they are more likely to arrange for private adoption of their child, especially if they are among the older age group.[43] In general, the maternity home appears, from the

[41] Albert J. Reiss, "Sex Offenses: The Marginal Status of the Adolescent," *Law and Contemporary Problems* (Durham, N.C.: Duke University School of Law, 1960).

[42] See Vincent, "The Adoption Market and the Unwed Mother's Baby."

[43] *Ibid.*

case studies available in the literature, to attract the lower-middle-class girl, and particularly the severely disturbed individual. The well-known documentation by Dorothy Levy[44] in her follow-up study of fifty-four former residents of Inwood House, showing that release of the child is more conducive to the mother's happy adjustment after the birth (a significant relationship although she did not test it), makes it appear likely that most maternity homes encourage their residents to release their children for adoption.

Lower-class women stay where they are, receiving little prenatal care, relying often on public assistance and the hospital ward, and returning with their child to the slums.[45] Particularly for the Negro unwed mother, few services, either in terms of maternity homes or adoption, are open. (A perusal of entrance requirements of maternity homes included in the study of illegitimacy in Delaware,[46] for example, reveals that many exclude Negroes.) The prevalence of psychological and physical problems contained in the case histories of ADC families indicates that the Negro unwed mother undoubtedly faces innumerable problems. And yet the Cook County study in 1952[47] showed that caseworkers reported fewer needs among the nonwhites. This is probably correctly identified as an example of differential perception due in part to the differential services available to the white and nonwhite.

The greater threat of pregnancy or any violation of societal norms to the family status among middle-class families results in a higher incidence of rejection of the girl by her family. The absence of status open to threat may well result in less rejection of the girl in the lower social classes. While adequate documentation of middle-class rejection exists in the literature, however, few studies have attempted to document the familial relationships of the lower-class unwed mother. Generally, the reliance of most studies upon maternity

[44] Levy, *op. cit.*

[45] See, for instance, previously cited ADC studies and Ruth Reed, *Negro Illegitimacy in New York City.*

[46] Committee on Unmarried Mothers, *op. cit.*, pp. 39–59.

[47] Welfare Council of Metropolitan Chicago, *A Study of Cook County Health and Welfare Services for Unmarried Mothers and Their Children in November, 1952* (Chicago: Research Department, Welfare Council of Metropolitan Chicago, 1955).

home populations results in a keenly felt lack of knowledge about the lower-class woman and her problems.

In the area of placement of the child, the work of Meyer, Borgatta, Fanshel, and Jones[48] deserves particular emphasis. In this work, nineteen variables measuring background characteristics of unwed mothers who place or retain their child have been factor analyzed. Five factors describing the dimensions of the characteristics relating to the mother's decision about her child have been isolated. The factors represent: social class, appropriate handling of the situation, rural-urban background, emancipation, and social mobility. This study is unique in being one of the few attempts to apply powerful statistical analysis to the problems involved in unwed maternity. Thus, this analysis represents the first move toward the knowledge about the unwed mother that will perhaps make accurate prediction possible.

SUMMARY

To summarize the major points of this paper: Some increase in the rate of illegitimacy in the last few decades may have occurred, although it is probably less than is immediately apparent. The incidence of illegitimacy is higher in the lower socioeconomic classes, in part because of differential access to and use of contraceptive knowledge and differential use of abortion and forced marriage, and also because of subcultural variation in mating patterns. The adolescents, both in terms of dating patterns and involvement with the father, provide a separate subgroup of unmarried mothers. With regard to race, however, recent studies indicate that it may not be an important variable in explaining the occurrence of pregnancy and birth out of wedlock. By contrast, patterns of behavior, from the motivation for involvement with the puta-

[48] Henry J. Meyer, Wyatt Jones, and Edgar F. Borgatta, "The Decision by Unmarried Mothers To Keep or Surrender Their Babies," *Social Work*, I, No. 2 (1956), 103–109; and Henry J. Meyer, Edgar F. Borgatta and David Fanshel, "Unwed Mothers' Decisions About Their Babies: An Interim Replication Study," *Child Welfare*, XXXVIII, No. 2 (1959), 1–6.

tive father to the arrangements for birth and disposition of the child, vary with social class. Case studies document the importance of psychological disturbance for some women, although the data are too scattered and selective to permit generalization about the nature and the importance of this dimension of the problem. The validity of the general tendency to generalize from individual case studies of unwed mothers to tendencies among the unwed-mother group remains to be established.

Clearly, research to date on the problem of unwed mothers has begun the task of identifying related variables. This task has been hindered by the reliance upon sample populations representing only a small portion of the total population; by a narrow and argumentative approach to the problem itself, an approach guided by popular concern rather than the requirements for conceptual formulation of a research problem; and by a generally unsophisticated research approach to their solution. If the recent works of Vincent, Borgatta, and Meyer are taken as an example of current work, there is evidence that the current trend is toward more rigorous and fruitful investigation of this area. It is essential that future work consider carefully the problem to be researched, and that in examining the general problems, it consider the broader relations between pregnancy out of wedlock as a form of social behavior and other forms of behavior, as well as between pregnancy out of wedlock and the wider social structure. Research should establish the relative importance or the magnitude of the relations among the variables investigated, thus moving closer to a knowledge of causative factors as a basis for the prediction of human behavior. At present, we have a multiplicity of explanations for the behavior, with few, if any, rules for choosing among them.

The Unwed Mother
and Sampling Bias

CLARK E. VINCENT

⤬ A preliminary survey of the available data on unwed
motherhood reveals that historically a variety of etiological
factors have been emphasized. Studies made during the
1920's stressed such causal factors as "immorality" and
"mental deficiency."[1] During the 1930's the findings pointed
to the factors of a "broken home," "poverty," "little education," and "domestic occupation."[2] Within the past two decades, unwed motherhood has been explained increasingly as

REPRINTED FROM *The American Sociological Review*, Vol. 19, No. 5
(October, 1954), pp. 562–567, by permission of the author and the publisher. (Copyright, 1954, by The American Sociological Association.)

[1] See W. E. McClure, "Intelligence of Unmarried Mothers," *Psycho
logical Clinic*, XX (1931), pp. 154–157; W. E. McClure and B. Gold
berg, "Intelligence of Unmarried Mothers," *Psychological Clinic*, XVII
(1929), pp. 119–127; P. G. Kammerer, *The Unmarried Mother*, Boston
Little, Brown and Company, 1918; Willystine Goodsell, *Problems of the
Family*, rev. ed., New York: 1936, p. 365; and G. B. Mangold, *Children
Born Out of Wedlock*, Columbia: University of Missouri Studies, III
No. 3, June 1921, p. 41.

[2] See Ruth Nottingham, "A Psychological Study of Forty Unmarried
Mothers," *Genetic Psychology Monographs*, XIX (May, 1937), pp. 155-
228; Ruth Reed, *The Illegitimate Family in New York City*, New York
Columbia University Press, 1934, pp. 138–139; and D. F. Puttee and M
R. Colby, *The Illegitimate Child in Illinois*, Chicago: University of Chi
cago Press, 1937, pp. 119–120.

an accepted pattern of life in a given sub-culture.[3] However, the most frequent emphasis at the present time appears to be upon psychological processes. The majority of current studies conclude that unwed motherhood is a product of unresolved parent-child conflict and represents an "unrealistic way out of inner difficulties."[4]

Equally evident from such a survey is the fact that in the majority of investigations reported, the samples of unwed mothers were taken from public institutions, welfare agencies or psychiatric clinics. Out of 48 studies surveyed, 39 or 81.3 per cent used samples of unwed mothers taken from psychiatric clinics, social agencies, charity institutions and private therapy cases. Another 10.4 per cent of the studies drew samples from a particular socio-economic or ethnic subgroup, and the remaining 8.3 per cent comprised statistical analyses of available data from a national or international level of incidence.

This method of sampling has prolonged the picture of the unwed mother as being an extremely young, poor, uneducated or psychologically disturbed female. This portrayal has persisted despite the impressions of many professional people working with the unwed mother that this is a phenomenon

[3] See Franklin Frazier, *The Negro in the United States,* New York: Macmillan Company, 1949, pp. 318–321; Hortense Powdermaker, *After Freedom: A Cultural Study in the Deep South,* New York: Viking Press, 1939, pp. 166–170, 204–206; C. S. Johnson, *Growing Up in the Black Belt,* Washington, D.C.: American Council on Education, 1941, Chapter 8; and H. Hertz and S. W. Little, "Unmarried Negro Mothers in a Southern Urban Community," *Social Forces,* XXIII (October, 1944), pp. 73–79.

[4] See Florence Clothier, "Psychological Implications of Unmarried Parenthood," *American Journal of Orthopsychiatry,* XIII, (July, 1943), pp. 531–549; Helene Deutsch, *The Psychology of Women, A Psychoanalytic Interpretation,* Vol. II, New York: Grune and Stratton, 1945, Chapter 10; C. Donnell and S. J. Glick, "Background Factors in 100 Cases of Jewish Unmarried Mothers," *The Jewish Social Service Quarterly,* XXIX (Winter, 1952), pp. 152–160; Leontine Young, *Out of Wedlock,* New York: McGraw-Hill, 1954; B. Hutchinson, "Unmarried Mothers as Patients of a Psychiatric Clinic," *Smith College Studies in Social Work,* XIX (February, 1949), pp. 102–103; Norman Reider, "The Unmarried Father," *American Journal of Orthopsychiatry,* XVIII (1948), pp. 230–237; and J. Kasanin and Sieglinde Handschin, "Psychodynamic Factors in Illegitimacy," *American Journal of Orthopsychiatry,* XI (January, 1941), pp. 66–84.

occurring quite frequently among middle-income, normal and well-educated women.

In an effort to examine unwed motherhood on the basis of a non-agency, non-psychiatric and non-institutional sample, the following study was undertaken.

THE SAMPLE

A questionnaire was sent to all surgeons, obstetricians, gynecologists, general practioners and osteopaths listed in the 1952 medical directory of Alameda County, California. The questionnaire requested data on the mothers of all babies born out of wedlock which the doctors had delivered during 1952 in *private practice* (i.e., not delivered in a county hospital, clinic or public institution). Of the 576 questionnaires mailed, 409 or 71 per cent were returned. Of the 409 doctors who responded, 31.8 per cent had delivered in private practice during 1952 a total of 252 babies born out of wedlock.

These 252 cases of illegitimate births were further divided into three categories: (a) 171 unwed mothers who had never been married, (b) 51 mothers who were divorced or separated from their husbands, and (c) 30 mothers who were married but the baby was fathered by a man other than the mother's legal husband. The data being reported concern 137 unwed mothers of category "a" for whom data were reported by the doctors.[5] Of these 137 unwed mothers, 83.9 per cent were white, 13.1 per cent Negro, 2.2 per cent Oriental, and for 0.7 per cent no data were given. This represented the first child born out of wedlock for 87.6 per cent of the 137 unwed mothers, the second for 8.0 per cent, the third for 2.9 per cent, and for 1.5 per cent no data were given.

SOCIO-ECONOMIC STATUS

The extreme youth of the unwed mother, which has been pointed out in the majority of previous studies, would ap-

[5] In the other 34 cases of category "a" the doctors had indicated delivering such an unwed mother but did not complete the questionnaire.

pear from Table 1 to be more typical of the institutional case than of the private practice case (hereafter referred to as PR). Rather than cite the findings of other studies using institutional samples, comparisons are limited to the Booth Memorial Hospital data since they occurred during the same year within the same county. Booth Memorial Hospital is the Salvation Army Hospital. Whereas 80.4 per cent of the

TABLE 1. Age of the Unwed Mothers and Their Alleged Sexual Mates Recorded in PR Deliveries, as Compared with the Age of the Unwed Mothers and Their Alleged Sexual Mates Recorded in Booth Hospital Deliveries

	Unwed Mothers			Alleged Sexual Mates	
Ages[a]	PR Cases N = 137	Booth Cases[b] N = 270	Ages[a]	PR Cases N = 137	Booth Cases N = 270
	Per Cent	Per Cent		Per Cent	Per Cent
13–17	15.4	46.3	14–16	1.5	1.9
18–21	32.8	34.1	17–20	11.7	29.3
22–25	33.6	11.1	21–25	14.6	32.2
26–30	13.1	5.9	26–30	18.2	16.6
31 and over	5.1	2.6	31 and over	27.0	9.3
No information	—	—	No information	27.0	10.7
	100.0	100.0		100.0	100.0

[a] Age categories are divided for purposes of comparison with the available data from Booth.
[b] The writer is indebted to Brigadier Cox for the Booth data.

unwed mothers delivered at Booth were 21 years of age or younger, 51.8 per cent of the PR cases were 22 years of age or older. This difference would be even more striking if the Booth cases were not inclusive of divorced and widowed mothers, since the PR sample includes only unwed mothers who have never been married. The alleged sexual mate reported in PR cases also tends to be older than the alleged sexual mate reported in institutional studies.

Table 2 further illustrates how investigations using unwed mothers from institutions and agencies may reveal factors which are more closely related to a screening process than they are related specifically to unwed motherhood. Of the unwed mothers delivered in private practice, 38 per cent had attended or completed college and 26.2 per cent had not completed high school. For the unwed mothers delivered at

TABLE 2. Education of Unwed Mothers and Their Alleged Sexual Mates Recorded in PR Deliveries, Compared with the Education of Unwed Mothers and Their Alleged Sexual Mates Recorded in Booth Hospital Deliveries

Education	Unwed Mothers		Alleged Sexual Mates	
	PR Cases N = 137	Booth Cases N = 270	PR Cases N = 137	Booth Cases N = 270
	Per Cent	Per Cent	Per Cent	Per Cent
Attended or completed college	38.0	12.2	35.8	21.0
Completed high school	29.2	29.3	18.2	27.9
Less than 12th grade	26.2	52.2	8.8	27.4
No information or other	6.6	6.3	37.2	23.7
	100.0	100.0	100.0	100.0

Booth the percentages were 12.2 per cent and 52.2 per cent respectively. A comparison of the educational attainment of the alleged sexual mates in the two groups also indicates a higher educational attainment for the alleged father of the baby delivered in private practice than for the alleged father of the baby delivered at Booth.

The educational attainment of the unwed mothers' parents (Table 3), as well as the occupation of their fathers (Table 4), suggests that the educational and occupational level of many of these unwed mothers is less indicative of recent social climbing and more indicative that they come from "established" middle-class homes.

TABLE 3.   Education of the Parents of 137 Unwed Mothers

Education	Unwed Mother's Father N = 137	Unwed Mother's Mother N = 137
	Per Cent	Per Cent
College graduate	21.1	14.5
Some college	13.2	10.3
High school graduate	13.2	18.2
Less than 12th grade	8.0	5.9
No information	44.5	51.1
	100.0	100.0

TABLE 4.   The Occupations of 137 Unwed Mothers, the Occupations of their Fathers, and the Occupations of their Alleged Sexual Mates[a]

Occupational Category	Unwed Mothers N = 137	Fathers of Unwed Mothers N = 137	Alleged Sexual Mate of Unwed Mothers N = 137
	Per Cent	Per Cent	Per Cent
Professional	11.0	14.6	16.8
Semi-professional	3.6	0.7	—
Managerial	0.7	9.5	8.8
College students	15.3	—	8.8
Clerical	27.7	—	—
Sales	2.2	7.4	5.8
Armed services	—	—	5.8
High school and grammar school	11.0	—	5.1
Skilled	3.0	9.0	7.3
Semi-skilled	5.2	7.4	7.3
Unskilled	3.6	2.1	5.1
Not working	6.5	—	—
No information	10.2	49.3	29.2
	100.0	100.0	100.0

[a] Occupational classification is taken from *Dictionary of Occupational Titles Vol. II Occupational Classifications*, 2nd ed., Washington: U. S. Government Printing Office, 1949.

RESIDENCE AS A FACTOR IN
BIASED SAMPLING

The policy which many welfare agencies and public institutions observe of not accepting "non-residents" appears to be operative as an additional factor in biasing the samples of unwed mothers taken from such agencies and institutions. For example, in the present study, as indicated in Table 5,

TABLE 5. The Residence and Educational Attainment of
137 Unwed Mothers

Educational Attainment	Permanent Residence		
	Alameda County N = 73	County in California Other than Alameda N = 27	State Other than California N = 37
	Per Cent	Per Cent	Per Cent
Attended or completed college	19.2	33.3	78.4
Completed high school	32.8	33.3	13.5
Less than 12th grade	39.8	22.2	8.1
No information	8.2	11.2	—
	100.0	100.0	100.0

the higher the educational attainment of the unwed mother, the more likely that she came from out of the state to have her baby in Alameda County. The lower her educational attainment, the more likely she was to have her baby in the county in which she resides. Thus the studies which rely on agency and institutional samples tend to miss the unwed mother who is presumably in an educational and financial position to travel to another state in order to have her baby delivered away from home in the secrecy of a doctor's private practice.

AGE DIFFERENCES AND EDUCATIONAL ATTAINMENT

There were 94 cases for which age data were given for both the alleged father and the unwed mother. Table 6 shows that the age difference between the unwed mother and the alleged father tends to increase with the increase in the unwed mother's educational attainment. It is frequently as-

TABLE 6. Education of 94 Unwed Mothers Compared With the Age Difference Between Her Alleged Sexual Mate and Herself

Age Differences	Attended or Completed College N = 44	Completed High School N = 30	Less Than 12th Grade N = 20
	Per Cent	Per Cent	Per Cent
Female older	4.5	—	5.0
Same age as man or man is 1–2 years older	16.0	13.3	70.0
Man is 3–6 years older	29.5	66.7	15.0
Man is 7 or more years older	50.0	20.0	10.0
	100.0	100.0	100.0

sumed that the unwed mother is usually a very young girl who is exploited by a man much older than she, and that the less education she has the more likely she is to be exploited by an older man. However, the table indicates that 70 per cent of the unwed mothers who had less than a 12th grade education were mated sexually with a man who was at the most two years older than themselves. Only 50 per cent of the unwed mothers who had attended or completed college had as the father of their baby a man who was seven or more years older than themselves. Some psychiatric and psychological analyses have interpreted this age difference to mean that the unwed mother is using the sexual mate to work through earlier unresolved emotional relationships with

her own father. On the basis of the above data the question
arises as to why this age difference does not apply equally
to the less and the better educated unwed mother.

EDUCATIONAL RELATIONSHIPS

There were 86 cases for which data were also available
on the education of both the alleged father and the unwed
mother. The data from Tables 6 and 7 suggest that the less

TABLE 7.   Education of 86 Unwed Mothers Compared with the
Education of the Alleged Sexual Mate in Each Case[a]

	Unwed Mother's Education		
Alleged Father's Education	Attended or Completed College N = 40	Completed High School N = 30	Less than 12th Grade N = 16
	Per Cent	Per Cent	Per Cent
Attended or completed college	90.0	30.0	25.0
Completed high school	7.5	60.0	25.0
Less than 12th grade	2.5	10.0	50.0
	100.0	100.0	100.0

[a] Chi-square for this table is 49.02 with p less than .001. The association thus
appears highly significant, even though the expected values are less than 5 in some
cells.

educated unwed mother is more often mated with a sexual
mate who is the same age but who has more education than
she has. The better educated unwed mother is more often
mated with a sexual mate who is older than she, but who has
the same educational attainment.

OCCUPATIONAL ASSOCIATION

There are 89 cases for which data were available on the
occupation of both the unwed mother and the alleged sexual

mate. This is in rather sharp contrast to the findings from investigations of unwed mothers taken from clinics and institutions, which emphasize that the unwed mother knows very little or at least gives very little information about the alleged sexual mate. This may again suggest that the apparent disinterest in the alleged sexual mate is true of only certain samples of unwed mothers. In view of Durkheim's prediction

TABLE 8.   Occupations of 89 Unwed Mothers and Their Alleged Sexual Mates

Number of Cases	Occupation of Unwed Mother	Occupation of Alleged Sexual Mates
11	college student	college student
6	high school student	high school student
6	stenographer and secretary	executive or office manager
4	teacher	teacher
3	nurse	physician
3	sales clerk	salesman
2	legal stenographer	lawyer
2	medical receptionist	dentist
2	beauty operator	hair stylist and barber
2	cashier	cafe owner and butcher
2	waitress	cafe owner and bartender
2	bus driver	bus driver
2	PBX and telephone operator	lineman and installer
2	factory worker	factory worker
1	waitress	waiter
1	reporter	reporter
1	office clerk	store manager
1	domestic	her employer
1	usher	theater manager
1	lab technician	chemist
1	actress	musician
1	servicewoman	serviceman
1	buyer (clothing)	merchandiser
1	stenographer	accountant
1	secretary	dentist
1	designer (clothes)	store manager
1	secretary	chemist
27	no apparent relationship	
89		

that the occupational group would become the "primary" group in the industrialized and urbanized society, it is interesting that occupational association appears to be operative as a situational factor in some of these cases of unwed motherhood.

SUMMARY

A preliminary survey of the investigations of unwed motherhood indicated that the majority of the samples studied have been taken from public institutions, welfare agencies and psychiatric clinics. This method of sampling has prolonged the picture of the unwed mother as being an extremely young, poor, uneducated or psychologically disturbed female. This sampling procedure is in part related to the ease with which such groups can be studied. It is also related to, and in turn reinforces, a like-causes-like approach which tends to regard unwed motherhood as bad and then emphasizes bad or pathological etiological factors.[6] Historically, the factors emphasized have ranged from mental deficiency in the 1920's to psychological disturbances at the present time.

The findings reported in the present paper resulted from a deliberate attempt to sample unwed mothers who do not go to agencies, clinics or institutions. The data were based on a 71 per cent response from 576 doctors who provided information on 137 unwed mothers delivered in private practice in Alameda County, California, during 1952.

The following findings suggest the need for more inclusive samples in studies of unwed motherhood and raise additional questions for future research. Of the 137 unwed mothers delivered in private practice:

83.9 per cent were white;
51.8 per cent were 22 years of age or older;
. 38.0 per cent had attended or completed college and 34.3, 24.8, and 35.8 per cent respectively of their fathers, mothers and alleged sexual mates had attended or completed college;

[6] See the excellent discussion by Kingsley Davis of the "evil causes evil" fallacy in "Illegitimacy and the Social Structure," *American Journal of Sociology*, XLV (September, 1939), pp. 215–233.

60.5 per cent were employed in professional or white collar jobs or were college students, and only 8.8 per cent were employed in semi-skilled or unskilled jobs;

36.5 per cent of 74 who were working, received a salary of 251.00 dollars or more per month;

78.4 percent of those who came from out of the state to have their baby in California had attended or completed college;

50.0 per cent of those who had attended or completed college were mated sexually with a man seven or more years their senior;

70.0 per cent of those with less than a 12th grade education were mated sexually with a man the same age or not more than two years their senior;

90.0 per cent of those who had attended or completed college were mated with an alleged sexual mate who had attended or completed college.

Occupational association appeared to be operative as a situational factor in some of the 89 cases for which occupational data were available for both the unwed mother and the alleged sexual mate.

Index